ZEN CULTURE

ZEN CULTURE
Thomas Hoover

Vintage Books
A Division of Random House
New York

FIRST VINTAGE BOOKS EDITION, April 1978

Grateful acknowledgment is made to the following for permission to reprint previously published material:
AMS Press, Inc.: Two three-line poems from page 75 of *Diaries of Court Ladies of Old Japan*. Doubleday & Company, Inc.: Eight Haiku poems from *An Introduction to Haiku* by Harold G. Henderson. Copyright © 1958 by Harold G. Henderson; The Hokuseido Press Co. Ltd.: Poem on page 35 of *The Kokin Waka-Shu*, translated by H. H. Honda. Poem on page 82 of *History of Haiku*. Vol. II by R. H. Blyth: Penguin Books Ltd.: A tanka from 'Ise Monogatari' by Ariwara Narihira. Reprinted from page 71 of *The Penguin Book of Japanese Verse*, translated by Geoffrey Bownas and Anthony Thwaite (1964). Copyright © 1974 by Geoffrey Bownas and Anthony Thwaite; Shambhala Publications, Inc. (Berkeley, California): Poems on pages 15 and 18 of *The Sutra of Hui-Neng*; Stanford University Press: Poem on page 91 of *An Introduction to Japanese Court Poetry* by Earl Miner; Charles E. Tuttle Company, Inc.: Three lines of verse from page 130 of *The Noh Drama*; University of California Press: Four-line Haiku poem from page 104 of *The Year of My Life: A Translation of Issa's Oraga Haru*, translated by Nobuyuki Yuasa. Copyright © 1960, 1972 by The Regents of the University of California.

Library of Congress Cataloging in Publication Data

Hoover, Thomas, 1941-
Zen culture.

Bibliography: p.
Includes index.
1. Japan—Civilization—Zen influences. I. Title
[DS821.H8126 1978]   952   77-12768
ISBN 0-394-72520-4

Picture Sources and Credits

Sources for the illustrations in this book are given after their page numbers. Gratitude is expressed by the author to all concerned.

Throughout the entire Far East of China, Korea, and Japan, we see the system of a unique culture which originated in the sixth century, reached its meridian in the thirteenth and fourteenth centuries and began to decline in the seventeenth century, but which is still kept up in Japan even in this day of materialism and mechanization. It is called Zen Culture.

SOHAKU OGATA, *Zen for the West*

Acknowledgments

THE AUTHOR'S THANKS go to Anne Freedgood for editing the manuscript and for her many helpful suggestions; to Professor Ronald F. Miller for critical advice on things Western, ranging from art to aesthetics; to Professor Gary D. Prideaux for introducing the author to both Japan and Japanese linguistics; to Tatsuo and Kiyoko Ishimoto for assistance in interpreting Japanese architecture; and to others who have graciously reviewed the manuscript at various stages and provided helpful suggestions, including Julie Hoover, Lynne Grifo, Anna Stern and Ellen O'Hara. I am also grateful for guidance from Professors Shigeru Matsugami and Takashi Yoshida, formerly of Tottori University, and from the garden artist Masaaki Ueshima. The insights of yet others, lost in years of questioning and research, are acknowledged here in spirit if not, unfortunately, in name.

Foreword

ANYONE WHO EXAMINES the Zen arts is immediately struck by how modern they seem. Many of the most famous stone gardens are abstract expressionism pure and simple, created out of found objects. The ceramics of the sixteenth-century Zen artists could be interchanged with the rugged pots of our own contemporary crafts movement and few people would notice a difference. Ancient Zen calligraphies, bold and slashing, suggest the monochromes of Franz Kline or Willem de Kooning, and if the word "impressionistic" has any real meaning left, the spontaneous, intuitive, impulsive Zen painters should have first claim to it. The apparent nonsense and illogic of Zen parables established the limitations of language long before the theater of the absurd decided to ridicule our modern doublespeak; indeed, our new-found skepticism about language as a medium for communication was a commonplace to Japanese artists who created both a drama (the Nō) and a poetry (the Haiku) that neatly circumvent reliance on mere words for expression—and in two entirely different ways. Four-hundred-year-old Zen architecture appears to be virtually a copy of contemporary design ideas: modular sizing, exposed woods and materials, movable partitions, multifunctional rooms, bare walls and uncluttered space, indirect lighting effects, and a California marriage of house and garden. The celebrated tea ceremony might be considered an early form of Japanese group therapy, while Zen landscape gardens are nothing less than a masterful deception masquerading as the "natural" look.

If all this were not coincidence enough, consider for a moment our present-day artistic conventions and aesthetic ideals. Like much of what we consider "modern," Zen arts tend to be as simple as possible, with clean, even severe, lines. Decoration for its own sake is virtually nonexistent; Zen artists had no more taste for the ornate than we do today. The works of medieval

Contemporary Zen calligraphy in traditional style, painted by Zen artist at Ryōan-ji, Kyōto.

Zen artists were rough and asymmetrical, with a skillful exploitation of deliberate imperfections and blemishes to make the viewer aware of both the materials used and the process of creation. If it is true that classic art makes one aware of the form and romantic art makes one aware of the artist, Zen art makes one aware of the work of art itself.

We have absorbed into our Western culture almost unawares such Zen cultural forms and aesthetic principles as Japanese ideas of architecture, gardens, and flower arranging. Other forms, such as Haiku poetry and Zen-style ceramics, we have borrowed in a more open-handed way, freely acknowledging the source. Actually, none of the Zen arts is really out of our reach, and a critical following has developed in the West for almost all of them. The great Irish poet and dramatist William Butler Yeats embraced the Zen-inspired Nō drama, although he probably knew next to nothing about Zen. (For that matter, we should recall that no English-language books were written on Zen until well into the twentieth century.) It seems fair to say that the Zen arts have touched us because they express some view of the world that we have, several hundred years later, quite independently come to share.

Yet for all the seeming familiarity, there remains an alien quality. We are not always aware of the really quite extraordinary mind manipulation inherent in Zen art. Why, for instance, does a Japanese garden often seem much larger than it really is? How does the Japanese-style room alter human perception in such a way that people's experience of each other is intensified? Why do Zen ceramics always manage to make one take special notice of their surface? This subtle manipulation of perception is all done by ingenious but carefully hidden tricks. But since the Zen arts *appear* so modern, we are lulled out of looking below the surface to find the fundamental differences.

Most important of all, it is easy to miss what is surely the most significant quality of Zen arts—their ability to unlock our powers of *direct* perception. Since Zen teaches that categories and systematic analysis hinder real understanding of the outer (or inner) world, many Zen arts are specifically designed to awaken our latent ability to perceive directly. They appear innocent enough on the surface, but they involve a subtle mind-massage not obvious to a casual observer. It is this added dimension of Zen art that truly sets it apart from anything we have produced in the twentieth century.

In these pages I will attempt to trace the history and characteristics of both Zen and the Zen arts—to explain where they came from, why they arose, what they were intended to do, and how they go about doing it. I have also included some Western-style analysis of their very non-Western qualities. The aesthetic ideas embedded in Zen culture and its perception-inducing works of art are among the most stunning achievements in world art history. Zen culture, concerned as it is with the process of perception as much as with actual works of art, can open our senses so that we experience anew the arts of both East *and* West, ancient *and* modern.

Chronology

JŌMON CULTURE (2000 B.C. [?]–ca. 300 B.C.)

YAYOI PERIOD (ca. 300 B.C–ca. A.D. 300)

MOUND TOMB ERA (ca. A.D. 300–552)

ASUKA PERIOD (552–645)

Buddhism introduced (552)
Chinese government and institutions copied

EARLY NARA PERIOD (645–710)

LATE NARA PERIOD (710–794)

Japan ruled from replica of Chinese capital of Ch'ang-an built
    at Nara (710)
Bronze Buddha largest in world dedicated at Nara (752)
Compilation of early poetry anthology, Manyōshū (780)
Scholarly Buddhist sects dominate Nara

HEIAN PERIOD (794–1185)

Capital established at Heian-kyō (Kyōto) (794)
Saichō (767–822) introduces Tendai Buddhism from China
    (806)

Kūkai (774–835) introduces Shingon Buddhism from China (808)

Last mission to T'ang court ends direct Chinese influence (838)

Tale of Genji written by Lady Murasaki (ca. 1002–1019)

Hōnen (1133–1212) establishes Pure Land, or Jōdo, sect (1175)

Taira clan takes control of government, ousting aristocracy (1159–1185)

Minamoto clan replaces Taira (1185)

KAMAKURA PERIOD (1185–1333)

Warrior outpost in Kamakura becomes effective capital (1185)

Eisai (1141–1215) introduces *kōan*-oriented Rinzai sect of Zen on Kyūshū (1191)

Minamoto Yoritomo (1147–1199) becomes shōgun (1192)

Hōjō clan assumes real power in Kamakura (1205)

Shinran (1173–1262) founds rival Amidist sect called True Pure Land, or Jōdo Shin (1224)

Dōgen (1200–1253) founds temple for *zazen*-oriented Sōtō sect of Zen (1236)

Nichiren (1222–1282) founds new sect stressing chants to Lotus Sūtra (1253)

ASHIKAGA PERIOD (1333-1573)

Hōjō regency ended; Kamakura destroyed (1333)

Emperor Godaigo briefly restores imperial rule (1334)

Ashikaga Takauji (1305–1358) ousts Godaigo, who establishes rival court (1336)

Takauji becomes shōgun, beginning Ashikaga era proper (1338)

Musō Soseki (1275–1351) convinces Takauji to found sixty-six Zen temples throughout Japan (1338)

Landscape gardens evolve to reflect Zen aesthetic ideals

Ashikaga Yoshimitsu (1358–1408) establishes relations with Ming China (1401)

Zeami (1363–1443), encouraged by Yoshimitsu, creates the classic Nō theater

Golden Pavilion built by Yoshimitsu (begun 1394)
Sung monochromes imported, inspiring re-creation of Chinese
  schools (fourteenth century)
Yoshimasa (1435–1490) becomes shōgun (1443)
Ōnin War begins, destined to devastate Kyōto for ten years
  (1467)
Silver Pavilion built by Yoshimasa; Zen architecture (1482)
Tea ceremony begins to take classic shape as a celebration of
  Zen aesthetics
Sesshū Tōyō (1420–1506), greatest Japanese landscape artist
Abstract stone gardens appear (ca. 1490)
General anarchy envelops country (ca. 1500)
Portuguese discover Japan, introduce firearms (1542)
Francis Xavier arrives to preach (1549)
Ashikaga shōgunate overthrown by Oda Nobunaga (1534–1582)

Momoyama Period (1573–1615)

Nobunaga begins unification of Japan (1573)
Nobunaga assassinated (1582)
Hideyoshi (1536–1598) assumes control and continues unifica-
  tion (1582)
Sen no Rikyū (1520–1591) propagates Zen aesthetics through
  tea ceremony
City of Edo (Tokyo) founded (1590)
Hideyoshi unsuccessfully invades Korea, returns with Korean
  ceramic artists (1592)
Momoyama Castle built by Hideyoshi, giving name to the age
  (1594)
Rise of elaborate arts in opposition to Zen aesthetic ideals
Tokugawa Ieyasu (1542–1616) appointed shōgun (1603)
Ieyasu defeats forces supporting Hideyoshi's heir (1615)

Tokugawa Period (1615–1868)

Ieyasu founds Tokugawa shōgunate (1615)
Daimyō forced to begin system of attendance on Tokugawa
  in Edo

Bashō (1644–1694), greatest Haiku poet
Popular arts of Kabuki and woodblock prints arise in Edo
Classic Zen culture no longer supported by shōgunate
Hakuin (1685–1768) revives Zen and broadens appeal
Zen culture influences popular arts and crafts

MAJOR CHINESE PERIODS

Han dynasty (206 B.C.–A.D. 220)
Six Dynasties (220–589)
Sui dynasty (589–618)
T'ang dynasty (618–907)
Five Dynasties (907–960)
Northern Sung dynasty (960–1127)
Southern Sung dynasty (1127–1279)
Yuan (Mongol) dynasty (1279–1368)
Ming dynasty (1368–1644)

Contents

Part I

THE BEGINNINGS: PREHISTORY TO 1333

CHAPTER 1
Zen Culture and the Counter Mind

Consider the lilies of the field, how they grow.

Matthew 6:28

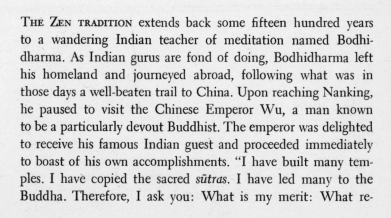

THE ZEN TRADITION extends back some fifteen hundred years to a wandering Indian teacher of meditation named Bodhidharma. As Indian gurus are fond of doing, Bodhidharma left his homeland and journeyed abroad, following what was in those days a well-beaten trail to China. Upon reaching Nanking, he paused to visit the Chinese Emperor Wu, a man known to be a particularly devout Buddhist. The emperor was delighted to receive his famous Indian guest and proceeded immediately to boast of his own accomplishments. "I have built many temples. I have copied the sacred *sūtras.* I have led many to the Buddha. Therefore, I ask you: What is my merit: What reward have I earned?" Bodhidharma reportedly growled, "None whatsoever, your Majesty." The emperor was startled but persisted, "Tell me then, what is the most important principle or teaching of Buddhism?" "Vast emptiness," Bodhidharma replied, meaning, of course, the void of nonattachment. Not knowing what to make of his guest, the emperor backed away and inquired, "Who exactly *are* you who stands before me now?" To which Bodhidharma admitted he had no idea.

Sensing that the emperor was not yet prepared for such teachings, Bodhidharma left the palace and traveled to a mountain monastery to begin a long career of meditation. Over the years his reputation for wisdom gradually attracted many followers—dissident Chinese who rejected classical Buddhism and all its rigmarole in favor of Bodhidharma's meditation, or *dhyāna*, a Sanskrit term they pronounced as *Ch'an*—later to be called Zen by the Japanese. This teaching of meditation and vast emptiness shared very little with other branches of Chinese Buddhism. Ch'an had no sacred images because it had no gods to worship, and it de-emphasized the scriptures, since its central dogma was that dogma is useless. Handed down from master to pupil was the paradoxical teaching that nothing can be taught. According to Ch'an (and Zen), understanding comes only by ignoring the intellect and heeding the instincts, the intuition.

Thus Zen became the religion of the antirational, what might be called the counter mind. The counter mind has taken on more concrete significance in recent years with the discovery that the human mind is not a single entity but is divided into two quite different functional sections. We now know that the left hemisphere of the brain governs the logical, analytical portion of our lives, whereas the right hemisphere is the seat of our intuitive, nonverbal perception and understanding. As far back as the ancient Greeks, we in the West have maintained an almost unshakable belief in the superiority of the analytical side of the mind, and this belief may well be the most consistent distinguishing quality of Western philosophy. By contrast, the East in general and Zen in particular have advanced the opposite view. In fact, Zen masters have deliberately developed

techniques (like illogical riddles or *kōan*) to discredit the logical, verbal side of the mind so that the intuitive perceptions
of the right hemisphere, the counter mind, may define reality.

What is the counter mind really like? What is there about
it that has caused Western thinkers to disavow its functions
for so many centuries? The answer to these questions is not
simple, but the path leading to it is directly before us. Zen has
produced a rich culture which we may now examine at length.
As the scholar-diplomat Sir George Sansom has pointed out,
"The influence of [Zen] upon Japan has been so subtle and
pervading that it has become the essence of her finest culture."
And in the classical culture of Japan it is possible to find the
most revealing examples of the arts of the counter mind. Zen
culture invites us to experience reality without the intervening
distractions of intellect, categories, analysis. Here we may find
the best evidence of what the intuitive side of the mind can
produce—evidence all the more fascinating because it repudi-
ates many of the most cherished assumptions of Western civilization.

When examined closely, Zen culture in Japan reveals at least
three interrelated aspects or faces. First there are the fine arts,
creations of beauty but also devices whereby the Zen masters
transmit otherwise inexpressible insights. Interestingly enough,
the Zen masters did not trouble to invent new art forms but
rather co-opted existing Japanese (and sometimes Chinese)
forms and revised them to suit Zen purposes. During medieval
times, the Chinese-style gardens so favored by the Japanese
aristocracy were adopted for use around Zen temples, but not
before they were first converted into small-scale landscape
"paintings" and later into monochrome abstractions. Chinese
ink painting, both that of the Sung academy and that of eccentric Chinese Ch'an monks, was imported and made the official
art of Zen. Ideas from Shintō architecture were combined with
design details from mainland Ch'an monasteries to produce the
Zen-inspired classic Japanese house. Various types of rustic
dramatic skits popular among the Japanese peasants were converted by Zen aesthetes into a solemn theater experience called

the Nō, whose plays and narrative poetry are so austere, symbolic, and profound as to seem a kind of Zen Mass.

In the later years of popular Zen culture, poets revised the standard Japanese poetic form, which might be compared loosely to the Western sonnet, into a shorter, epigrammatic expression of the Zen outlook—the seventeen-syllable Haiku. Zen ceramics are a curious mixture of Japanese folk craft and Chinese technical sophistication; flower arranging is a link between Zen and the Japanese love of nature, blossoms and beauty; even formal Japanese cuisine is often more a celebration of Zen ideals than a response to hunger. The famous Japanese tea ceremony evolved from a Chinese party game into a solemn episode for the celebration of ideal beauty, inner calm, and the Zen concept of living.

The second face of Zen culture is best seen in the way in which Japanese life differs from our own. This is not to suggest that every Japanese is a living exemplar of Zen, but rather that many of the peculiarities—both good and bad—of the way of life we now think of as Japanese are traceable to attitudes stemming from Zen. In the military sphere, Zen influence began as a special approach to swordsmanship and archery and ended as a disciplined contempt for death beyond what any other religion has inspired, save possibly in a few saints. In the military arts, as in other areas of life, Zen both led and followed Japanese culture—molding that culture and also presenting a vehicle for the expression of tendencies far older than Zen, among them the historic Japanese love of nature, the acceptance of hardship as uplifting to the spirit, the refusal to distinguish between the religious and the secular, and the capacity for the most unpleasant sorts of self-discipline. It might be said that the ideals of Zen struck a respondent chord in the Japanese character, bringing harmony where once there had been random notes.

Zen also brought something new to the Japanese which might be described as a religion of tranquility, or the idea that tranquility is the main objective of religion. The underside of this tranquility is its sense of humor. Zen, with its absurdist *kōan*, laughs at life much the way the Marx brothers did. What exactly can you make of a philosophical system whose teacher answers the question, "How do you see things so clearly?" with the seeming one-liner, "I close my eyes"? Zen has long used the comic view of life to deflate those who start believing in their own systems and categories. It is easier to be tranquil about existence when you recognize the pointlessness of solemnity.

The other side of the religion of tranquility is the need to maintain peace of mind in the face of chaos. Sitting quietly in meditation is the traditional mainstay of Eastern religion, but Zen manages to carry the mental repose born of meditation back into daily life. This equanimity is the product of inner resources brought into being by spiritual training. You need not study Zen to have it, but it is Zen's most tangible goal. The Japanese, whose ability to ignore external distractions in a hectic world is possibly their best-known national trait, have deliberately used Zen and Zen arts (such as the tea ceremony, flower arranging, or ink painting) to counteract the stresses of modern life.

The follower of Zen is protected from the incursions of the world by an inverted (in our Western terms) understanding of what is real and what illusory. One of the all-time favorite *kōan* helps to make this clear. The *kōan* describes three monks watching a banner flutter in the breeze. One monk observes, "The banner is moving," but the second insists, "The wind is moving." Finally, the third monk says, "You are both wrong. It is your mind that is moving." The point here is that, in modern times, most Westerners view the physical world as the operative reality and the unseen, nonphysical world as an abstraction (comforting or not, depending upon our beliefs or immediate needs; the spiritual world is said to grow less abstract to those in foxholes). But Zen takes the opposite tack; it holds that true reality is the fundamental unity of mind and matter, inner spirit and external world. When life is viewed in such terms, there can be no success or failure, happiness or unhappiness; life is a whole, and you are simply part of it. There are no dualities, hence there is nothing to worry about. The result is perfect tranquility.

Of course, one small thread remains to be tied. What do you do about daily life, where the world carries on as though it really does exist, dualities and all? Quite simply, Zen would have you treat the physical world exactly as followers of Western religions sometimes treat the spiritual world—as a convenient fiction whose phenomena you honor *as though* they existed, although you know all the while that they are illusions. The world of strife and relative values may trouble those who mistake it for the real thing, but the Zen-man echoes the words of Hamlet, "We that have free souls, it touches us not." The world is in fact meaningless. It is one's mind that is moving.

However startling such a doctrine may be to Western rationalists, it has engendered such Japanese phenomena as the *samurai* swordsmen and the *kamikaze* pilot, both of whom could, in the Japanese phrase, live as if already dead. On a less dramatic scale, it allows the modern Japanese to be spiritually content and enjoy mental repose in a crowded subway, or to find solitude in a paper-walled house amid noisy neighbors. They wrap their cocoon of tranquility about them and become spiritually apart. Again, it is possible to enjoy this inner repose without Zen, but only in a Zen culture could it become a national trait.

The third face of Zen, the deep concern with and understanding of what constitutes beauty, also preceded Zen culture in Japan to some degree. As with many of the existing Japanese art forms, the native sense of taste was co-opted by Zen culture and bent to the rules of Zen. Aesthetic discernment was as important for social advancement in medieval, pre-Zen Japan as good grammar is in the West today, and the characteristic attention to small details, the genuine ability to *notice* things, from the feathered pastel hues of a partially opened blossom to the colored refractions in a drop of dew, was already well developed. In the centuries before Zen, the notion that aesthetics in Japan could reflect a philosophical point of view would have seemed strange. But to the taste-makers of Zen culture the arts were the handmaiden of spiritual ideas; their arts had to make a statement, and as a result art became an expression of religion, not so much a direct, point-blank depiction of religious motifs as in Christian art, but rather a belief that art itself is an inherently religious concern—an idea Zen shares with the ancient Greeks. But whereas the Greeks strove for perfect form as an exemplification of man's kinship with the gods, the Zen artist carefully avoids final perfection, not wishing to idealize a physical world whose very existence he finds problematical.

Perhaps the most noticeable principle of Zen art is its asymmetry; we search in vain for straight lines, even numbers, round circles. Furthermore, nothing ever seems to be centered. Our first impulse is to go into the work and straighten things up—which is precisely the effect the artist intended. Symmetrical art is a closed form, perfect in itself and frozen in completeness; asymmetrical art invites the observer in, to expand his imagination and to become part of the process of creation. The absence of bilateral symmetry mysteriously compels the observer to reach past surface form and touch the individuality of a work. Even more important, Zen asymmetry forcefully draws one away from any mental connection one might have between completed form and notions of completion and timelessness in material things. Zen denies the significance of the external world and underscores the point by never depicting it in static, stable, or closed terms. Greek art was a tribute to perfection; Zen art is a statement, if only implicit, that the objective world should never be taken too seriously.

The ideas taught by asymmetry in the visual arts are paralleled in the literary arts by the device of suggestion. This quality, first seen in pre-Zen aristocratic poetry, was brought to new heights by the Zen Haiku poets. Among other things, a Haiku poem sets you up for the last line, which kicks your imagination spinning into imagery. The most famous Haiku poem of all probably demonstrates this quality as well as any:

> An ancient pond;
> A frog leaps in:
> The sound of water.

Try to stop yourself from hearing that splash in your imagination, or try to stifle the images and details your mind wants to fill in. Just as with the off-balance picture or garden, the Zen poet has forced you to be a part of his creation. But more significantly, he has achieved a depth and reverberation impossible with mere words. Explicit art ends with itself; suggestive art is as limitless and profound as one's imagination can make it.

Another obvious quality of Zen art is its simplicity. Again one thinks of the spareness and purity in Greek art, and again the connection is wrong. A more useful comparison would be with the diverse, textured arts of India, whether sensuous statuary or fabrics decorated over every square inch. Indian art is a celebration of life and vigor, whereas Zen, with its philosophy that categories and distinctions do not exist, is naturally unsympathetic to decorative multiplicity. The happy result of this rather sober outlook is that Zen art seems surprisingly modern; it is never cluttered, busy, gaudy, overdone. The forms —whether in the classic Japanese house, the stone garden, or a simple ceramic pot—are invariably clean and elegant. And by avoiding overstatement, the Zen artist manages to convey the impression of disciplined restraint, of having held something in reserve. The result is a feeling of strength, the sense that one has only glimpsed the power of the artist rather than experienced everything he had to offer. The Zen artist may deny one voluptuousness, but in the empty spaces one senses a hidden plenitude.

Along with simplicity goes naturalness and lack of artifice. Zen art always seems spontaneous and impulsive, never deliberate, thought-out, or contrived. To achieve this, the artist must so master his technique that it never interferes with his intentions. Again the lesson is contempt for the material world; one must never give the impression of having taken one's art, or indeed life itself, too seriously. This deceiving sense of naturalness is particularly striking in the later Zen ceramic art, in which potters went out of their way to give their bowls a coarse, uneven finish. They tried very hard to give the impression that they were not trying at all. The joinery of the Japanese house is first assembled with the care even an early European cabinetmaker might find excessive; and then it is left unpolished, to age naturally! Such is the inverted snobbery of Zen aesthetics.

Another quality of Zen art is its understatement or restraint. It does not yield all its secrets on first viewing; there are always depths which become apparent with further study. This storehouse of latent profundity is frequently found in the narrative poetry of the Nō drama, which, although suggestive in something like the manner of the lighter Haiku poems, has a cutting edge capable of slowly penetrating the deeper emotions. Through language seemingly concerned only with externalities, the characters of the Nō give us the full sense of their inner anguish, somehow communicating to us sorrows too deep for words. In the same way, Zen-inspired stone gardens have hidden qualities. Unlike formal European or Persian gardens, which are mainly surface and reward the viewer with all their decorative beauty on the first visit, Zen gardens present you with new pleasures and insights each time you study them. Because it conceals its profundity, Zen art is never fully knowable on first acquaintance; there is always something more when one is prepared to receive it.

Perhaps the most puzzling, yet curiously rewarding, aesthetic principle in Zen art is its seeming celebration of the ravages of time. The Zen Japanese consider a taste for newness the mark of the aesthetic parvenu. To be sure, Westerners who have acquired a preference for antiques are sometimes looked upon as more sophisticated than those preferring the latest machine-made item; yet Zen taste has an important difference —the Japanese would never "restore" an antique. The signs of age and wear are to them its most beautiful qualities. This convoluted attitude actually began in pre-Zen aristocratic times, when courtiers concluded that the reason cherry blossoms or autumn leaves were so beautiful was their short season. Soon, the more perishable something was, the more aesthetically satisfying it became. (One unfortunate result of this point of view was a lot of mediocre poetry about the dew.) Later, Zen took over this attitude, extending it to things that perish slowly, and before long, things old and worn out—already perished, in a sense—were thought the most beautiful of all. This idea fitted well with the Zen notion that material things were dross and should not be accorded excessive importance. The curious thing is that the idea works; old objects, dessicated and apparently used up, have a nobility that makes one contemplate eternity and scorn the fashions of the moment. Broken and patched tea bowls or frayed scrolls seemingly falling apart are indeed more beautiful than they were when new. The patina of age is a lesson that time is forever and that you, creature of an hour, would do well to know humility in the face of eternity.

Finally, the aesthetic principles of Zen culture's third face also reflect the practical concerns of its second face, tranquility. Zen art exudes an unmistakable calm and repose of the spirit. Contemplating a stone garden or viewing the measured movements of the tea ceremony, one realizes that Zen art is certain of itself, and it imparts this certainty, this gentle voice of inner calm, to one's spirit. The things that matter are settled, and those that do not are winnowed out like chaff in the wind. And here you realize that Zen art is, last and foremost, a virile creation of strength and surety.

Perhaps the most startling thing about the Zen creations of the counter mind is that few Japanese are willing even to discuss them, let alone analyze them. Zen is the enemy of analysis, the friend of intuition. Analysis is to art what grammar is to a living language, the dull afterthought of the scholar, and Zen culture despises excessive interpretation as a leech on the spirit of life. The Zen artist understands the ends of his art intuitively, and the last thing he would do is create categories; the avowed purpose of Zen is to eliminate categories! The true Zen-man holds to the old Taoist proverb, "Those who know do not speak. Those who speak do not know." Ask a Japanese to "explain" a Zen rock garden and he will inspect you blankly, uncomprehending. The question will never have occurred to him, and he may try to spare you embarrassment by pretending you never asked or by changing the subject. Should you persist, he may go out and take its dimensions for you, thinking by this objective, modern response to satisfy your Western requirements. When you stop asking and surrender to a kind of intuitive osmosis, you will have begun the journey into the culture of the counter mind.

CHAPTER 2

The Prelude to Zen Culture

It was a clear, moonlit night . . . Her Majesty . . . sat by the edge of the veranda while Ukon no Naishi played the flute for her. The other ladies in attendance sat together, talking and laughing; but I stayed by myself, leaning against one of the pillars between the main hall and the veranda.

'Why so silent?' said Her Majesty. 'Say something. It is so sad when you do not speak.'

'I am gazing into the autumn moon,' I replied.

'Ah yes,' she remarked, 'That is just what you should have said.'

From *The Pillow Book of Sei Shōnagon*, ca. A.D. 995

ZEN CULTURE did not spring upon the Japanese islands as an alien force, dislodging native beliefs, ideals, and values. It could indeed be argued that precisely the opposite happened, that the Japanese actually used Zen as a framework over which to organize their own eclectic beliefs about reverence toward nature, aesthetics, anti-intellectualism, artistic forms and ideals, and basic attitudes toward life. The truth, however, lies somewhere between: Zen did not reshape Japan, but neither did Japan reshape Zen. Rather, the two melted together, with the resulting amalgam often seeming to be all Zen, while actually being, in many instances, merely older Japanese beliefs and ideals in a new guise.

Some of the most fundamental qualities of Japanese civilization had their origins in high antiquity, when the Japanese had no writing and worshiped gods found among fields and groves. These early Japanese had no religious doctrines other than respect for the natural world and the sanctity of family and community. There were no commandments to be followed, no concept of evil. Such moral teachings as existed were that nature contains nothing that can be considered wicked, and therefore man, too, since he is a child of nature, is exempt from this flaw. The only shameful act is uncleanliness, an inconsiderate breach of the compact between man and nature.

The early Japanese left no evidence that they brooded about nature or required rituals to subdue it. Rather, the natural world was welcomed as a joyous if unpredictable companion to life, whose beauty alone was sufficient to inspire love. This reverence for nature, which lay deep within the Japanese psyche, was in later centuries to become a fundamental part of Zen culture Like the early Japanese, .the followers of Zen believed the world around them was the only manifestation of god and did not bother with sacred icons or idols, preferring to draw religious symbolism directly from the world as it stood.

The first arrivals on the Japanese archipelago were a Stone Age people, known today as "Jōmon," who left artifacts across a time span beginning in the fourth millennium B.C. and lasting until the early Christian Era. Arriving in Japan from northeast Asia via a land bridge now submerged, they remained primarily in the north, where they lived in covered pits, buried their dead in simple mounds, and, most importantly for the later Japanese, developed a ceramic art of low-fired vessels and figurines whose loving awareness of material and form re-emerged centuries later as a characteristic of Zen art.

The free, seminomadic life of the Jōmon was disrupted around the time of Aristotle by the arrival of various groups of invaders known collectively as the "Yayoi." These Bronze Age warriors eventually replaced the Jōmon, first driving them farther into the north and finally eradicating them entirely. The gods and culture of the Yayoi indicate a tropical origin, perhaps the vicinity of South China. They settled in the southern islands, where they erected tropical dwellings and began the cultivation of rice. Soon they were making implements of iron, weaving cloth, and molding pottery using the wheel and high-temperature kilns. The descendants of the Yayoi became the Japanese people.

For the first several hundred years of Yayoi hegemony, their ceramics, although technically more sophisticated, showed less artistic imagination than those of the Jōmon. In the fourth century A.D., however, after the consolidation of their lands into a unified state, a new era of artistic production began. From this time until the introduction of Buddhism in the sixth century, an interlude known as the Mound Tomb era, the arts of Japan blossomed, producing some of the finest sculpture in the ancient world. The Yayoi mound tombs, often many acres in size, were filled with the implements of their aristocratic owners (much as were the pyramid tombs of Egyptian pharaohs), and around their perimeters were positioned hollow clay statues, presumably as symbolic guardians. These realistic figures, ordinarily two or three feet in height, are today known as *haniwa*. Fashioned in soft brown clay, they portrayed virtually all the participants in early Japanese life: warriors in armor, horses standing at the ready, courtiers, rowdy farmers, fashionable ladies-in-waiting, and even wild boar.

The making of *haniwa* died out after the sixth century, as Chinese Buddhist culture gradually took hold among the Japanese aristocracy, but the underlying aesthetic values were too fundamental to perish. When Zen culture came to flower in medieval times, all the early artistic values awoke from what seems to have been only a slumber; monk-artisans returned to an emphasis on natural materials—whether in soft clay tea bowls, in unworked garden rocks, in the architecture of unfinished woods, or in a general taste for unadorned simplicity. These men created their art and architecture from seemingly rough and imperfect materials out of deliberate choice rather

A haniwa *clay statue from the pre-Buddhist culture in Japan, revealing the sensitivity to material and form that later re-emerged in Zen ceramic art.*

than necessity—a preference rare if not unique in human experience.

During the years following the introduction of pre-Zen Buddhism, the Japanese disowned their native values and artistic instincts as they slavishly copied Chinese culture and reproduced the ornate and elaborate arts of mainland Buddhism. The nature-worshiping tribes of Japan were awed by the seemingly powerful religion of China. They were no less impressed by the manner in which the Chinese emperor ruled his land, and shortly after becoming acquainted with China they set about copying the Chinese form of government. Equally important, the previously illiterate Japanese adopted a

Chinese system of writing—a confusing arrangement whereby Chinese symbols were used for their phonetic value rather than for their meaning. This lasted for several centuries, until the Japanese finally gave up and created a simplified system which included their own syllabary or alphabet.

Having borrowed Chinese administration and Chinese writing, the Japanese next decided to re-create a Chinese city, and in the year 710 they consecrated Nara, a miniature replica of the T'ang capital of Ch'ang-an. The city was soon overflowing with Chinese temples and pagodas. Newly ordained Japanese priests chanted Buddhist scriptures they scarcely understood, while the native aristocracy strode about in Chinese costume reciting verses of the T'ang poets.

Japan had never really had a city before Nara, and its population quickly rose to some 200,000. Yet less than a century after its founding it was abandoned by the court—possibly because the new Buddhist priesthood was getting out of hand—and a new capital was laid out on the site of present-day Kyōto. This new city, founded at the beginning of the ninth century and known as Heian, was deliberately kept free of Buddhist domination, and within its precincts the first truly native high culture arose as Chinese models were gradually transcended. No longer copiers, the aristocrats of Heian turned inward to bring forth a highly refined secular civilization.

To understand the foundations of Zen beauty, it is necessary to examine this Heian culture in some detail, for many of the Zen arts and the aesthetic rules later associated with Zen arose in these early aristocratic years. If civilization may be gauged by the extent to which relations are mediated by artificiality, this would surely be the finest example in all history. Etiquette and sentimentality were the touchstones. The courtiers occupied their days with elaborate ceremonies, extravagant costumes, and lightweight versifying, and their nights with highly ritualized amorous intrigues, conducted in a fashion so formal that the courtly love of Provence seems brusque in comparison. Initially the court had modeled its behavior on the T'ang dynasty, but in the year 894, a hundred years after the founding of Heian, relations with the T'ang court were suspended. There were few formal contacts with China until the coming of Zen several centuries later. Since the country was unified and at peace, interest in affairs of state gradually disappeared altogether, freeing the aristocracy to create a misty, artificial world all its own.

This period, whose aesthetic values were the precursor of Zen art, was also Japan's great age of literature. The idleness of the court provided an abundance of free time and equally abundant boredom—circumstances that brought into being rich, textured psychological novels, some of the earliest and most revealing diaries of the world's literature, and a concern with poetry never equaled elsewhere, before or since. These works of literature depict a society preoccupied with beauty, where life and art merged, and founded on a conviction, later to become ingrained in Japanese life and Zen art, that the ability to appreciate beauty was the most important characteristic an individual could possess.

Perhaps the most unusual aspect of this great age of literature is the fact that the work was produced almost entirely by women. Theirs was the aesthetic legacy that later became the foundation for Zen taste, including the overwhelming importance of brushstroke calligraphy, the subtle sense of what constitutes beauty and what excess, the vocabulary of aesthetics, the elaborate concern with the use of color, and the refinement of the poetic form that eventually led to Zen Haiku.

Taste in the use of color is an excellent place to begin examining the Heian heritage, for in later years the Zen arts would be characterized by muted, carefully matched natural shades whose application followed sophisticated rules of taste. The seriousness with which colors were matched by Heian courtiers is revealed in a famous diary of the era:

One [of the court ladies' dresses] had a little fault in the color combination at the wrist opening. When she went before the royal presence to fetch something, the nobles and high court officials noticed it. Afterwards, [she] regretted it deeply. It was not so bad; only one color was a little too pale.[1]

Episodes in another diary reveal the importance attached to properly matched shades:

It is dawn and a woman is lying in bed after her lover has taken his leave. She is covered up to her head with a light mauve robe that has a lining of dark violet. . . . The woman . . . wears an unlined orange robe and a dark crimson skirt of stiff silk. . . . Near by another woman's lover is making his way home in the misty dawn. He is wearing loose violet trousers, an orange hunting costume, so lightly coloured that one can hardly tell whether it has been dyed or not, a white robe of stiff silk, and a scarlet robe of glossy, beaten silk.[2]

This interest in the colors (and textures) of materials remains a Japanese characteristic to this day, perpetuated by Zen and post-Zen aesthetes, who sensibly realized that this outgrowth of their culture surpassed that found anywhere else in the world.

As may be gathered from the passage above, celibacy was not part of the fashionable world of Heian Japan. Marriages were sanctioned only after the sexual compatibility of the couple had been established, a ritual carried out by a young man calling at a young lady's quarters for several nights running before officially announcing his intentions to her parents. The secret visits were, of course, secret to no one, and at times a young lady might initiate the test by an open invitation. Such a letter also allowed the man to judge her handwriting in advance and thus not waste his time courting a girl wanting in accomplishment. The following diary passage reveals the curious Heian association of penmanship and sex:

I remember a certain woman who was both attractive and good-natured and who furthermore had excellent hand-writing. Yet when she sent a beautifully written poem to the man of her choice, he replied with some pretentious jottings and did not even bother to visit her. . . . Everyone, even people who were not directly concerned, felt indignant about this callous behaviour, and the woman's family was much grieved.[3]

In a society where brushwork was a primary test of social acceptability, it is not hard to find the roots of Japan's later great age of Zen monochrome painting, for, as Sir George Sansom has pointed out, to write beautifully is to solve certain fundamental problems of art—particularly when that writing is executed with the brush.

The writing materials used by Heian courtiers and the calligraphy they set down became important tools for the Zen arts. Writers made use of what the Chinese called the "Four Treasures": a brush of animal hair or bristle, a block of solid ink made of lampblack and glue, a concave inkstone for grinding and wetting the dried ink, and a paper or silk writing surface. These materials are all thought to have been introduced into Japan by a Korean Buddhist priest sometime near the beginning of the seventh century, but they already had a long history in China—possibly as much as a thousand years.

With these materials the Heian calligrapher—and later the Zen monochrome artist—created a subtle world of light and shade. The preparation for writing (and later, painting) is itself a ritual of almost religious significance. The ink, called *sumi,* must be prepared fresh each time it is used: a small amount of water is introduced into the concave portion of the inkstone, and the slightly moistened ink block is slowly rubbed against the stone until the proper shade is realized. The brush is soaked thoroughly in water, dried by stroking it on a scrap of paper, dipped into the new ink, and applied directly to the writing surface. The writer or artist holds the brush perpendicular to the paper and spreads the ink in quick strokes, which allow for no mistakes or retouching.

Where the male scholars of the Heian period labored with complex Chinese ideograms, the female artists and calligraphers were able to work in a new, simplified syllabary of approximately fifty symbols, which had been invented by a Buddhist priest in the early Heian era. Since this new script was less angular and geometrically formal than Chinese writing, it lent itself to a sensuous, free style of calligraphy whose rules later spilled over into Zen aesthetics. The new "women's script" called for brushstrokes that were a pirouette of movement and dynamic grace, requiring the disciplined spontaneity

Page from a twelfth-century (Heian era) manuscript with a delicate brushwork calligraphy whose disciplined spontaneity was a forerunner of Japanese Zen painting.

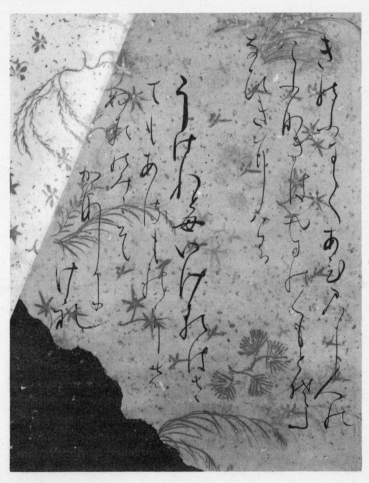

that would become the essence of Zen painting. Indeed, all the important technical aspects of later Zen monochrome art were present in early Heian calligraphy: the use of varying shades of ink, the concentration on precise yet spontaneous brushwork, the use of lines flexible in width and coordinated with the overall composition, and the sense of the work as an individual aesthetic vision. The lines record the impulse of the brush as it works an invisible sculpture above the page; the trail of the brush—now dry, now flushed with ink—is a linear record of nuances in black across the white space beneath. The total mastery of brushwork and the ink line gave the monochrome artists a foundation of absolute technical achievement, and the Zen calligrapher-poets a tradition of spontaneity in keeping with Zen ideals.

Another legacy to Zen artists was the creation of spontaneous verse, which also sharpened the faculties and required a sure mastery of technique. Since virtually all communication was in the form of poems, to move in polite circles a man or woman had to be able to compose a verse on any subject at a moment's notice. A famous female novelist and diarist recalled a typical episode:

The Lord Prime Minister . . . breaks off a stalk of a flower-maiden which is in full bloom by the south end of the bridge. He peeps over my screen [and] says, "Your poem on this! If you delay so much the fun is gone" and I seized the chance to run away to the writing box, hiding my face—

> Flower-maiden in bloom—
> Even more beautiful for the bright dew,
> Which is partial, and never favors me.

"So prompt!" said he, smiling, and ordered a writing box to be brought [for himself]. His answer

> The silver dew is never partial.
> From her heart
> The flower-maiden's beauty.[4]

The quality of such impromptu verse is necessarily strained, but the spirit of impulsive art revealed in this episode survived to become an important quality of Zen creations.

The Heian era bequeathed many artistic forms and techniques to later Zen artists, but even more important was the *attitude* toward beauty developed by the Heian courtiers. Their explicit contributions were a sense of the value of beauty in life and a language of aesthetics by which this value could be transmitted. One of the more lasting attitudes developed was the belief that transience enhanced loveliness. (The idea of transience seems to be one of the few Buddhist concepts that entered Heian aesthetics.) Beauty was all the more arresting for the certainty that it must perish. The perfect symbol for this, naturally enough, was the blossom of the cherry tree, as may be seen from a poem taken at random from a Heian-period compilation.

> O cherry tree, how you resemble
> this transitory world of ours,
> for yesterday you were abloom
> and gone today your flowers.[5]

Many of the later verities of Zen art can be traced to this first philosophical melancholy over life's transience which developed in the Heian era. The vehicle for this heritage was a special vocabulary of aesthetic terms (providing distinctions few Westerners can fully perceive) which could describe subtle outer qualities of things—and the corresponding inner response by a cultivated observer—by the use of fine-grained aesthetic distinctions.[6] The word that described the delicate discernment of the Heian courtiers was *miyabi*, which was used to indicate aspects of beauty that only a highly refined taste could appreciate: the pale shades of dye in a garment, the fragile geometry of a dew-laden spiderweb, the delicate petal of a purple lotus, the texture of the paper of a lover's letter, pale yellow clouds trailing over a crimson sunset. If the beauty were more direct and less muted, it was described as *en,* or charming, a term marking the type of beauty as sprightly or more obvious. The most popular aesthetic term was *aware,* which refers to a pleasant emotion evoked unexpectedly. *Aware* is what one *feels* when one sees a cherry blossom or an autumn maple. (This internalization of aesthetic qualities was later to have great import for the Zen arts, whose reliance on suggestiveness shifted a heavy responsibility to the perceiver.) As the notion of beauty's transience became stronger, the term also came to include the feeling of poignancy as well as pleasure and the awareness that delight must perish.

These terms of refined aristocratic discernment became thoroughly ingrained in Japanese life and were passed on to Zen aesthetics, which added new terms that extended the Heian categories to reverence for beauty past its prime and for objects that reflect the rigors of life. The Zen aesthetes also added the notion of *yūgen,* an extension of *aware* into the region of poignant foreboding. At a brilliant sunset one's mind feels *aware,* but as the shadows deepen and night birds cry, one's soul feels *yūgen.* Thus the Zen artists carried the Heian aesthetic response into the inner man and turned a superficial emotion into a universal insight.

The most important aspect of the Japanese character to surface during the Heian era, at least from the standpoint of later Zen culture and ideals, was faith in the emotions over the intellect. It was during this period that the Japanese rejected for all time a rigorously intellectual approach to life. As Earl Miner wrote in his description of pre-Zen Heian society, "The respect accorded to correct or original ideas in the West has always been given in Japan to propriety or sincerity of feeling. And just as someone without an idea in his head is archetypally out of our civilization, so the person without a true feeling in his heart is archetypally out of the Japanese."[7] From such an attitude it is not far to the Zen intuitive approach to understanding.

The early years of Japanese isolation saw a people with a rich nature religion whose arts revealed deep appreciation for material and form. The coming of Chinese culture brought with it Buddhism, which became a national religion and provided a vehicle for the dissemination of Zen. Finally, the aristocratic civilization of the Heian era developed Japanese sensitivity to remarkable levels, providing later generations with a valuable framework of taste and standards. The court civilization of Heian was ultimately dethroned by medieval warriors, who themselves soon came under the sway of Zen. Although the Zen artist-monks of the medieval era brought into being a new culture with its own rules of taste and behavior, they were always in the debt of the earlier ages.

CHAPTER 3

The Rise of Japanese Buddhism

The new doctrine of the Buddha is exceeding excellent, although difficult to explain and comprehend.

Message accompanying the first image
of the Buddha to enter Japan, ca. A.D. 552

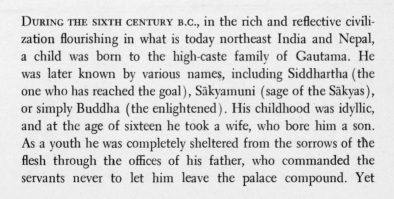

DURING THE SIXTH CENTURY B.C., in the rich and reflective civilization flourishing in what is today northeast India and Nepal, a child was born to the high-caste family of Gautama. He was later known by various names, including Siddhartha (the one who has reached the goal), Sākyamuni (sage of the Sākyas), or simply Buddha (the enlightened). His childhood was idyllic, and at the age of sixteen he took a wife, who bore him a son. As a youth he was completely sheltered from the sorrows of the flesh through the offices of his father, who commanded the servants never to let him leave the palace compound. Yet finally, the legends relate, he managed to escape this benign prison long enough to encounter old age, sickness, and death. Understandably distressed, he began pondering the questions of human mortality and suffering, a search which led him to a holy man, whose devoutness seemed to hold the answers.

True to his convictions, he renounced wealth, family, and position and embarked upon the life of an ascetic. A spiritual novice at the age of twenty-nine, he traveled for the next six years from sage to sage, searching for the teachings that might release him from the prison of flesh. Finally, with disciples of his own, he left all his teachers and devoted himself to meditation for another six years, at the end of which he was close to death from fasting and privation. But he was no nearer his goal, and abandoning the practices of traditional religion, he set out to beg for rice. Although his disciples immediately deserted him as unworthy to be a teacher, he was undeterred and enjoyed his first full meal since leaving his father's palace. He then had a deep sleep and learned in a dream that realization would soon be his. He proceeded to a wood and began his final meditation under the now legendary Bodhi tree—where he at last found enlightenment. Gautama had become the Buddha.

For the next forty-nine years he traveled the length of India preaching a heretical doctrine. To appreciate what he taught, one must grasp what he preached against. At the time, the predominant religious system was Brahmanism, which was based upon the Upanishads, a collection of early Vedic writings. According to this system, the universe was presided over by the Brahman, an impersonal god-form which was at once a pantheistic universal soul and an expression of the order, or *dharma*, of the cosmos. This universal god-form was also thought to reside in man, in the form of the *ātman*, roughly translatable as the soul; and the individual was believed to be able to rise above his physical existence and experience the uniting of this *ātman* with the larger god-form through practice of a rigorous physical and mental discipline, which became known as yoga. Not surprisingly, all formal communications with the universal god-form had to be channeled through a special priest class, who called themselves Brāhmans.

The Buddha disputed these beliefs. He taught that there was no universal god and hence no internal soul, that there is, in fact, no existence in the world. All perception to the contrary is illusory. Enlightenment therefore consists not of merging one's *ātman* with the greater god-head, but rather in recognizing that there actually is nothing with which to merge. Consequently the aim is to transcend the more troublesome aspects of perception, such as pain, by turning one's back on the world —which is nonexistent in any case—and concentrating on inner peace. The Buddha stressed what he called the "Four Noble Truths" and the "Eightfold Path." The Four Noble Truths recognized that to live is to desire and hence to suffer, and the Eightfold Path (right views, right resolve, right speech, right conduct, right livelihood, right effort, right mindfulness, right concentration) provided a prescription for the resolution of this suffering. Followers of the Eightfold Path understand that the external world is illusory and that its desires and suffering can be overcome by a noble life, guided by mental fixation on the concept of nonexistence.

The original teachings of the Buddha are more a philosophy than a religion, for they admit no supreme god, nor do they propose any salvation other than that attainable through human diligence. The aim is temporal happiness, to be realized through asceticism—which was taught as a practical means of turning one's back on the world and its incumbent pain. There were no scriptures, no sacred incantations, no soul, no cycle of rebirth, nothing beyond one's existential life.

Since the Buddha left no writings or instructions regarding the establishment of a religion in his name, his followers called a council some ten years after his death to amend this oversight. This first council produced the earliest canon of Buddhist teachings, a group of *sūtras* or texts purporting to reproduce various dialogues between the Buddha and his disciples. A second council was held exactly one hundred years later, supposedly to clarify points raised in the first meeting. But instead of settling the disagreement which had arisen, the meeting polarized the two points of view and shattered monolithic Buddhism once and for all.

As Buddhism spread across India into Ceylon and Southeast Asia, a distinct sectarian split developed, which might be described as a controversy between those who strove to preserve the teachings of the Buddha as authentically as possible and those who were willing to admit (some might say compromise with) other religions. The purer form, which was established in Southeast Asia, came to be called Hīnayāna, or the Lesser Vehicle (purportedly because of the exclusionary strictness of its views). The other branch, comprising the beliefs that spread to China and thence to Japan, was described as Mahāyāna, or the Greater Vehicle.

This division also resulted in two versions of the *sūtras* being canonized. That revered by the Hīnayānists is known as the Pali Canon and was set down in the Pali language (a dialect of Indian Sanskrit) around 100 B.C. The *sūtras* of the eclectic Mahāyānists grew over the centuries, with additions in Sanskrit, Tibetan, and, later, Chinese. In addition to the original thoughts of the Buddha, they included large sections of commentary or secondary material. The Chinese, particularly, had strong speculative minds and thought nothing of amending the teachings of a simple Indian teacher. The Indians also found the Buddha's thought a shade too austere for their tastes, but instead of embellishing it as the Chinese did, they gradually plowed it back into the theological mélange of pantheistic Hinduism until it finally lost any separate identity.

Buddhism is said to have officially reached China during the first century A.D., and after some three hundred years of adjusting it to suit their established teachings of Confucianism and Taoism, the Chinese embraced it as their own. (It was the admittance of Taoist beliefs into Chinese Buddhism that laid the foundations for the school of Ch'an Buddhism, the parent of Japanese Zen.) Buddhism did not replace the two earlier Chinese religions but, rather, provided an alternative spiritual framework wherein the Chinese, structured, Confucianist bent of mind could be merged with their Taoist yearning for mystical philosophy to produce a native religion at once formal and introspective. During the third, fourth, and fifth centuries a virtual parade of Indian Mahāyāna Buddhist teachers traveled north around the high Himalayas and into China, there to dispense their own respective brands of the Buddha's thought. The Chinese, on their part, set about importing Indian Sanskrit *sūtras* and translating them via a process whereby Indian philosophical concepts were rendered directly by pre-existing Chinese terms—the literal pounding of round Indian pegs into square Chinese holes. Since no more effective way has yet been found to destroy the originality of foreign ideas than to translate them word for word into the nearest native approximation, Chinese Buddhism became, in many ways, merely a rearrangement of existing Chinese philosophies.

The date Chinese Buddhism was introduced to Japan has traditionally been set at A.D. 552. In that year, the records state, a Korean monarch, fearful of belligerent neighbors, appealed to the Japanese for military assistance, accompanying his plea with a statue of the Buddha and a missal of *sūtras*. Since the Japanese had for many centuries reserved their primary allegiance for their sun-goddess, whose direct descendant the emperor was thought to be, they were wary of new faiths that might jeopardize the authority of the native deities. After much high-level deliberation it was decided to give the Buddha a trial period to test his magical powers, but unfortunately no sooner had the new image been set up than a pestilence, apparently smallpox, swept the land. The new Buddha was swiftly consigned to a drainage canal by imperial decree.

Twenty years later a new emperor came to the throne, and he was persuaded to give the Buddha another try by a political faction which thought a new religion might undermine the theological position of the established nobility. By odd coincidence, no sooner had a new Buddha been imported than another plague broke out. The new Buddha statue and all accompanying trappings were disposed of, but the plague only worsened, allowing the pro-Buddhist faction to turn the tragedy to their advantage by blaming those who had desecrated the statue. After more political maneuvering, this faction took the somewhat unprecedented step of assassinating the hesitant emperor in order to ensure a place for Buddhism in Japanese life. Finally the faith did catch hold, and, by the beginning of the seventh century, temples and pagodas were being built.

As interest grew in both the doctrines of the Buddha and the political innovations of the new T'ang dynasty, which had come to power in China in 618, the Japanese aristocracy began to copy Chinese civilization, gradually abandoning much of their indigenous culture. Although new Japanese monks were soon writing and reciting Chinese *sūtras*, Buddhist ideas, now twice removed from their Indian origins, were grasped imperfectly if at all by most Japanese. Indeed, few of the early aristocracy who professed Buddhism viewed it as anything other than a powerful new form of magic—a supplement to the native gods, or *kami*, who presided over harvests and health. Given the difficulty Japanese scholars had in understanding Chinese texts, it is easy to sympathize with later Zen monks who claimed the *sūtras* were mainly a barrier to enlightenment.

Three fundamental types of Buddhism preceded Zen in Japan: the early scholarly sects which came to dominate Nara; the later aristocratic schools whose heyday was the noble Heian era; and, finally, popular, participatory Buddhism, which reached down to the farmers and peasants. The high point of Nara Buddhism was the erection of a giant Buddha some four stories high whose gilding bankrupted the tiny island nation but whose psychological impact was such that Japan became the world center of Mahāyāna Buddhism. The influence of the Nara Buddhist establishment grew to such proportions that the secular branch of government, including the emperor himself, became nervous. The solution to the problem was elegantly simple: the emperor simply abandoned the capital, leaving the wealthy and powerful temples to preside over a ghost town. A new capital was established at Heian (present-day Kyōto), far enough away to dissipate priestly meddling.

The second type of Buddhism, which came to prominence in Heian, was introduced as deliberate policy by the emperor. Envoys were sent to China to bring back new and different sects, enabling the emperor to fight the Nara schools with their own Buddhist fire. And this time the wary aristocracy saw to it that the Buddhist temples and monasteries were established well outside the capital—a location that suited both the new Buddhists' preference for remoteness and the aristocracy's new cult of aesthetics rather than religion.

The first of the Heian sects, known as Tendai after the Chinese T'ien-t'ai school, was introduced into Japan in 806 by the Japanese priest Saichō (767–822). The Tendai stressed the authority of the Lotus Sūtra, which recognized the Buddha as both an historical person and the realization in human form of the universal spirit—an identity implying the oneness of the latent Buddha nature in all matter, animate and inanimate. Although the school was avowedly eclectic, embracing all the main Mahāyāna doctrines, it was bitterly opposed by the Nara schools, which campaigned unsuccessfully to convert Tendai novices. Saichō countered their opposition by pointing out that his Buddhism was based on an actual *sūtra*, purportedly the Buddha's own words, whereas the schools of Nara had contented themselves primarily with wrangling over commentaries or secondary interpretations of the Buddha's teachings. Saichō also introduced the question of individual morality, a concern conspicuously absent in Nara Buddhism.

The Tendai sect became dominant during the ninth and tenth centuries, when its center on Mt. Hiei (on the outskirts of Kyōto) swelled to over three thousand buildings. Although Saichō himself appears to have been benign in nature, practicing the principles of morality he taught, in later years the Mt. Hiei Tendai complex became the base for an army of irascible monks who frequently descended upon Kyōto to harass courtiers and citizens alike. In the late sixteenth century, the entire complex was burned to the ground and thousands of monks slaughtered by a fierce shōgun who was determined to stop the intervention of Tendai monks in public affairs. Tendai survives today as a religion primarily of the upper classes, with a membership of something over a million, but even by the end of the Heian era it had become mainly ceremonial.

The other Buddhist sect to gain prominence during the Heian era was Shingon, founded by a younger contemporary of Saichō named Kūkai (774–835). He also went to China, where he studied teachings of the Chên-yen school, a type of Buddhism known as "esoteric" because of its kinship to the mystical Tantrism of Tibet. The elaborate rituals of the Japanese Shingon temples were an immediate success with the ceremonially minded Heian aristocracy. Shingon was superb theater, with chants, incantations, sacred hand signs (*mūdra*), and meditation on the sacred *mandala*—geometrical diagrams purportedly containing the key to the cosmological meaning of reality. The headquarters for the Shingon school was established on Mt. Kōya, near Kyōto but sufficiently removed that the monks were not tempted to dabble in state affairs. Nevertheless, in later years it too became a stronghold for mercenary warrior-monks, with the result that it also was chastened by an outraged shōgun. Today there are Shingon monasteries in remote mountain areas, standing regal and awesome in their forested isolation, and the sect still claims over nine million practitioners, scattered among a host of offshoots.

The popular, participatory Buddhism which followed the aristocratic sects was home-grown, although it reflected Chinese prototypes. Much of it centered around one particular figure in the Buddhist pantheon, the benign, sexless Amida, a Buddhist saint who presided over a Western Paradise or Pure Land of milk and honey accessible to all who called on his name. Amida has been part of the confusing assemblage of deities worshiped in Japan for several centuries, but the simplicity of his requirements for salvation made him increasingly popular with the Heian aristocrats, who had begun to tire of the elaborate rigmarole surrounding magical-mystery Buddhism. And as times became more and more unstable during the latter part of the Heian era, people searched for a messianic figure to whom they could turn for comfort. So it was that a once minor figure in the Japanese Buddhist hierarchy became the focus of a new and widespread cult.

The figure of Amida, a gatekeeper of the Western Paradise, seems to have entered Buddhism around the beginning of the Christian Era, and his teachings have a suspiciously familiar ring: Come unto me all ye who are burdened and I will give you rest; call on my name and one day you will be with me in Paradise. In India at this time there were contacts with the Near East, and Amida is ordinarily represented as one of a trinity, flanked by two minor deities. However, he is first described in two Indian *sūtras* which betray no hint of foreign influence. During the sixth and seventh centuries, Amida became a theme of Mahāyāna literature in China, whence he entered Japan as part of the Tendai school. In the beginning, he was merely a subject for meditation and his free assist into Paradise did not replace the personal initiative required by the Eightfold Path. Around the beginning of the eleventh century, however, a Japanese priest circulated a treatise declaring that salvation and rebirth in the Western Paradise could be realized merely by pronouncing a magic formula in praise of Amida, known as the *nembutsu*: *Namu Amida Butsu*, or Praise to Amida Buddha.

This exceptional new doctrine attracted little notice until the late twelfth century, when a disaffected Tendai priest known as Hōnen (1133–1212) set out to teach the *nembutsu* across the length of Japan. It became an immediate popular success, and Hōnen, possibly unexpectedly, found himself the Martin Luther of Japan, leading a reformation against imported Chinese Buddhism. He preached no admonitions to upright behavior, declaring instead that recitation of the *nembutsu* was in itself sufficient evidence of a penitent spirit and right-minded intentions. It might be said that he changed Buddhism from what was originally a faith all ethics and no god to a faith all god and no ethics.

What Hōnen championed was actually a highly simplified version of the Chinese Jōdo school, but he avoided complicated theological exercises, leaving the doctrinal justifications for his teachings vague. This was intended to avoid clashes with the priests of the older sects while simultaneously making his version of Jōdo as accessible as possible to the uneducated laity. The prospect of Paradise beyond the River in return for minimal investment in thought and deed gave Jōdo wide appeal, and this improbable vehicle finally brought Buddhism to the Japanese masses, simple folk who had never been able to understand or participate in the scholarly and aristocratic sects which had gone before.

Not surprisingly, the popularity of Hōnen's teachings aroused enmity among the older schools, which finally managed to have him exiled for a brief period in his last years. Jōdo continued to grow, however, even in his absence, and when he returned to Kyōto in 1211 he was received as a triumphal hero. Gardens began to be constructed in imitation of the Western Paradise, while the *nembutsu* resounded throughout the land in mockery of the older schools. The followers of Jōdo continued to be persecuted by the Buddhist establishment well into the seventeenth century, but today Jōdo still claims the allegiance of over five million believers.

An offshoot of the Jōdo sect, destined to become even more popular, was started by a pupil and colleague of Hōnen called Shinran (1173–1262), who also left the Tendai monastery on Mt. Hiei to become a follower of Amida. His interpretation of the Amida *sūtras* was even simpler than Hōnen's: based on his studies he concluded that only *one* truly sincere invocation of the *nembutsu* was enough to reserve the pleasures of the Western Paradise for the lowliest sinner. All subsequent chantings of the formula were merely an indication of appreciation and were not essential to assure salvation. Shinran also carried the reformation movement to greater lengths, abolishing the requirements for monks (which had been maintained by the conciliatory Hōnen) and discouraging celibacy among priests by his own example of fathering six children by a nun. This last act, justified by Shinran as a gesture to eliminate the division between the clergy and the people, aroused much unfavorable notice among the more conservative Buddhist factions.

Shinran was also firm in his assertion that Amida was the only Buddha that need be worshiped, a point downplayed by Hōnen in the interest of ecumenical accord.

The convenience of only one *nembutsu* as a prerequisite for Paradise, combined with the more liberal attitude toward priestly requirements, caused Shinran's teachings to prosper, leading eventually to an independent sect known as Jōdo Shin, or True Pure Land. Today the Jōdo Shin, with close to fifteen million followers, enjoys numerical dominance over other forms of Japanese Buddhism.

The Amidist salvation movement was confronted by its only truly effective detractor in the person of the extremist Renchō (1222–1282), who later took for himself the name of Nichiren, or Sun Lotus. An early novice in the Tendai monastery, he took a different tack from the Amida teachers, deciding that all essential Buddhist truth was contained in the Lotus Sūtra itself. Although the Tendai school had originally been founded on the study of the Lotus Sūtra, he believed the school had strayed from the *sūtra's* precepts. Denouncing all sects impartially, he took a fundamentalist, back-to-the-Lotus text for his sermons. Sensing that most of his followers might have trouble actually reading a *sūtra*, he produced a chanting formula of his own which he claimed would do just as well. This Lotus *"nembutsu"* was the phrase *namu myōhō renge-kyō*, or Praise to the Lotus Sūtra. The chanting Amidists had met their match.

The Tendai monks on Mt. Hiei did not receive this vulgarization of their teachings kindly, and their urgings, together with his intemperate pronouncements regarding imminent dangers of a Mongol invasion, led in 1261 to Nichiren's banishment to a distant province. Three years later the truth of his warnings became all too apparent and he was recalled by the government. But on his return he overplayed his hand, offering to save the nation only if all other Buddhist sects were eliminated. This was too much for the Japanese ruling circles; they turned instead to a new band of warriors trained in Zen military tactics who promptly repelled the invasion without Nichiren's aid.

Persecution of his sect continued, reaching a high point in the mid-sixteenth century, when a band of rival Tendai monks burned twenty-one Nichiren temples in Kyōto, slaughtering all the priests, including a reputed three thousand in the last temple.

The sect has survived, however, and today Nichiren Shōshū and its lay affiliate, the Sōka Gakkai, or Value Creation Society, claim the membership of one Japanese in seven and control of the country's third largest political party. The Sōka Gakkai recently dedicated a vast new temple at the foot of Mt. Fuji, said to be the largest religious structure in existence. With services that often resemble political conventions, the Nichiren sect has achieved what might once have been thought impossible: it has simplified even further the ingenuous philosophy of its founder, embellishing the praise of the Lotus Sūtra with marching bands and gymnastic displays in sports-stadium convocations.

The Japanese reformation represented by Amidism and Nichiren was a natural outcome of the contempt for the average man that characterized the early sects. It also opened the door for Zen, which found an appeal among the nonaristocratic warrior class to equal that of the popular Buddhist sects among the peasantry and bourgeoisie. As it happened, the warriors who became fired with Zen also took control of the government away from the aristocracy after the twelfth century, with the result that Zen became the unofficial state religion of Japan during its great medieval period of artistic activity.

CHAPTER 4

The Chronicles of Zen

A special transmission outside the sūtras;
No reliance upon words and letters;
Direct pointing to the very soul;
Seeing into one's own essence.

Traditional Homage to Bodhidharma

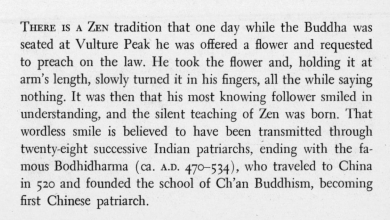

THERE IS A ZEN tradition that one day while the Buddha was seated at Vulture Peak he was offered a flower and requested to preach on the law. He took the flower and, holding it at arm's length, slowly turned it in his fingers, all the while saying nothing. It was then that his most knowing follower smiled in understanding, and the silent teaching of Zen was born. That wordless smile is believed to have been transmitted through twenty-eight successive Indian patriarchs, ending with the famous Bodhidharma (ca. A.D. 470–534), who traveled to China in 520 and founded the school of Ch'an Buddhism, becoming first Chinese patriarch.

What Bodhidharma brought to China was the Indian concept of meditation, called *dhyāna* in Sanskrit, *Ch'an* in Chinese and *Zen* in Japanese. Since the transmission of the wordless insights of meditation through a thousand years of Indian history must, by definition, have taken place without the assistance of written scriptures or preaching, the identity and role of the twenty-eight previous Indian patriarchs must be approached with caution. It has been suggested that the later Chinese Ch'an Buddhists, striving for legitimacy of their school in the eyes of colleagues from more established sects, resurrected a line of "patriarchs" from among the names of obscure Indian monks and eventually went on to enshroud these faceless names with fanciful biographies. These Indian patriarchs reportedly transmitted one to the other the wordless secrets of *dhyāna,* thereby avoiding any need to compose *sūtras,* as did the lesser-gifted teachers of the other schools.

Although Bodhidharma clearly was an historical figure, he made no personal claims to patriarchy and indeed was distinguished more by individuality than by attempts to promulgate an orthodoxy. Arriving from India to teach meditation, he was greeted by an emperor's boasts of traditional Buddhism's stature in China. Bodhidharma scoffed and marched away, reportedly crossing the Yangtze on a reed to reach the Shao-lin monastery, where he sat in solitary meditation facing a cliff for the next nine years. This famous interview and Bodhidharma's response were the real foundation of Zen.

Bodhidharma seems to have gone essentially unnoticed by his contemporaries, and in the first record of his life—*Biographies of the High Priests,* compiled in 645—he is included simply as one of a number of devout Buddhists. He is next mentioned in *The Transmission of the Lamp,* a sourcebook of Zen

---

Bodhidharma (d. ca. 534) in a fifteenth-century portrait by a Japanese monk which catches the legendary personality of Zen's First Patriarch in a few suggestive, bold strokes.

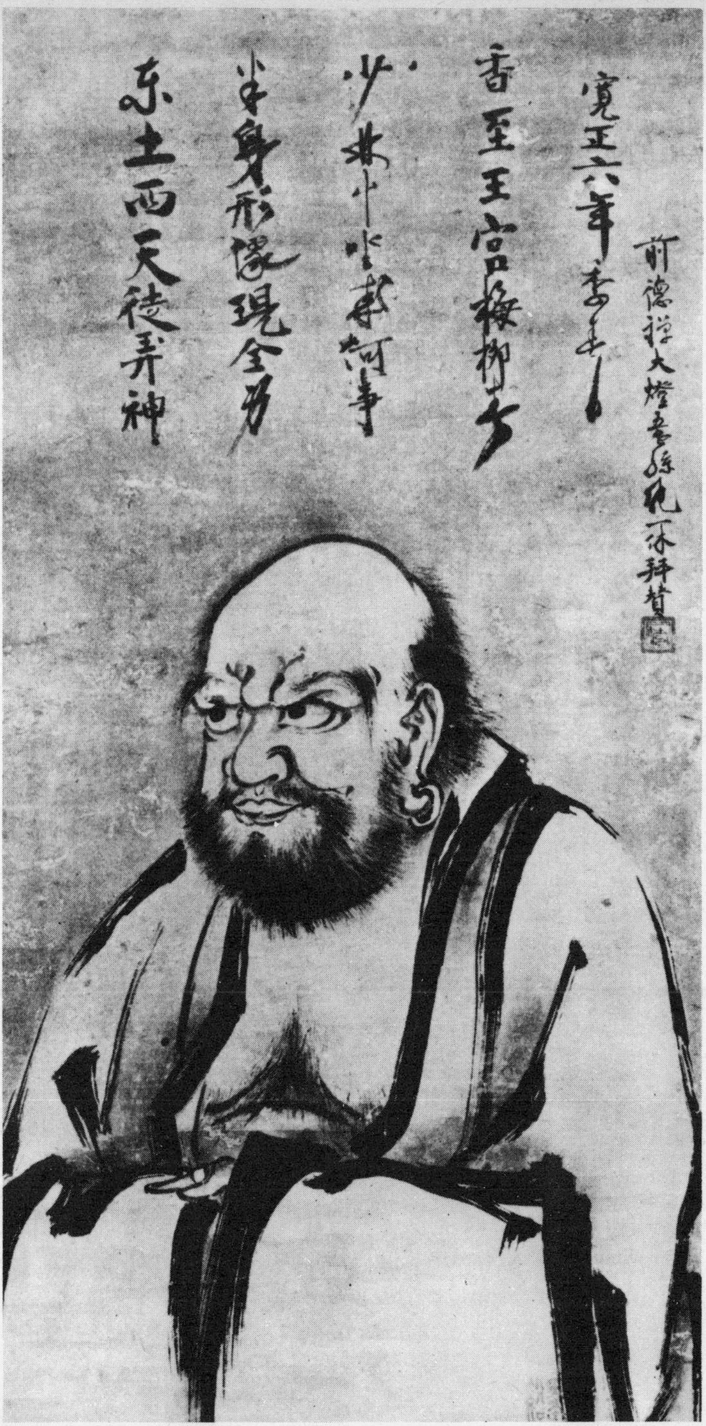

writings and records assembled in the year 1004. In point of fact, Bodhidharma, like the Buddha, seems not to have left a written account of his teachings, although two essays are extant which are variously attributed to him and which probably maintain the spirit if not necessarily the letter of his views on meditation. The most quoted passage from these works, and one which encapsulates the particular originality of Bodhidharma, is his praise of meditation, or *pi-kuan*, literally "wall gazing." This term supposedly refers to the legendary nine years of gazing at a cliff which has become part of the Bodhidharma story, but it also may be taken as a metaphor for staring at the impediment that reason places in the path of enlightenment until at last the mind hurdles the rational faculties. His words are reported as follows:

> When one, abandoning the false and embracing the true, and in simpleness of thought abides in *pi-kuan*, one finds that there is neither selfhood nor otherness. . . . He will not then be guided by any literary instructions, for he is in silent communication with the principle itself, free from conceptual discrimination, for he is serene and not-acting.[1]

This emphasis on meditation and the denial of reason formed the philosophical basis for the new Chinese school of Ch'an. By returning to first principles, it was a denial of all the metaphysical baggage with which Mahāyāna Buddhism had burdened itself over the centuries, and naturally enough there was immediate opposition from the more established sects. One of Bodhidharma's first and most ardent followers was Hui-k'o (487–593), who, according to *The Transmission of the Lamp*, waited in vain in the snows outside Shao-lin monastery, hoping to receive an audience with Bodhidharma, until at last, in desperation, he cut off his arm to attract the Master's notice. Some years later, when Bodhidharma was preparing to leave China, he left this pupil his copy of the *Lankāvatāra Sūtra* and bade him continue the teachings of meditation. Today the one-armed Hui-k'o is remembered as the Second Patriarch of Ch'an.

It seems odd that one who scorned literary instruction should have placed such emphasis on a *sūtra*, but on careful reading the *Lankāvatāra*, a Sanskrit text from the first century, proves to be a cogent summary of early Ch'an teachings on the function of the counter mind. According to this *sūtra*,

> Transcendental intelligence rises when the intellectual mind reaches its limit and, if things are to be realized in their true and essence nature, its processes of mentation . . . must be transcended by an appeal to some higher faculty of cognition. There is such a faculty in the intuitive mind, which as we have seen is the link between the intellectual mind and the Universal Mind.[2]

Regarding the achievement of self-realization by meditation, the *sūtra* states,

> [Disciples] may think they can expedite the attainment of their goal of tranquilisation by entirely suppressing the activities of the mind system. This is a mistake . . . the goal of tranquilisation is to be reached not by suppressing all mind activity but by getting rid of discriminations and attachments. . . .[3]

This text, together with the Taoist ideas of the T'ang Chinese, became the philosophical basis for early Ch'an. Indeed, traditional Zen owes much of its lighthearted irreverence to the early Taoists, who combined their love of nature with a wholesome disregard for stuffy philosophical pronouncements, whether from scholarly Confucianists or Indian *sūtras*.

The Taoists were also enemies of attachments, as exemplified by an admonition of the famous Chuang Tzŭ, the fourth-century B.C. Taoist thinker who established much of the philosophical basis for this uniquely Chinese outlook toward life:

> Do not be an embodier of fame; do not be a storehouse of schemes; do not be an undertaker of projects; do not be a proprietor of wisdom. . . . Be empty, that is all. The Perfect Man uses his mind like a mirror—going after nothing, welcoming nothing, responding but not storing.[4]

Bodhidharma, practitioner of "wall-gazing" meditation, probably knew nothing of Taoism, but he seems to have sensed correctly that China would provide a home for his Buddhism of nonattachment. The Chinese of the T'ang era (618–907) did indeed find in his teachings a system remarkably congenial to their own thousand-year-old philosophy of *tao*, or The Way. Even the practice of *dhyāna*, or meditation, resembled in a sense the Chinese tradition of the ascetic, solitary hermit, musing on the essence of nature in a remote mountain retreat. Whether Ch'an was really Buddhism masquerading as Taoism or Taoism disguised as Buddhism has never been fully established: it contains elements of both. But it was the first genuine merging of Chinese and Indian thought, combining the Indian ideas of meditation and nonattachment with the Chinese practice of nature reverence and nature mysticism (something fundamentally foreign to the great body of Indian philosophy, either Hindu or Buddhist).

The Third Patriarch after Bodhidharma was also a wandering mendicant teacher, but the Fourth chose to settle in a monastery. This introduction of monastic Ch'an coincided roughly with the beginning of the T'ang dynasty, and it brought about a dramatic rise in the appeal of Ch'an to the Chinese laity. It made the new faith respectable and an acceptable alternative to other sects, for in the land of Confucius, teachers who wandered the countryside begging had never elicited the respect that they enjoyed in India. Before long, the Fourth Patriarch had a following of some five hundred disciples, who constructed monastery buildings and tilled the soil in addition to meditating on the *sūtras*. The ability to combine practical activities with the quest for enlightenment became a hallmark of later Zen, accounting for much of its influence in medieval Japan.

The Fifth Patriarch, Hung-jên (605–675), continued the monastery, although at another spot, which was to be the location of an historic turning point in the history of Ch'an. Out of it was to come the Sixth Patriarch, Hui-nêng (638–713), sometimes known as the second founder of Chinese Ch'an, whose famous biographical treatise, *The Sūtra of Hui-nêng*, is revered as one of the holy books of Zen. In this memoir he tells of coming to the monastery of the Fifth Patriarch as an illiterate but precocious youth, having been spiritually awakened by happening to hear a recitation of the *Vajracchedikā Sūtra*, better known as the Diamond Sūtra. He made the mistake of revealing his brilliance and was immediately banished by the Fifth Patriarch to pounding rice, lest he embarrass the more experienced brothers and be in peril of his safety. According to his account, he lived in obscurity for many months until one day the Fifth Patriarch called an assembly and announced that the disciple who could compose a stanza which would reveal an understanding of the essence of Mind would be made the Sixth Patriarch.

All the monks assumed that the leading scholar of the monastery, Shên-hsiu, would naturally win the contest, and all resolved not to bother composing lines of their own. The story tells that Shên-hsiu struggled for four days and finally mounted his courage to write an unsigned verse on a wall corridor at midnight.

> Our body is the Bodhi-tree,
> And our mind a mirror bright.
> Carefully we wipe them hour by hour,
> And let no dust alight.[5]

This verse certainly demonstrated the concept of the mind's nonattachment to phenomena, but perhaps it showed an attachment of the mind to itself. In any case, it did not satisfy the Fifth Patriarch, who recognized its author and advised Shên-hsiu privately to submit another verse in two days. Before he had a chance, however, the illiterate Hui-nêng, between sessions of rice pounding, chanced along the hallway and asked that the verse be read to him. Upon hearing it, he dictated a stanza to be written next to it.

> There is no Bodhi-tree,
> Nor stand of a mirror bright.
> Since all is void,
> Where can the dust alight?[6]

The story says that all were amazed, and the Fifth Patriarch immediately rubbed away the stanza lest the other monks become jealous. He then summoned Hui-nêng late at night, expounded the Diamond Sūtra to him, and presented him with the robe and begging bowl of Bodhidharma—together with advice to flee south in the interest of safety.

Thus Hui-nêng became the Sixth Patriarch, began the Southern school of Ch'an, which would later be transmitted to Japan, and established the Diamond Sūtra as the faith's primary scripture. And so it was that the *Lankāvatāra Sūtra* of Bodhidharma, a rich moral and spiritual treatise, was replaced by the more easily understood Diamond Sūtra, a repetitive and self-praising document whose message is that nothing exists:

> notions of selfhood, personality, entity, and separate individuality, as really existing, are erroneous—these terms are merely figures of speech. . . . Develop a pure, lucid mind, not depending upon sound, flavor, touch, odor, or any quality . . . develop a mind which alights upon no thing whatsoever.[7]

With this *sūtra* as text, the Southern Ch'an masters turned ever farther away from intellectual inquiry, since even the mind itself does not exist. (It has even been suggested that the biography of the founder of Southern Ch'an was revised in later years to render him as unschooled and illiterate as possi-

---

Hui-nêng (638–713), Sixth Patriarch and founder of antischolastic modern Zen, in a thirteenth-century Chinese Ch'an painting (a zenki-zu, or "Zen activity picture" glorifying menial tasks) later brought to Japan as a model by Zen monks who admired its studied impulsiveness.

ble, the better to emphasize the later Ch'an's contempt for scholars and scholarship.)

By the time of Hui-nêng's death, China was basking in the cultural brilliance of the T'ang dynasty. Oddly enough, the sect of Southern Ch'an, which was at odds with the intellectual life of the T'ang, was the Buddhist sect most prospering. The T'ang became the golden age of Ch'an, producing the vast majority of great Zen thinkers as well as the classic techniques for teaching novices. Perhaps the fact that Ch'an was outside the mainstream of Chinese culture during the T'ang period contributed to the independent character of its teachers; during the later Sung dynasty, when Zen became fashionable among scholars and artists, few dynamic teachers were to be found.

The main objective of the Ch'an teachers was to inculcate a basically Taoist view of the world using a Buddhist framework. Such famous Taoists as Chuang Tzŭ had long demonstrated the irrelevance of logical inquiry into the mind through the use of absurdist stories which confounded conventional under-standing. To this the Ch'an teachers added the Buddhist teach-ing that the mind cannot understand external reality because it is itself the only reality. The hand cannot grasp itself; the eye cannot see itself; the mind cannot perceive itself. Quite obviously, no amount of logical introspection can elicit this truth; therefore the mind must abandon its pointless questing and simply float with existence, of which it is merely an un-differentiated part.

But how can such a truth be taught? Teaching ideas is the transmission of logical constructions from one mind to another, and the essence of Zen is that logical constructions are the greatest impediment to enlightenment. In answer, the Zen masters took a page from the Taoists and began using non-sense conundrums, later known as *kōan*, as well as frustrating quesion-and-answer sessions, known as *mondō*, to undermine a novice's dependence on rational thought. A new monk would be presented with an illogical question or problem by the head of a monastery, who would then monitor his response. (Exam-ples might include: Why did Bodhidharma come from the

West, that is, from India to China? Does a dog have Buddha-nature? What was your face before your mother was born?) If the novice struggled to construct a response using logical thought processes, he failed; if he intuitively and nondiscursively grasped the truth within the *kōan*, he passed.

This pass-or-fail technique differentiated Ch'an from all previous Buddhist sects; Ch'an allowed for no gradual progress upward in the spiritual hierarchy through the mastery of rituals. In the early days of the T'ang dynasty, when the number of initiates was small, the great masters of Ch'an directly tested the nonrational understanding of novices; in the later years of the Sung dynasty it was necessary to develop a more impersonal procedure, such as handing out the same *kōan* to a number of novices during a lecture. The more effective exchanges between the old T'ang masters and their pupils began to be reused by later teachers in the Sung, who had neither the genius to create new challenges for their novices nor the time to tailor-make a special problem for each new face appearing at the monastery. Out of this there was gradually canonized what are now the classic *kōan* of Zen. Late in the T'ang and early in the Sung period the *kōan* themselves began to be written down and used as the scriptures, resulting in a catalog said to number around seventeen hundred today. The *kōan* is a uniquely Zen creation, a brilliant technique developed by the T'ang masters for transmitting a religion which revered no scriptures and had no god. It appears nowhere else in the vast literature of world mysticism.

Several of the greatest masters of the T'ang developed their own schools of Ch'an, and the two most successful—the Lin-chi (Japanese Rinzai) and the Ts'ao-tung (Japanese Sōtō)—were later transmitted to Japan. The Rinzai school pursued a technique of "sudden" enlightenment; the Sōtō school, "gradual" enlightenment. These terms can be misleading, however, for sudden enlightenment may require more time than gradual. The gradual school taught that by sitting in meditation (Japanese *zazen*) for long periods of time—kept awake by thrashings if necessary—one's mind slowly acquires a detachment from the world of false reality perceived by one's discriminating senses and thus achieves enlightenment. It is a slow, cumulative process. By contrast, the sudden school de-emphasizes *zazen* in favor of study of *kōan*. The student struggles with *kōan*, building up a kind of hopeless tension which may last for years, until at last his logical processes suddenly short-circuit and he attains enlightenment. Practitioners of the sudden school also use shouts and beatings to jolt novices out of their linear, sequential thought patterns. Students of the gradual school are also invited to study *kōan*, and those in the sudden school are encouraged to practice *zazen*, but each school believes its own approach is best.

Although the latter T'ang era saw the persecution of Buddhism in China, with the coming of the Sung dynasty, Ch'an basked in the official encouragement of the court. The *kōan* of T'ang masters were compiled and studied, while the *sūtras* of orthodox Buddhism suffered from neglect. But the real future of Ch'an Buddhism was to lie with the Japanese. In the latter part of the twelfth century a Japanese Tendai monk named Eisai (1141–1215), concluding that Japanese Buddhism had become stagnant and lifeless, journeyed to China to learn the developments that had taken place during the years that Japan had isolated herself. He naturally went to a T'ien-t'ai monastery, which had been the source of so much Japanese Buddhism, but there he discovered Chinese Buddhists immersed in Ch'an. The new faith seemed a healthy answer to Japanese needs, and on a second visit he studied Ch'an until he received the seal of enlightenment. A fully accredited Zen master, he returned to Japan in 1191 to found the first Rinzai temple, on the southern island of Kyūshū.

Although his introduction of a new sect inspired the customary opposition from the Tendai monks on Mt. Hiei, the new faith challenging the usefulness of scholarship found a receptive audience among the newly emergent warrior class. Basically illiterate, the warriors often felt themselves intellectually inferior to the literary aristocracy, and they were delighted to be informed that a scholarly mind was an impediment rather than an asset in life. They also found Zen's emphasis on the quick, intuitive response agreeably in accord with their approach to armed combat. Eisai soon found himself invited to head a temple in Kyōto and later in the new warrior capital of Kamakura. Perhaps his most practical move was the composition of a treatise designed to win for Zen a place in the hearts of the nationalistic military establishment and at the same time to conciliate the Tendai monks on Mt. Hiei. In his *Propagation of Zen for the Protection of the Country* he described Zen as follows:

> In its rules of action and discipline, there is no confusion of right and wrong. . . . Outwardly it favors discipline over doctrine, inwardly it brings the Highest Inner Wisdom.[8]

Although it may seem paradoxical that a pacifist religion like Zen found immediate favor with the rough warrior class of medieval Japan, it had an obvious appeal. As Sir George Sansom has explained it,

> For a thoughtful warrior, whose life always bordered on death, there was an attraction, even a persuasion, in the belief that truth comes like the flash of a sword as it cuts through the problem of existence. Any line of religious thought that helped a man understand the nature of being without arduous literary studies was likely to attract the kind of warrior who felt that the greatest moments in life were the moments when death was nearest.[9]

The Japanese warriors were captured by the irreverent, antischolastic qualities of Rinzai, with its reliance upon anecdotal *kōan* and violent jolts of enlightenment. Thus the ruling warriors of Japan began studying *kōan*, even as the peasantry at large was chanting praises to Amida and the Lotus Sūtra.

The aristocratic priest Dōgen (1200–1253), who also left the Tendai monastery for China and returned to establish the meditative, gradual school of Sōtō Zen, is generally considered the second founder of Japanese Zen. Although he grudgingly acknowledged the usefulness of *kōan* as an aid to instruction, Dōgen considered *zazen* meditation the time-proven method of the Buddha for achieving enlightenment. For scriptural support, he preferred to go back to the earlier Hīnayāna *sūtras* for their more authentic accounts of the words of the Buddha, rather than to rely on Mahāyāna sources, which had been corrupted over the centuries by an elaborate metaphysics and polytheism. Dōgen had not originally planned to start a school of Zen but merely to popularize *zazen*, to which end he wrote a small treatise, *General Teachings for the Promotion of Zazen*, which has become a classic. This was followed a few years later by a larger, more generalized work which was to become the bible of Japanese Sōtō Zen, *Shōbōgenzō*, or *Treasury of Knowledge Regarding the True Dharma*. In this work he tried to stress the importance of *zazen* while at the same time acknowledging the usefulness of instruction and *kōan* where required.

There are two ways in which to set body and mind right: one is to hear the teaching from a master, and the other is to do pure *zazen* yourself. If you *hear* the teachings the conscious mind is put to work, whilst *zazen* embraces both training and enlightenment; in order to understand the Truth, you need both.[10]

Unlike the conciliatory Eisai, Dōgen was uncompromising in his rejection of the traditional schools of Buddhism, which he felt had strayed too far from the original teachings of Gautama. He was right, of course; the chanting, savior-oriented popular Buddhists in Japan were, as Edwin Reischauer has noted, practicing a religion far closer to European Christianity of the same period than to the faith started by the Buddha—an atheistic self-reliance aimed at finding release from all worldly attachments. Dōgen's truths did not rest well with the Buddhist establishment of his time, however, and for years he moved from temple to temple. Finally, in 1236, he managed to start a temple of his own, and gradually he became one of the most revered religious teachers in Japanese history. As his reputation grew, the military leaders invited him to visit them and teach, but he would have no part of their life. Possibly as a result of Dōgen's attitude, Sōtō Zen never became associated with the warrior class, but remained the Zen of the common people. Today Sōtō (with approximately six and a half million followers) is the more popular version of Zen, whereas Rinzai (with something over two million followers) is the Zen of those interested in theological daring and intellectual challenge.

Historically a religion at odds with the establishment—from Bodhidharma to the eccentric T'ang masters—Zen in Japan found itself suddenly the religion of the ruling class. The result was a Zen impact in Japan far greater than any influence Ch'an ever realized in China.

CHAPTER 5

Zen Archery and Swordsmanship

(THE KAMAKURA ERA—1185–1333)

The anti-scholasticism, the mental discipline—still more the strict physical discipline of the adherents of Zen, which kept their lives very close to nature—all appealed to the warrior caste. . . . Zen contributed much to the development of a toughness of inner fiber and a strength of character which typified the warrior of feudal Japan. . . .

Edwin Reischauer, *Japan: Past and Present*

THE BEGINNINGS of the Zen era are about the middle of the twelfth century, when the centuries-long Heian miracle of peace came to an end. The Japanese aristocracy had ruled the land for hundreds of years practically without drawing a sword, using diplomatic suasion so skillful that Heian was probably the only capital city in the medieval world entirely without fortifications. This had been possible partly because of the ruling class's willingness to let taxable lands slip from their control—into the hands of powerful provincial leaders and rich monasteries— rather than start a quarrel. For occasions when force was required, they delegated the responsibility to two powerful military clans, the Taira and the Minamoto, who roamed the land to collect taxes, quell uprisings, and not incidentally to forge allegiances with provincial chieftains. The Taira were in charge of the western and central provinces around Kyōto, while the Minamoto dominated the frontier eastern provinces, in the region one day to hold the warrior capital of Kamakura. The astounding longevity of their rule was a tribute to the aristocrats' skill in playing off these two powerful families against each other, but by the middle of the twelfth century they found themselves at the mercy of their bellicose agents, awakening one day to discover ruffians in the streets of Kyōto as brigands and armed monks invaded the city to burn and pillage.

The real downfall of the *ancien régime* began in the year 1156, when a dispute arose between the reigning emperor and a retired sovereign simultaneously with a disagreement among the aristocracy regarding patronage. Both sides turned to the warriors for support—a formula that proved to be extremely unwise. The result was a feud between the Taira and Minamoto, culminating in a civil war (the Gempei War) that lasted five years, produced bloodshed on a scale previously unknown in Japan, and ended in victory for the Minamoto. A chieftain named Minamoto Yoritomo emerged as head of a unified state and leader of a government whose power to command was beyond question. Since Yoritomo's position had no precedent, he invented for himself the title of shōgun. He also moved the government from Kyōto to his military headquarters at Kamakura and proceeded to lay the groundwork for what would be almost seven hundred years of unbroken warrior rule.

The form of government Yoritomo instituted is generally, if somewhat inaccurately, described as feudalism. The provincial warrior families managed estates worked by peasants whose role was similar to that of the European serfs of the same period. The estate-owning barons were mounted warriors, new figures in Japanese history, who protected their lands and their family honor much as did the medieval European knights. But instead of glorifying chivalry and maidenly honor, they respected the rules of battle and noble death. Among the fiercest fighters the world has seen, they were masters of personal combat, horsemanship, archery, and the way of the sword. Their principles were fearlessness, loyalty, honor, personal integrity, and contempt for material wealth. They became known as *samurai*, and they were the men whose swords were ruled by Zen.

Battle for the *samurai* was a ritual of personal and family honor. When two opposing sides confronted one another in the field, the mounted *samurai* would first discharge the twenty to thirty arrows at their disposal and then call out their family names in hopes of eliciting foes of similarly distinguished lineage. Two warriors would then charge one another brandishing their long swords until one was dismounted, whereupon hand-to-hand combat with short knives commenced. The loser's head was taken as a trophy, since headgear proclaimed family and rank. To die a noble death in battle at the hands of a worthy foe brought no dishonor to one's family, and cowardice in the face of death seems to have been as rare as it was humiliating. Frugality among these Zen-inspired warriors was as much admired as the soft living of aristocrats and merchants was scorned; and life itself was cheap, with warriors ever ready to commit ritual suicide (called *seppuku* or *harakiri*) to preserve their honor or to register social protest.

Yoritomo was at the height of his power when he was killed accidentally in a riding mishap. Having murdered all the competent members of his family, lest they prove rivals, he left no line except two ineffectual sons, neither of whom was worthy to govern. The power vacuum was filled by his in-laws of the Hōjō clan, who very shortly eliminated all the remaining members of the Minamoto ruling family and assumed power. Not wishing to appear outright usurpers of the office of shōgun, they invented a position known as regent, through which they manipulated a hand-picked shōgun, who in turn manipulated a powerless emperor. It was an example of indirect rule at its most ingenious.

Having skillfully removed the Minamoto family from ruling circles, the Hōjō Regency governed Japan for over a hundred years, during which time Zen became the most influential reli-

gion in the land. It was also during this time that Zen played
an important role in saving Japan from what was possibly the
greatest threat to its survival up to that time: the invasion attempts of Kublai Khan. In 1268 the Great Khan, whose Mongol armies were in the process of sacking China, sent envoys to
Japan recommending tribute. The Kyōto court was terrified, but
not the Kamakura warriors, who sent the Mongols back empty-
handed. The sequence was repeated four years later, although
this time the Japanese knew it would mean war. As expected, in
1274 an invasion fleet of Mongols sailed from Korea, but after
inconclusive fighting on a southern beachhead of Kyūshū, a
timely storm blew the invaders out to sea and inflicted enough
losses to derail the project. The Japanese had, however, learned
a sobering lesson about their military preparedness. In the century of internal peace between the Gempei War and the Mongol landing, Japanese fighting men had let their skills atrophy.
Not only were their formalized ideas about honorable hand-to-
hand combat totally inappropriate to the tight formations and
powerful crossbows of the Asian armies (a *samurai* would ride
out, announce his lineage, and immediately be cut down by a
volley of Mongol arrows), the Japanese warriors had lost much
of their moral fiber. To correct both these faults the Zen monks
who served as advisers to the Hōjō insisted that military training, particularly archery and swordsmanship, be formalized,
using the techniques of Zen discipline. A system of training
was hastily begun in which the *samurai* were conditioned psychologically as well as physically for battle. It proved so successful that it became a permanent part of Japanese martial
tactics.

The Zen training was urgent, for all of Japan knew that
the Mongols would be back in strength. One of the Mongols'
major weapons had been the fear they inspired in those they
approached, but fear of death is the last concern of a *samurai*
whose mind has been disciplined by Zen exercises. Thus the
Mongols were robbed of their most potent offensive weapon,
a point driven home when a group of Mongol envoys appear-

ing after the first invasion to proffer terms were summarily be-
headed.

Along with the Zen military training, the Japanese placed
the entire country on a wartime footing, with every able-
bodied man engaged in constructing shoreline fortifications. As
expected, in the early summer of 1281 the Khan launched an
invasion force thought to have numbered well over 100,000
men, using vessels constructed by Korean labor. When they
began landing in southern Kyūshū, the *samurai* were there and
ready, delighted at the prospect of putting to use on a common
adversary the military skills they had evolved over the decades
through slaughtering one another. They harassed the Mongol
fleet from small vessels, while on shore they faced the invaders
man for man, never allowing their line to break. For seven
weeks they stood firm, and then it was August, the typhoon
month. One evening, the skies darkened ominously in the south
and the winds began to rise, but before the fleet could with-
draw the typhoon struck.

In two days the armada of Kublai Khan was obliterated,
leaving hapless onshore advance parties to be cut to ribbons
by the *samurai*. Thus did the Zen warriors defeat one of the
largest naval expeditions in world history, and in commemora-
tion the grateful emperor named the typhoon the Divine Wind,
Kamikaze.

The symbols of the Zen *samurai* were the sword and the
bow. The sword in particular was identified with the noblest
impulses of the individual, a role strengthened by its historic
place as one of the emblems of the divinity of the emperor,
reaching back into pre-Buddhist centuries. A *samurai*'s sword
was believed to possess a spirit of its own, and when he experienced disappointment in battle he might go to a shrine to
pray for the spirit's return. Not surprisingly, the swordsmith
was an almost priestly figure, who, after ritual purification,
went about his task clad in white robes. The ritual surrounding
swordmaking had a practical as well as a spiritual purpose; it
enabled the early Japanese to preserve the highly complex

formulas required to forge special steel. Their formulas were carefully guarded, and justifiably so: not until the past century did the West produce comparable metal. Indeed, the metal in medieval Japanese swords has been favorably compared with the finest modern armorplate.

The secret of these early swords lay in the ingenious method developed for producing a metal both hard and brittle enough to hold its edge and yet sufficiently soft and pliable not to snap under stress. The procedure consisted of hammering together a laminated sandwich of steels of varying hardness, heating it, and then folding it over again and again until it consisted of many thousands of layers. If a truly first-rate sword was required, the interior core was made of a sandwich of soft metals, and the outer shell fashioned from varying grades of harder steel. The blade was then heated repeatedly and plunged into water to toughen the skin. Finally, all portions save the cutting edge were coated with clay and the blade heated to a very precise temperature, whereupon it was again plunged into water of a special temperature for just long enough to freeze the edge but not the interior core, which was then allowed to cool slowly and maintain its flexibility. The precise temperatures of blade and water were closely guarded secrets, and at least one visitor to a master swordsmith's works who sneaked a finger into the water to discover its temperature found his hand suddenly chopped off in an early test of the sword.

The result of these techniques was a sword whose razor-sharp edge could repeatedly cut through armor without dulling, but whose interior was soft enough that it rarely broke. The sword of the *samurai* was the equivalent of a two-handed straight razor, allowing an experienced warrior to carve a man into slices with consummate ease. Little wonder the Chinese and other Asians were willing to pay extravagant prices in later years for these exquisite instruments of death. Little wonder, too, that the *samurai* worshiped his sidearm to the point where he would rather lose his life than his sword.

Yet a sword alone did not a *samurai* make. A classic Zen anecdote may serve to illustrate the Zen approach to swordsmanship. It is told that a young man journeyed to visit a famous Zen swordmaster and asked to be taken as a pupil, indicating a desire to work hard and thereby reduce the time needed for training. Toward the end of his interview he asked about the length of time which might be required, and the master replied that it would probably be at least ten years. Dismayed, the young novice offered to work diligently night and day and inquired how this extra effort might affect the time required. "In that case," the master replied, "it will require thirty years." With a sense of increasing alarm, the young man then offered to devote all his energies and every single moment to studying the sword. "Then it will take seventy years," replied the master. The young man was speechless, but finally agreed to give his life over to the master. For the first three years, he never saw a sword but was put to work hulling rice and practicing Zen meditation. Then one day the master crept up behind his pupil and gave him a solid whack with a wooden sword. Thereafter he would be attacked daily by the master whenever his back was turned. As a result, his senses gradually sharpened until he was on guard every moment, ready to dodge instinctively. When the master saw that his student's body was alert to everything around it and oblivious of all irrelevant thoughts and desires, training began.

Instinctive action is the key to Zen swordsmanship. The Zen fighter does not logically think out his moves; his body acts without recourse to logical planning. This gives him a precious advantage over an opponent who must think through his actions and then translate this logical plan into the movement of arm and sword. The same principles that govern the Zen approach to understanding inner reality through transcending the analytical faculties are used by the swordsman to circumvent the time-consuming process of thinking through every move. To this technique Zen swordsmen add another vital element, the complete identification of the warrior with his weapon. The sense of duality between man and steel is erased by Zen training, leaving a single fighting instrument. The *samurai* never has a sense that his arm, part of himself, is holding a sword, which is a separate entity. Rather, sword, arm, body, and mind become one. As explained by the Zen scholar D. T. Suzuki:

> When the sword is in the hands of a technician-swordsman skilled in its use, it is no more than an instrument with no mind of its own. What it does is done mechanically, and there is no [nonintellection] discernible in it. But when the sword is held by the swordsman whose spiritual attainment is such that he holds it as though not holding it, it is identified with the man himself, it acquires a soul, it moves with all the subtleties which have been imbedded in him as a swordsman. The man emptied of all thoughts, all emotions originating from fear, all sense of insecurity, all desire to win, is not conscious of using the sword; both man and sword turn into instruments in the hands, as it were, of the unconscious. . . .[1]

Zen training also renders the warrior free from troubling frailties of the mind, such as fear and rash ambition—qualities lethal in mortal combat. He is focused entirely on his opponent's openings, and when an opportunity to strike presents itself, he requires no deliberation: his sword and body act automatically. The discipline of meditation and the mind-dissolving paradoxes of the *kōan* become instruments to forge a fearless, automatic, mindless instrument of steel-tipped death.

The methods developed by Zen masters for teaching archery differ significantly from those used for the sword. Whereas swordsmanship demands that man and weapon merge with no acknowledgment of one's opponent until the critical moment, archery requires the man to become detached from his weapon and to concentrate entirely upon the target. Proper technique is learned, of course, but the ultimate aim is to forget technique, forget the bow, forget the draw, and give one's concentration entirely to the target. Yet here too there is a difference between Zen archery and Western techniques: the Zen archer gives no direct thought to hitting the target. He does not strain for accuracy, but rather lets accuracy come as a result of intuitively applying perfect form.

Before attempting to unravel this seeming paradox, the equipment of the Japanese archer should be examined. The Japanese bow differs from the Western bow in having the hand grip approximately one-third of the distance from the bottom, rather than in the middle. This permits a standing archer (or a kneeling one, for that matter) to make use of a bow longer than he is tall (almost eight feet, in fact), since the upper part may extend well above his head. The bottom half of the bow is scaled to human proportions, while the upper tip extends far over the head in a sweeping arch. It is thus a combination of the conventional bow and the English longbow, requiring a draw well behind the ear. This bow is unique to Japan, and in its engineering principles it surpasses anything seen in the West until comparatively recent times. It is a laminated composite of supple bamboo and the brittle wood of the wax tree. The heart of the bow is made up of three squares of bamboo sandwiched between two half-moon sections of bamboo which comprise the belly (that side facing the inside of the curve) and the back (the side away from the archer). Filling out the edges of the sandwich are two strips of wax-tree wood. The elimination of the deadwood center of the bow, which is replaced by the three strips of bamboo and two of waxwood, produces a composite at once powerful and light. The arrows too are of bamboo, an almost perfect material for the purpose, and they differ from Western arrows only in being lighter and longer. Finally, the Japanese bowstring is loosed with the thumb rather than the fingers, again a departure from Western practice.

If the equipment differs from that of the West, the technique, which verges on ritual, differs far more. The first Zen archery lesson is proper breath control, which requires techniques learned from meditation. Proper breathing conditions the mind in archery as it does in *zazen* and is essential in developing a quiet mind, a restful spirit, and full concentration. Controlled breathing also constantly reminds the archer that his is a religious activity, a ritual related to his spiritual character as much as to the more prosaic concern of hitting the target. Breathing is equally essential in drawing the bow, for the arrow is held out away from the body, calling on muscles much

less developed than those required by the Western draw. A breath is taken with every separate movement of the draw, and gradually a rhythm settles in which gives the archer's movements a fluid grace and the ritual cadence of a dance.

Only after the ritual mastery of the powerful bow has been realized does the archer turn his attention to loosing the arrows (not, it should be noted, to hitting the target). The same use of breathing applies, the goal being for the release of the arrow to come out of spontaneous intuition, like the swordsman's attack. The release of the arrow should dissolve a kind of spiritual tension, like the resolution of a *kōan*, and it must seem to occur of itself, without deliberation, almost as though it were independent of the hand. This is possible because the archer's mind is totally unaware of his actions; it is focused, indeed riveted in concentration, on the target. This is not done through aiming, although the archer does aim—intuitively. Rather, the archer's spirit must be burned into the target, be at one with it, so that the arrow is guided by the mind and the shot of the bow becomes merely an intervening, inconsequential necessity. All physical actions—the stance, the breathing, the draw, the release—are as natural and require as little conscious thought as a heartbeat; the arrow is guided by the intense concentration of the mind on its goal.

Thus it was that the martial arts of Japan were the first to benefit from Zen precepts, a fact as ironic as it is astounding. Yet meditation and combat are akin in that both require rigorous self-discipline and the denial of the mind's overt functions. From its beginning as an aid in the arts of death, Zen soon became the guiding principle for quite another form of art. In years to come, Zen would be the official state religion, shōguns would become Zen patrons *extraordinaire*, and a totally Zen culture would rule Japan.

A Zen monk, who has mastered the oversized Japanese bow so that its mechanics live in him, freeing his mind from distractions and allowing it to merge with the target.

Part II

THE AGE OF HIGH CULTURE: ASHIKAGA (1333-1573)

CHAPTER 6
The Great Age of Zen

For we are lovers of the beautiful, yet simple in our tastes, and we cultivate the mind without loss of manliness.

Pericles, ca. 430 B.C.

THE MEDIEVAL FLOWERING of Zen culture might be described as the Periclean age of Japan. As with fifth-century Greece, this was the era that produced Japan's finest classical art at the same time that rampant plagues and internecine warfare bled the land as never before. Government, such as it was, rested in the hands of the Ashikaga clan, men ever ready to sacrifice the general good in furtherance of personal interests. That these interests happened to include Zen and the Zen arts probably brought scant solace to their subjects, but today we can weigh their selfishness against the culture they sponsored. In any case, all who admire the classic Zen cultural forms should be aware that their price included the heartless taxation of and disregard for the entire peasant population of medieval Japan.

The historical backdrop for the Ashikaga era reads like a Jacobean tragedy peopled by cutthroat courtiers ever alert to advantage in chambers or in battle. The political shape of the Ashikaga era began to emerge in the early years of the fourteenth century as the once invincible Kamakura rule of the Hōjō family dissolved, plunging Japan into a half-century of war and feuding over the identity of the rightful emperor. Throughout much of the century the provincial *daimyō* warlords and their *samurai* soldiers warred up and down the length of the land, supporting first one emperor, then another. It was during this time and the two centuries following that Zen became the official state religion and Zen monks served as foreign diplomats, domestic advisers, and arbiters of taste.

The political troubles that ended the Kamakura warrior government and unseated the Hōjō seem to be traceable to the war against the Mongols. It was a long and costly operation which left most of the *samurai* impoverished and angered at a government that could give them only cheerful thanks rather than the lands of the vanquished as was traditional medieval practice. The general discontent found a focus in the third decade of the fourteenth century when a Kyōto emperor named Godaigo attempted to unseat the Hōjō and re-establish genuine imperial rule. After some minor skirmishes, the Hōjō commissioned an able general named Ashikaga Takauji (1305–1358) from an old Minamoto family to march on Godaigo and settle the difficulty. Along the way Takauji must have thought things over, for when he reached Kyōto instead of attacking the emperor's forces he put the Hōjō garrison to the sword. Shortly thereafter, another general supporting the imperial cause marched out to Kamakura and laid waste the Hōjō capital. The last few hundred Hōjō supporters committed suicide en masse, and the Kamakura age was ended.

Godaigo gleefully set up the new Japanese government in Kyōto, and soon it was like old times, with aristocrats running everything. In a serious miscalculation, he assumed that the provincial warlords had joined his cause out of personal loyalty rather than the more traditional motive of greed, for he gave the Hōjō estates to his favorite mistresses while regarding warriors like Takauji as hardly more than rustic figures of fun. As might have been expected, another war soon broke out. This time the conflict lasted for decades, with almost unbelievable convolutions, including a number of decades in which Japan had two emperors. At one point Takauji found it necessary to poison his own brother, and it has been estimated that his military exploits cost some sixty thousand lives, not to mention the general ruin of the country at large. The end result was that the forces of Godaigo were defeated, leaving Japan in the hands of the Ashikaga family.

For all his bloodletting, Takuji was also a patron of the Zen sect, giving it a formal place in the national life and encouraging its growth and dissemination. One of his closest advisers was the great Zen prelate Musō Soseki (1275–1351), whose influence made Rinzai Zen the official religion of the Ashikaga era. An astutely practical man, Musō established the precedent for doctrinal flexibility which allowed Zen to survive while emperors and shōguns came and went:

> Clear-sighted masters of the Zen sect do not have a fixed doctrine which is to be held to at any and all times. They offer whatever teaching the occasion demands and preach as the spirit moves them, with no fixed course to guide them. If asked what Zen is, they may answer in the words of Confucius, Mencius, Lao Tzŭ or Chuang Tzŭ, or else in terms of the doctrines of the various sects and denominations, and also by using popular proverbs.[1]

Like many Zen teachers, Musō enjoyed the company of the powerful. He began his career in statecraft as a supporter and confidant of the ill-fated Emperor Godaigo. When Godaigo was deposed, he adjusted his allegiance and became the high priest of the Ashikaga house. He was soon the constant companion of Takauji, advising him on policy, flattering his taste in Zen art, and secretly trying to give him a bit of polish. Although Takauji could scarcely have had time for extensive meditation amid his continual bloodletting, Musō preached to him in odd moments and soothed his occasionally guilty conscience.

Since Takauji was clearly haunted by his treatment of Godaigo, Musō suggested that the former emperor's ghost might find repose if a special Zen temple was built in his memory. The project was well underway when funds ran low, whereupon the resourceful Musō suggested sending a trading vessel to China to raise foreign-exchange cash. The venture was so successful that before long regular trade was established— naturally enough under the guidance of Zen monks. In later years a special branch of government was established devoted exclusively to foreign trade and directed by well-traveled prelates of Zen. (The Chinese regarded this trade as the exchange of Chinese gifts for Japanese tribute, but the Japanese were willing to overlook the insult in the interest of profit.) Musō's other lasting contribution to the growth of Zen influence was persuading Takauji to build a Zen temple in each of the sixty-six provinces, thereby extending state support of the religion outside of Kyōto ruling circles.

Takauji was the founder of a line of Ashikaga shōguns who gave their name to the next two centuries of Japanese history. His entire life was spent on the battlefield, where he concentrated his energies on strengthening the shōgunate through the liberal application of armed might. In a sense he prefigured the attitude of John Adams, who once lamented that he must study war so that his grandsons might fashion art and architecture. Indeed, Takauji's grandson was the famous aesthete Ashikaga Yoshimitsu (1358–1408), who ascended to shōgun in 1368 and soon thereafter brought to flower a renaissance of the Zen artistic tradition of Sung China.

Yoshimitsu was only nine years of age when he became shōgun, so the early years of his reign were guided by regents of the Hosokawa clan, who put to rest any remaining dissidence. Consequently, when Yoshimitsu came of age, he felt secure enough in his office to tour the country, visiting religious shrines and establishing his place in the pageant of Japanese history. More significantly for the rise of Zen culture, he also turned his eyes abroad, encouraging the trade with China by stabilizing political relations and becoming the best customer for the silks, brocades, porcelains, and—most important—Sung paintings brought back by the Zen monks.

In a very short time, Yoshimitsu had become addicted to the Chinese finery and antique Ch'an art of the Sung which his monks were importing. He was fortunate that the country was stable and peaceful enough to allow him his whims, especially since he almost entirely lost interest in all functions of government save taxation, which he found necessary to apply to the peasants in ever greater measure in order to support his patronage of the arts. Absorbed with aesthetics and Zen art, he became a cloistered sovereign whose luckless subjects were left on their own to weather fortunes that alternated between starvation and the plague, leavened by intermittent wars among provincial chieftains. The peasantry, however, was not blind to his callous priorities, and it is said that his reputation survived into the nineteenth century, maintained by country folk who would trek to a certain temple to revile an old statue of the Ashikaga shōgun.

His personal failings notwithstanding, Yoshimitsu was the key figure in bringing about the rise of Zen art. His contributions were manifold: he founded a Zen monastery which became the school for the great landscape painters of the era; his personal patronage was largely responsible for the development of the Nō drama; his example and encouragement did much to bring into being the identification of Zen with landscape garden art; his own practice of *zazen* under the guidance of a famous Zen monk set an example for the warrior court; his interest in tea and poetry served both to set the stage for the development of the tea ceremony as an aesthetic phenomenon and to temper the literary tastes of his warrior followers; and, finally, his interest in Zen-inspired architecture was responsible for the creation of one of the most famous Zen chapels in Japan.

When Yoshimitsu retired in 1394 to enter Zen orders, leaving the government to his nine-year-old son, he ensconced himself in a palace in the Kyōto suburbs and proceeded to build a chapel for Zen meditation. The Golden Pavilion, or *Kinkaku-ji*, as it came to be known, was a wooden teahouse three stories high whose architectural beauty is now legendary.

There were few if any previous examples of this type of multistory structure, although it has been suggested that the idea may have been copied from a comparable temple in southern China. (The turn-of-the-century American critic Ernest Fenollosa suggested that it was modeled after the structure Kublai Khan constructed for a garden in Shang-tu, which Coleridge called Xanadu, after the translation of the name by Marco Polo: "In Xanadu did Kubla Khan/A stately pleasure-dome decree.") Whatever its origins, the building superficially resembled a low-rising pagoda—each successive story was a more or less smaller version of the one below. The two lower floors were used for evening entertainments of music, poetry, and incense, while the top floor was a tiny meditation chapel (whose ceiling was covered with gold leaf, thereby giving the building its name). Set in the midst of a beautiful landscape garden, the sweeping roofs, painstaking wooden joinery, and exquisite unpainted woods of the Golden Pavilion were a landmark of Zen taste destined to influence the course of Japanese architecture for centuries.

The Golden Pavilion was the crowning act of Yoshimitsu's career, a fitting monument to the man who, more than any other, was responsible for the rise of Zen culture. Under his rule, Japanese monks first brought back from China the finest examples of Ch'an-inspired art, from which they derived and mastered the artistic principles of the vanished Sung era and went on to re-create if not surpass the great Sung age of artistic production. The momentum for Zen culture produced by Yoshimitsu lasted through the reign of his grandson Yoshimasa (1435–1490), the last great Ashikaga patron of Zen art.

As a shōgun, Yoshimasa was even more distracted by Zen than his famous grandfather. He concentrated on encouraging

The Golden Pavilion of Ashikaga Yoshimitsu in a contemporary reconstruction that re-creates the combination of elegance and delicacy that made it the glory of Zen architecture.

the school of Sung-style ink painting, the Zen ritual of ceremonial tea, the art of flower arranging, and new styles of Zen-influenced architecture. Unfortunately, his apparently hereditary absence of interest in affairs of state ultimately brought about the disintegration of the Japanese political fabric. As the office of shōgun weakened to the point of symbolism, Yoshimasa's power to tax became so frail that he was finally forced to borrow from the Zen monasteries. The real power in the land passed to the local feudal lords, or *daimyō*, men who governed entire domains, raised their own armies, and exercised far greater power than the *samurai* of earlier times.

What remained of Yoshimasa's power came to be exercised by his mistresses and his scheming wife, Tomi-ko. By his late twenties he was ready to retire entirely, the better to pursue Zen and its arts, but none of the women in the palace had yet presented him with a son who could become titular shōgun. By 1464 Yoshimasa's patience was exhausted and he turned to one of his brothers who was in monastic orders and persuaded him to begin an apprenticeship for the shōgunate. The brother wisely hesitated, pointing out that Tomi-ko, who was still in her twenties, might yet produce a son; but Yoshimasa won him over with solemn assurances that all sons who arrived would be made priests.

Less than a year later Tomi-ko did indeed bear a son, setting the stage for the struggle that would eventually destroy Kyōto and signal the decline of the Ashikaga age of Zen culture. As it happened, there was already an animosity between Yoshimasa's principal adviser, Hosokawa Katsumoto, and Hosokawa's father-in-law, Yamana Sōzen. When the child was born, Hosokawa, a member of the historic family of Ashikaga regents, favored retaining Yoshimasa's brother as shōgun, so the ambitious Tomi-ko turned to Yamana to enlist his aid in reverting the office of shōgun back to Yoshimasa and thence to her son. With a natural excuse for conflict finally at hand, the two old enemies Yamana and Hosokawa gathered their armies— both numbering near eighty thousand—outside Kyōto. The impending tragedy was obvious to all, and Yoshimasa tried vainly to discourage the combatants. By that time, however, his voice counted for nothing, and in 1467 the inevitable conflict, now known as the Ōnin War, began.

The war raged for a decade, until virtually all the majestic temples of Kyōto were burned and pillaged. Ironically, one of the few temples to escape destruction was Yoshimitsu's Golden Pavilion, which fortunately had been situated well outside the precincts of the main city. Although both Hosokawa and Yamana died in 1473, the fighting continued, as participants on both sides defected, changed leaders, and fought among themselves until no one could recall what the original war had been about. Finally, after ten full years of almost constant fighting, it became apparent that the carnage had accomplished nothing. One dark night the two armies folded their tents and stole away—and the war was no more. A remarkably senseless conflict, even by modern-day standards, the Ōnin War effectively obliterated all evidence in Kyōto of the marvelous Heian civilization, as well as the early Ashikaga, leaving nothing but a scorched palette for the final century of Zen art.

Yoshimasa, in the meantime, had long since removed himself from affairs of state. Since his shōgun brother had switched sides during the war and become a general for Yamana, the succession question was simplified. Tomi-ko took time out from her vigorous war-profiteering to prevail upon Yoshimasa to appoint her son, then four years old, shōgun. She thereby became de facto shōgun herself, encouraging Yoshimasa in his desire to retire while enriching herself handsomely with imaginative new taxes. The war proved a windfall for Tomi-ko, who lent funds to both sides to keep it going, and her cupidity played no small role in the final destruction of ancient Kyōto.

Immersed as he was in the world of Zen and Zen culture, Yoshimasa seemed oblivious to the sea of official corruption around him, and indeed there was probably little he could have done to prevent it. He loved the refined company of women and avoided warriors, whose rough manner offended him but in whose hands lay the only real power in the country. As the government disintegrated, he made his own contribution as a connoisseur and patron of the fine arts, bringing to culmination the movement in Zen art that left Japan a legacy far more lasting than any that mere diplomacy could have left. Like his European counterparts, the Medici, Yoshimasa balanced his failings in politics with faultless aesthetic judgment, endowing the Zen arts with new standards in architecture, painting, gardening, the Nō theater, the tea ceremony, and ceremonial flower arranging. Perhaps he should not be faulted for doing what he understood best.

Yoshimasa also left a physical monument intended to rival the Golden Pavilion. In 1466, as he contemplated retirement, he began plans to construct a villa for meditation. With the outbreak of war he was forced for a number of years· to devote his attentions to the repair of the imperial residence, but after the war he renewed his intentions to retire into Zen aesthetics. His decision was strengthened by family troubles, including Tomi-ko's displeasure with the number of his mistresses, a problem that finally exploded when her young son, the shōgun, demanded to marry one of them rather than a girl of Tomi-ko's choosing. In 1482, amid the general ruin and confusion, Yoshimasa resolved to begin the construction of his retirement villa. Financial circumstances had changed since his original plan eighteen years earlier, and his interest in Zen was even deeper, so instead of the sumptuous palace once planned, he built a small pavilion of exquisite taste and restraint. It stands today, a forerunner of the traditional house, and is known as the Silver Pavilion, or *Ginkaku-ji*, because of the popular belief that he originally planned to cover portions with silver leaf. *Ginkaku-ji* has two stories, the first in Zen temple style and the second in *shoin* style. The deliberately unpainted wood exterior of the two-story chapel has weathered to the color of bark, and it has all the dignity its five hundred years demand.

There were almost a dozen Ashikaga shōguns after Yoshimasa, but none had any influence on the course of history. The century after his retirement is known as the Age of the Country at War, and it is remembered for almost continuous civil strife among *daiymō*, the provincial chieftains who had swallowed up the *samurai*. In this period Japan was less a nation than several hundred small fiefdoms, each controlled by a powerful family and constantly in arms against its neighbors. Little wonder that many of the greatest Zen artists left Kyōto never to return; the capital was a desolate ruin, without power and without patrons. This condition prevailed until late in the six-

The Silver Pavilion of Ashikaga Yoshimasa, built in 1482, which combined Chinese Ch'an-influenced design elements with the Japanese preference for natural materials to become a forerunner of the Zen-inspired traditional Japanese house.

teenth century, when individuals of sufficient military genius to reunite the country again appeared.

The influence of Zen was probably as pervasive in medieval Ashikaga Japan as Christianity was in medieval Europe. A Zen monk was the first Ashikaga shōgun's closest adviser, and in later years Zen monasteries virtually took over foreign policy. (Indeed, Zen monks were the only Japanese educated enough to deal with the Chinese.) Yoshimitsu formalized the relationship between Zen and the state, setting up an official hierarchy among the Zen temples in Kyōto (the so-called "Five Mountains" or *Gozan*, of Tenryū-ji, Shōkoku-ji, Kennin-ji, Tōfuku-ji, and Manju-ji). These state temples became the resident schools for Zen painters and artists and also provided diplomats and government officials for the China trade. (They made Yoshimitsu so ardent a Sinophile that he once had some Japanese pirates who were troubling Chinese trading vessels captured and boiled alive.) Under the reign of Yoshimasa the China trade dwindled, but Zen monks continued to influence the government in directions that best suited their own interests. Wealthy from their commercial undertakings, they were in a position to finance some of Yoshimasa's more lavish projects, and in later years they helped him design the garden of the Silver Pavilion, including a detached building for tea drinking and meditation—the forerunner of the modern tea house. This was the finest hour of Zen influence in official circles, for Yoshimasa was the last Ashikaga shōgun whose preferences had any influence on the course of Japanese life. After his death, the artists who had surrounded him scattered to the provinces to find patrons. Within a decade the Silver Pavilion and its garden were virtually abandoned. Zen as a religion also went to the provinces, and gradually its following grew as sympathetic teachers who no longer cared for the company of the mighty were content to explain the rewards of nonattachment to the people at large.

The many faces of medieval Japanese Zen were paradoxical indeed. The Kamakura warriors turned to Zen for strength on the battlefield, whereas the Ashikaga court found in it aesthetic escapism and spiritual solace in a crumbling world. That an age such as the Ashikaga could have nourished high arts has puzzled historians for centuries, and no entirely satisfactory explanation has yet been advanced. Perhaps art flourishes best when social unrest uproots easy conventions. Fifth-century Athens produced its most enduring art at a time when the land was rent by the fratricidal Peloponnesian War and the city itself was haunted by the plague. Renaissance Florence is another example. Today Kyōto, like modern Athens and modern Florence, is a living museum, concerned more with traffic and tourist hotels than with the long-forgotten blood baths which once raged in its streets. Seemingly forgotten, too, are the warring Ashikaga, at whose behest the noble Zen arts of Japan were shaped.

CHAPTER 7
Zen and the Landscape Garden

To see a World in a grain of sand,
And a Heaven in a wild flower,
Hold Infinity in the palm of your hand,
And Eternity in an hour.

William Blake

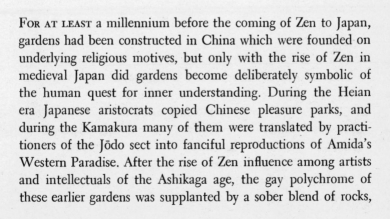

FOR AT LEAST a millennium before the coming of Zen to Japan, gardens had been constructed in China which were founded on underlying religious motives, but only with the rise of Zen in medieval Japan did gardens become deliberately symbolic of the human quest for inner understanding. During the Heian era Japanese aristocrats copied Chinese pleasure parks, and during the Kamakura many of them were translated by practitioners of the Jōdo sect into fanciful reproductions of Amida's Western Paradise. After the rise of Zen influence among artists and intellectuals of the Ashikaga age, the gay polychrome of these earlier gardens was supplanted by a sober blend of rocks, trees, sand, and water—Japanese copies of, first, Sung Chinese gardens and, later, Sung monochrome landscape paintings. In their landscape "painting" gardens, Zen artists captured the reverence for nature which, for them, was a cornerstone of Zen philosophy.

The origins of Far Eastern landscape gardens have been traced to an obscure Chinese legend which predates the Christian Era. It describes five holy islands, situated off the shores of Shantung province, whose peaks soared thousands of feet into the ocean mist and whose valleys were a paradise of perfumed flowers, snow-white birds, and immortals who plucked the trees for pearls. These islanders, who lived in palaces of precious metals, enjoyed eternal youth and had the capacity to levitate at will, although for extended journeys they might choose to ride on the backs of docile flying cranes. However, like Adam and Eve, these paradise dwellers wanted more. Since their islands were floating rather than attached to bedrock, they complained to the ruling deity, requesting more substantial support. The supreme ruler of ancient China was more understanding than the God of Mesopotamia; instead of evicting the island immortals, he obligingly sent out a flotilla of giant tortoises to hold the islands on their backs and secure them in place.

During the Han era (206 B.C.–A.D. 220) various Chinese emperors reportedly sent out expeditions to locate these islands, but they were always unsuccessful. Finally, the Han Emperor Wu hit upon the notion that if he were to construct an idealized landscape on his estate, the immortals might abandon their misty ocean isles for his park, bringing with them the secrets of eternal life. A garden park was built on a scale intended to rival that of paradise; and to make the immortals feel even more welcome, various rocks symbolizing cranes and tortoises were installed, items the Japanese would one day include in their gardens as symbols of longevity. No immortals materialized, but the Chinese landscape garden was launched in considerable style.

During the ensuing Six Dynasties era (A.D. 220–589), Chinese gardens began to reflect the beliefs of the new religion of

Buddhism. The lake-and-island gardens of the aristocracy ceased to represent the legend of the misty isles and became instead a symbol of the Western Paradise of Amida Buddha. As time passed, the growing influence of Taoism deepened the Chinese feeling for nature itself without reference to any particular legend. In later years, as scholars sought out mountain retreats in the rugged south of China, soaring peaks came to be part of the standard landscape garden, a need sometimes realized by situating the garden against a backdrop of distant mountains or by piling up rocks on the island in the garden lake.

The interest in garden art continued to grow during the T'ang dynasty (618–907), as poets and philosophers increasingly turned to nature for religious and artistic inspiration. Interestingly enough, their perception of nature was not idealized in the manner of the Florentine landscapists but rather emphasized the rugged, untamed qualities of the mountains and streams. It was this sense of nature as the embodiment of a free spirit that they tried to capture in their gardens. Theirs was a reverence for nature as it was in the wild; if it must be domesticated into a garden, the sense of freedom should be preserved as far as possible.

When the Shintō nature worshipers of Japan encountered the advanced civilization of China, they may have recognized in the Chinese Taoist feeling for nature a similarity to their own beliefs. It had never occurred to the Japanese to construct a domestic abstraction of nature for contemplation, but the new idea of a garden seems to have had its appeal. When a copy of the Chinese capital was created in Nara, the Japanese architects were careful to include a number of landscape gardens around the imperial palace. After the government moved to Kyōto and launched the regal Heian era, a rage for things Chinese became the consuming passion of the Japanese aristocracy; Heian nobles built Chinese-style houses and lake-and-island gardens, complete with Chinese-style fishing pavilions extending out over a lake. Since these pleasure parks were intended for parties of boaters and strollers, they had few religious overtones. Instead the lake became a thoroughfare for pleasure barges, on which idle courtiers cruised about dressed in Chinese costume, and reciting Chinese verses. These gardens were rich with plum and cherry trees, pines, willows, and flowering bushes, and often included a waterfall near at hand, in keeping with Chinese convention. The central island gradually lost its original symbolism as an Elysian holy isle as the nobles linked it to shore with stone footbridges. In these grand parks the Heian nobles gave some of the most sophisticated garden parties ever seen.

After relations with China fizzled to a stop around the beginning of the tenth century, the Japanese garden began to evolve on its own. It was always an emblem of power, making it essential that when the warrior government moved to Kamakura a leader no less imposing than Minamoto Yoritomo should oversee the creation of the main garden at the new capital. Significantly, the garden in Kamakura was constructed as part of the Buddhist establishment, rather than as an extension of Yoritomo's private estate. Perhaps this transformation of the garden into Buddhist temple art was a consequence of the Western Paradise beliefs of Amadism (a forerunner had been the late-Heian Western Paradise garden outside Kyōto at Ūji); perhaps it was the first implicit acknowledgment of the nature mysticism of Zen; or perhaps the Kamakura warriors simply believed that a private garden would smack too much of the decadence of Kyōto. Whatever the reason, the coming of Zen seems to have been coincidental with a new attitude toward the connection between gardens and religion. The frivolous polychrome of the Heian pleasure park was clearly a thing of the past; gardens became solemn and, as the influence of Zen grew, increasingly symbolic of religious ideas.

The monks who visited China to study Ch'an (as well as Ch'an monks who migrated to Japan) were, of course, familiar with the landscape gardens of the Sung Chinese. These gardens had purged many of the more decorative elements of the T'ang-period pleasure parks and reflected the reverential attitudes of the Taoists and Ch'an Buddhists toward the natural world. At least one of these Sung-style gardens was produced in Kyōto during the early years of renewed contacts with China.

Oddly enough, however, it was the Sung ink paintings that would eventually have the greatest influence on Zen landscape gardens. The Sung paintings captured perfectly the feeling Japanese Zen monks had for the natural world, leading them to conclude that gardens too should be monochromatic, distilled versions of a large landscape panorama.

Not surprisingly, the attitude that a garden should be a three-dimensional painting sparked the long march of Japanese garden art into the realm of perspective and abstraction. In fact, the manipulation of perspective advanced more rapidly in the garden arts than in the pictorial. Without going into the Chinese system of perspective in landscape painting, let it be noted that whereas the Chinese relied in part upon conventions regarding the placement of objects on a canvas to suggest distance (for example, the relative elevation of various tiers of landscape elements on the canvas was often an indication of their distance), the Zen artists learned to suggest distance through direct alteration of the characteristics our eye uses to scale a scene. And since many of these gardens were meant to be viewed from one vantage point, they became a landscape "painting" executed in natural materials.

The manipulation of perspective may be divided roughly into three main categories: the creation of artificial depth through overt foreshortening, thereby simulating the effects of distance on our visual sense; the use of psychological tricks that play on our instinctive presumptions regarding the existence of things unseen; and the masterly obliteration of all evidence of artifice, thereby rendering the deception invisible.

Zen gardeners' discovery of the use of foreshortening in a garden took place at almost the same time that the Florentine artist Uccello (1397–1475) began experimenting with natural perspective in his landscape oils. Although this example of artistic convergence can hardly be more than coincidence, certain of the devices were similar. As the American garden architect David Engel has observed, the Japanese learned that the apparent depth of a scene could be enhanced by making the objects in the distance smaller, less detailed, and darker than those in the foreground.[1] (In the garden of Yoshimitsu's Golden Pavilion, for example, the rocks on the spectator side of the garden lake are large and detailed, whereas those on the far side are smaller and smoother.) As time went by, the Japanese also learned to use trees with large, light-colored leaves at the front of a garden and dark, small-leafed foliage farther back. To simulate further the effects of distance, they made paths meandering toward the rear of a garden grow narrower, with smaller and smaller stones. The pathways in a Japanese garden curve constantly, disrupting the viewer's line of sight, until they are finally lost among trees and foliage set at carefully alternated levels; streams and waterfalls deceptively vanish and reappear around and behind rocks and plantings. Zen artists also found that garden walls would disappear completely if they were made of dark natural materials or camouflaged by a bamboo thicket, a thin grove of saplings, or a grassy hillock.

Many methods of psychological deception in a Zen garden exploit instinctive visual assumptions in much the same way that a judo expert uses his victim's body for its own undoing. A common trick is to have a pathway or stream disappear around a growth of trees at the rear of a garden in such a way that the terminus is hidden, leading the viewer to assume it actually continues on into unseen recesses of the landscape. Another such device is the placement of intermittent obstructive foliage near the viewer, causing the diminution in perception that the mind associates with distance. Japanese gardeners further enhance the sense of size and depth in a garden plot by leaving large vacant areas, whose lack of clutter seems to expand the vista. Dwarfing of trees is also a common practice, since this promotes the illusion of greater distance. And finally, flowers are rigidly excluded, since their appearance would totally destroy all the subtle tricks of perspective. Zen garden masters prefer to display their flowers in special vase arrangements, an art known as Ikebana.

The manipulation of perspective and the psychological deception of the Zen garden are always carefully disguised by giving the garden an appearance of naturalness and age. Garden rocks are buried in such a manner that they seem to be granite ice-bergs, extruding a mere tip from their ancient depths, while the edges of garden stones are nestled in beds of grass or obscured by applications of moss, adding to the sense of artless placement. Everything in the garden—trees, stones, gravel, grass —is arranged with a careful blending of areas into a seemingly natural relationship and allowed to develop a slightly unkempt, shaggy appearance, which the viewer instinctively associates with an undisturbed natural scene. It all seems as uncontrived as a virgin forest, causing the rational mind to lower its guard and allowing the garden to delude the viewer with its artificial depth, its psychological sense of the infinite.

The transformation in garden art the Zen artists wrought can perhaps best be emphasized by comparing the traditional Chinese garden with the abstract landscape created by Japanese artists of the Ashikaga and later eras. The Japanese regarded the garden as an extension of man's dwelling (it might be more accurate to say that they saw the dwelling as an extension of the garden), while the Chinese considered the garden a counterpoise for the formality of indoor life, a place to disown the obligations and conventions of society. It has been suggested that the average Chinese was culturally schizophrenic; indoors he was a sober Confucian, obedient to centuries-old dictates of behavior, but in his garden he returned to Taoism, the joy of splendor in the grass, of glory in the flower.

In spite of this, the Chinese garden was more formal than the type that developed in Japan, and it included numerous complicated corridors and divisions. The Chinese gardens of the T'ang aristocracy were intended for strolling rather than viewing, since the T'ang aesthetes participated in nature rather than merely contemplating it. Accordingly, Chinese gardens (and Heian copies of them) included architectural features not included in the later Zen landscapes. The Chinese apparently believed that if one is to duplicate the lakes and mountains, then all the items normally seen in the countryside should be there, including the artifacts of man. The Chinese garden wel-comed the physical presence of man, whereas the landscape

The Zen ideal of a closed yet infinite space may be seen in the garden of Renge-ji, where the light-leafed foreground tree and the darkened, shaded recesses on the left delude the viewer into assuming he has encountered merely an obstruction to vision rather than the back of the garden; the suggestion of a stream entering from just beyond view at the right rear is enhanced by a miniature stone bridge.

gardens developed in Japan are at their finest when viewed without people, if only because the presence of man acts as a yardstick to destroy the illusion of perspective and exaggerated distance. (However, a Zen-inspired form of Japanese stroll garden for use in connection with the tea ceremony did develop, as will be noted later.)

The plaster wall of a Chinese garden was often an integral element of the decoration, and its shape and topping were part of the overall aesthetic effect. The Japanese, on the other hand, chose to de-emphasize the presence of the wall. Stated differently, the purpose of the wall around a Chinese garden was to keep outsiders from seeing in, whereas the wall of a Japanese garden was to prevent those inside from having to see out—a fundamental difference in function and philosophy.

The dissimilarity in Chinese and Japanese attitudes toward garden rocks also deserves mention. The Japanese preferred interesting naturalness in their stones; they avoided blandness, but were wary of freakish, distracting shapes. The Chinese, in contrast, were charmed by curiosities, and they sought out garden rocks with fantastic, even grotesque contours. This preference seems to have grown out of a desire to duplicate the craggy mountainsides so often seen in Sung landscape paintings. They searched for unnaturally shaped stones in lake bottoms, where the action of water had honeycombed them. (In fact, this particular passion, which became known as "rockery," led to a bit of forgery during the latter part of the Ming era, when ordinary rocks were carved to the desired shape and then placed under a waterfall until they were smoothed sufficiently to disguise the deception.)

The presence of so many unnatural features in Chinese gardens tended to give them a rococo quality, which Zen artists were careful to avoid, and the hemispherical, symmetrical motif of Chinese gardens was transformed into the angular, asymmetrical style that suited Zen aesthetic theory. The fundamental impression a Chinese garden gives is that of skilled artifice, of being a magical, slightly fabulous landscape of dreams. Zen artists transformed this into a symbolic experience of the world at large, distilled into a controlled space but suggesting the infinite. The result was to change a form that had been essentially decorative into something as near to pure art as can be wrought with the primeval elements of tree, water, and stone. Gardens had been used before to approximate this or that monarch's conception of paradise, but never before had they been employed to express an otherwise ineffable understanding of the moral authority of the natural world.

Zen gardens differ even more greatly from Western garden

design. The geometrical creations of Europe, such as the palace garden at Versailles, were fashioned to provide wide-open vistas reaching toward the horizon, while the naturalistic Zen garden is closed in upon itself like a form of curved space, producing the illusion of an infinite wilderness in a few acres. It is intended primarily for viewing; there are no grassy dells for loitering. It is expected to serve functions ordinarily reserved for art in the West: it both abstracts and intensifies reality, being at once symbolic and explicit in design, and the emotion it evokes in the viewer gives him a deeper understanding of his own consciousness.

The four gardens in Kyōto that perhaps best demonstrate the principles of early Zen landscape were all constructed under the patronage of the Ashikaga: the first two, Saihō-ji (ca. 1339) and Tenryū-ji (ca. 1343), were designed by the Zen monk Musō under the reign of Takauji; the garden of the Golden Pavilion (1397) was executed under the influence of Yoshimitsu; and the garden of the Silver Pavilion (1484) was guided by Yoshimasa. All four were created on the sites of earlier gardens dating from the Heian or Kamakura eras which Zen artists both purified and modified, making changes roughly analogous to the reworking of a rococo marble statue of a rotund courtier into a free-standing muscular nude. It is also illustrative of the age that these one-time private estates were transformed into what were to become essentially public parks, albeit under the management of Zen temples.

The first of the gardens to be designed was the one at Saihō-ji, a temple on the western edge of Kyōto, popularly known as the "Moss Temple," or Kokedera. During the Heian and Kamakura eras this site belonged to a prominent family who constructed two temple gardens toward the close of the twelfth century in honor of Amida and his Western Paradise. Fashioned long after contacts with China had been broken, these Amida gardens already disowned many of the decorative motifs in the earlier, T'ang-style parks. They were self-contained and natural and had no pretense of being symbolic. This was to change, however, around the time that Ashikaga Takauji assumed power, when the owner hit upon the notion of converting these gardens of the Jōdo sect into something appropriate to the new school of Zen. The project was begun with the understanding that the famous Zen priest Musō Soseki would come to preside over the new temple as abbot, and work was begun under his guidance.

The resulting garden is on two levels, like the original dual garden of Amida, but the Zen designer used the levels to suggest many of the features of a larger universe. It was not yet a fully developed landscape, but rather a contemplative retreat for strolling which strove to emphasize minor aspects of the natural features of rocks, ponds, trees, grasses, and moss. Even so, many of the features of later landscape gardens are traceable to Musō's design here, particularly the rugged rockwork of the islands in the large lake on the lower level, which later

The main garden at Saihō-ji (ca. 1339), where an illusory sense of unattended nature is realized by painstaking design and maintenance.

inspired the rockwork of Yoshimitsu's Golden Pavilion garden. Located up the hill is a "dry cascade," suggested by the skillful arrangement of round, flat-topped stones carefully set in a place where water never ran. Already, the obligatory waterfall of the Chinese garden had been abstracted into a quiet symbolism. The garden bespeaks a sober, ancient grace and dignity—and reveals aesthetic concepts peculiar to Zen.

The garden of Tenryū-ji is at the temple founded by Takauji, at the suggestion of Musō, as a site for the repose of the soul of the Emperor Godaigo, whom Takauji had driven out of Kyōto. It will be recalled that the expense associated with building this temple was the occasion of Takauji's again opening trade with China, an act that led to the real explosion of Zen art. Musō also became the official abbot of the temple and is thought to have contributed to the redesign of its garden—it had previously been part of an imperial country villa. Musō's contribution is questionable, however, since the garden shows evidence of influence from the "landscape-painting" design of Sung China and the peculiarly Sung usage of "rockery." It may have been laid out earlier by some emigrant Chinese Ch'an monk who was aware of the latest Sung garden theory. The rock shapes are not grotesque, however, but rather show the crisp angularity later to become a Japanese trademark. A small islet of three stones suggests the three levels of a landscape painting, and at the back there is a simulated waterfall of rugged dry stones. The lake and its islands are monochromatic and severe, and the footbridge traditional to Sung landscape gardens is represented by three long flat stones crossing a narrow portion of the rear part of the lake. This garden is probably the only Sung-style creation in Japan, but its impact on Zen gardeners was considerable, since it showed the effects Ch'an Buddhism had had on Chinese garden art. Musō undoubtedly recognized the garden as a worthy model for Zen artists, and he probably did no more than put a few final Japanese touches on the work.

By the time of Ashikaga Yoshimitsu, builder of the third Zen landscape garden, Ch'an garden concepts were undoubtedly

The garden at Tenryū-ji (ca. 1343) with the temple-viewing veranda at the left, facing the near shore of the lake.

better understood in Japan than in China. Yoshimitsu had often gone to Saihō-ji to meditate in the garden, and he knew exactly what was required for the landscape garden to surround his Golden Pavilion. He selected a site known as the North Hill Villa, an estate originally built by an aristocratic family using funds they had got serving as spies to report the activities of the Kyōto aristocracy to the Kamakura warlords. Constructed in 1224, the original garden represented the last flowering of the Heian- (or T'ang Chinese) style garden; that is, it was a purely decorative boating pond. When Yoshimitsu acquired the site, he immediately demolished the Chinese-style residence with its fishing pavilion projecting out onto the lake. Then he turned his attention to the garden, paring down the central island and adding smaller islands by bringing in massive stones from the surrounding hills. To obtain the necessary trees, he simply selected those that caught his eye in the gardens of the powerless aristocracy.

Today the garden at the Golden Pavilion covers approximately four and a half acres (although it seems much larger), with a lake occupying about one-third of the total area. The pavilion sits at the lake's edge, but in past times before the waters shifted, it was in its midst. When viewed from the pavilion, as was the original intention, the garden seems a landscape vista. Several of the small islets scattered about the lake have their own dwarf pines, while others are no more than massive protruding stones, chosen for an abstract resemblance to a tortoise or crane. In the portion of the lake closest to the pavilion everything is wrought in great detail, whereas stones on the far side are vague and diffuse, so that the distant shoreline seems lost in misty recesses. The hillsides surrounding the gar-

The garden of the Golden Pavilion (ca. 1397) gives a sense of exaggerated perspective as the eye roams from the large foreground rocks past the small islets and deliberately dwarfed pines in the center to the distant reaches, where an absence of visual details subtly directs the focus back to the center and causes the mind to experience a sense of infinity confined in a curved space.

*In the garden of the Silver Pavilion (ca. 1484) an illusory cascade
at the rear seems to emerge from the recesses of the hillside and
pass under a stone bridge, which is itself a Zen-inspired abstraction
recalling the Heian-era garden footbridges.*

den are covered with foliage, and there is no clear demarcation
between the garden and the hills. Executed at a time when
resources were almost limitless, the garden of the Golden
Pavilion is one of the finest Zen landscape gardens ever created.
It stands as a watershed between the modification of Chinese
styles and the maturity of Japanese Zen art.

Yoshimasa, architect of the fourth great Zen landscape garden, was also fond of Saihō-ji and had studied its garden, as
well as that of the Golden Pavilion, with great care. But the
Silver Pavilion and its garden were built after the disastrous
Ōnin War, when the available resources were nothing like
those of the earlier Ashikaga shōguns. Although he was surrounded by a coterie of Zen aestheticians, it appears Yoshimasa
designed the garden himself, assisted by a new class of profes-

sional garden workers drawn from the outcast *eta* class (outcast because they were associated with the meat and hides industry and thus pariahs to all good Buddhists), who had been engaged by the Zen priests to take care of the heavy work involved in stone movement and placement. Many of these *eta* became famous for their artistic discernment, and one, the famous Zen-ami, is regarded as one of the foremost garden architects of the Ashikaga era.

The garden at the Silver Pavilion was modeled after the one at Saihō-ji and made the same use of bold, angular stones— a mixture of flat-topped, straight-sided "platform" rocks and tall slim stones reminiscent of Sung landscape paintings of distant mountains. Like Saihō-ji, the garden is on two levels, with the rear reminiscent of a mountain waterfall. At one side of the garden the pond is spanned by a stone footbridge connecting either side of the shore with the central island. Shaped dwarf pines abound, and the surface of the water, interrupted here and there with massive stones, is peaceful and serene. Little wonder Yoshimasa preferred his tasteful pavilion and its distilled microcosm of landscape to the ravaged ruins of Kyōto. Here he could rest in meditation, letting his eye travel over the placid waters, past the flowering trees which framed the symbolic waterfall, upward to the silhouette of the towering pines on the far hillside to watch the moon rise in the evening, bathing his world in silver. In this peaceful setting he could relish the last, closing years of the great Ashikaga age of Zen art.

The art of the landscape garden did not end with Yoshimasa, of course; rather, it shifted in its direction and purpose. Already beginning was the next phase of Zen garden art, the abstract sand-and-stone gardens.

CHAPTER 8

The Stone Gardens of Zen

And this our life, exempt from public haunt,
Finds tongues in trees, books in the running brooks,
Sermons in stones . . .

As You Like It

IN THE CLOSING decade of the fifteenth century, the long evening parties of Zen aesthetics were over; Kyōto lay in ruins after
the Ōnin War, and a new, sober mood gripped the land. Virtually all the temples and estates in Kyōto, together with their
gardens, were abandoned relics; and the once indulgent patronage of aristocrats and shōguns was gone forever. A reflective,
contemplative mood settled over the houses of Zen.

Out of this era of penurious disarray developed a style of
temple garden which many hold to be the most profound expression of Zen art: the dry landscape, or *kare sansui*. Fashioned
from the most austere materials, sand and stone, these water-

less vistas were the final step in the creation of three-dimensional reproductions of Sung ink paintings. They condensed the universe into a single span, and they were primarily, if not wholly, monochromatic. More importantly, they were intended exclusively for meditation. Whereas earlier landscape gardens had always striven for a quality of scenic beauty, these small temple gardens were meant to be a training ground for the spirit, a device wherein the contemplative mind might reach out and touch the essence of Zen. These later Zen gardens were also reduced in size and scope, since a temple yard in such diminished times could not accommodate the spacious parks once available to the aristocracy. Stylized, often abstract representations of nature, they dispensed with all decorative possibilities the better to promote the serious business of meditation.

Perhaps the best example of this type of monochrome "painting" garden is the famous creation at Daisen-in, a part of the Daitoku-ji temple compound in Kyōto. The sand-and-stone garden here is on all sides of the temple building, placing the viewer literally in the middle of a Sung landscape. The focus of the painting, however, is in one small corner of the grounds, where a pair of head-high vertical stones have been used to represent Sung mountain peaks while striated white sand placed around and among the larger background mountains, together with smaller flat-topped rocks in the foreground, suggest the inrush of water from a symbolic waterfall. The simulated stream of white sand winds among river rocks as it passes across the front of the viewing platform. Included in the design are a stone bridge crossing one portion of the sandy stream and a large boat-shaped stone enhancing the symbolism of water. The water seems to disappear under the temple veranda and emerge on the other side as a shimmering white sea. Adjacent to the tall mountain stones are several ancillary rocks approximately waist-high, over which flow rivulets of white sand, suggesting a cataract captured in monochrome. Just as an expert Zen painter extracts the details of a scene in a few strokes of the brush, so the master of Daisen-in succeeded in distilling from the natural world precisely those elements that excite the spirit.

The stone garden at Daisen-in (ca. 1513), a monochrome "paint-ing" in angular, often flat-topped stones meant to suggest the brushstrokes of an ink landscape, with distant mountains repre-sented by the two upright stones at the rear and the sense of rushing water captured in the raked gravel.

This classical *kare sansui* garden is thought to have been de-, signed around 1513, reconstructed from one of the run-down temples left after the Ōnin War. Credit for the design is traditionally (but probably erroneously) given to the artist Sō'ami (1472–1525), a well-known painter. The distinction between painting and garden art was necessarily blurred, since these gardens were in fact intended to copy paintings more than nature. The true mark of a Zen painter was his ability to handle rocks and mountains in the prescribed manner, with sharp, angular brushstrokes devoid of softness or sentimentality. Naturally enough, stones with this same quality were essential for the *kare sansui* gardens, but such stones were extremely rare and prized almost beyond price. Trees could be grown; stones had to be found in the mountains and moved somehow to Kyōto.

During the heyday of the Kamakura and Ashikaga glory, there were resources at hand to find, move, and position stones—and at times armies of over a thousand men were impressed into service for this task. After the Ōnin War no such battalions were available, but there was a ready source of superb stones: the burned-out temple and estate gardens of old Kyōto. Furthermore, monks from many of the earlier temples had systematically pillaged the estates of Heian nobles for stones, using the cream of the stone collections from earlier centuries to create their small gardens. So when the builders of Daisen-in began to collect stones, they had the finest examples of centuries of collecting at their disposal. Hence the magnificent stones at Daisen-in actually represent the *crème de la crème* of garden stonework, rising phoenixlike out of the destruction of older estates.

What were the qualities of these stones that they should have been hauled for hundreds of miles and prized by shōguns and Zen aesthetes alike? What did Zen artists look for when they scavenged the surrounding mountains for special rocks? They wanted rocks that looked like the mountains and crags in ink paintings. This meant light-colored stones with striated sides and sharp edges, with no hint of the hand of man about them. They looked not so much for odd formations as for natural shapes that possessed an authoritative, monumental quality. One particularly prized shape was flat-topped and vertical-sided, looking like a massive tree stump cut off about a foot above the ground. Another valuable stone was shaped like a steep-sided volcanic island which, nestled in a bed of sand, gave the impression of rising from the depths of the ocean. Oblong stones with lengthwise striations or incisions were valued for their similarity to towering vertical mountains; and rounded, flat-bottomed stones, for their resemblance to natural river rocks. The subjective "feel" of a stone was important; perfectly smooth stones or those with no memorable characteristics had no place in *kare sansui*. Those used must have the vigorous face of centuries, the weathered texture of antiquity.

Daisen-in was unquestionably the best of the Zen "painting" gardens: possibly designed by an experienced Zen painter, it contained the finest stones from an entire era of intensive collecting; and it was heir to centuries of garden mastery, from which was distilled the essence of landscape art. Its understated authority is the product of a long development of such Zen ideals as simplicity, starkness, austerity, and spareness. One would be tempted to declare it the finest example of the Zen *kare sansui* art were it not for an even more striking garden of the same era: Ryōan-ji.

Unlike Daisen-in, the garden at Ryōan-ji is not a symbolic mountain scene. It is instead a work of abstract art on a canvas of sand which goes beyond a symbolic representation of a landscape scene to provide a distillation of the very universe. It is internationally regarded as the very essence of Zen, and it is almost impossible to describe, in either words or pictures. It has a spirit that seems to rise up for those who come into its presence, evoking an immediate response even in someone who has no understanding of Zen.

Ryōan-ji was apparently built around 1490, which makes it roughly contemporaneous with Yoshimasa's Silver Pavilion. As early as 985 the site of Ryōan-ji had been used as the location of a private chapel for retired Heian emperors, and in the twelfth century a government minister of the Heian took it over and constructed a country villa, to which his grandson added a lavish Chinese-style lake and island garden in 1189. Thus the site had abundant water, something missing from other *kare sansui* gardens—although the style dictated that no water be used in the final Zen garden. After the fall of Heian and throughout the Kamakura deluge, the lake became a sort of lingering *ancien régime* touch, recalling the elegance of former days. (The remains of the lake, undoubtedly much modified through the centuries, still survive as part of the Ryōan-ji temple complex.)

The original Heian owners retained possession of the site until approximately 1450, when it was purchased by Katsumoto Hokusawa, adviser to the Ashikaga and one of the instigators of the Ōnin War. During his period of ownership, Katsumoto built a country villa overlooking the lake-and-island garden, and like Yoshimitsu, he requested that his villa be made into a Zen temple when he died. As it turned out, the Ōnin War caused his wishes to be executed sooner than he might have expected; shortly after the villa was built the estate was transferred to the Myōshin-ji branch of the Rinzai sect, which also controlled a nearby temple called Ryōan-ji. Not long after Katsumoto's death, his villa and other estate buildings were set on fire during the Ōnin War and joined the general ruin of much of the rest of Kyōto.

In the last decade of the fifteenth century the burned-out estate was restored by Katsumoto's son, but in replacing the buildings he chose a new style of Zen architecture known as *shoin*, which included a special bay window and desk modeled after those in Chinese Ch'an monasteries. The *shoin* style had been recently popularized in Kyōto by Yoshimasa, who chose the design for several buildings surrounding his Silver Pavilion. The *shoin* window overlooked the lake-and-island garden, but since the later Zen monks who controlled the estate had no interest in decorative landscape art, they walled off a small courtyard in front of the window and installed a flat *kare sansui* garden for contemplation, which soon eclipsed in interest the older lake-and-island landscape. Shortly thereafter the *shoin* building was in turn destroyed by fire, giving the monks an excuse to bring in a pavilion with a long viewing veranda from the neighboring Seigen-in temple. This veranda, which was positioned along the long axis of the *kare sansui* garden, now permits group meditation, something not possible from the single window of the earlier *shoin* structure.

The stone garden at Ryōan-ji (ca. 1490) with five clusters of stones awash in a sea of raked gravel whose expanses are a device to turn the viewer's mind inward.

Modern visitors to Ryōan-ji still pass through the older landscape garden en route to the main temple pavilion. From this vantage point only the outer wall of the sand-and-stone garden can be seen; there is no hint of what lies inside. On the temple steps the fragrance of incense mingles with the natural perfume of the ancient trees which line the pathways of the lake. As one enters the dimly lighted hallway of the temple, street shoes are replaced by noiseless, cushioned slippers. Shod in silence, visitors walk along the temple hallways onto the long *hōjō* veranda facing the garden, where the brilliance of the shimmering sand washes unexpectedly over the senses. The effect is sudden and striking.

What one sees, in purely prosaic terms, is an area of rippled sand about the size of a tennis court, set about with fifteen not particularly unusual (by Ashikaga standards) stones arrayed in five distinct clusters. The white sand is raked lengthwise (a routine task for a lay brother), and concentric circles are traced around each of the stones, imparting an illusion of ripples. In the garden proper there is not a tree, indeed not a blade of grass, to be seen; the only suggestion of living matter is the bed of ancient moss in which each group of stones lies nestled. On the three sides of the garden opposite the veranda stands the ancient courtyard wall, whose oil-stained earthen brown contrasts splendidly with the pure white sand. Above the wall, which is capped with black clay tile in Chinese fashion, one can see the tall trees of the landscape garden, obscuring what must once have been a grand view of old Kyōto to the south.

Each of the five clusters of stones seems balanced around its own center of gravity, and the clusters, in turn, appear to be balanced with one another—with the two groups of stones on the left being approximately equal in mass to the three groups on the right. As is the case in most Ashikaga gardens, each grouping is dominated by one obviously assertive member, against which the smaller, less authoritative stones strain for prominence, producing a sense of tension. Simultaneously, there is a feeling of strength about each of the groups, since each cluster is set on an island of mossy soil, which acts as a base to unite the assemblages. Aesthetic stability is also achieved by the placement of the stones at sufficient depth (or apparent depth) within their nest of moss so that only their tips seem to protrude above the floor of the garden.

The stones are set in two groups of two stones, two groups of three, and one group of five. Each of these groupings displays one or another of the various Ashikaga garden conventions. Both groups of two stones make explicit use of contrasting shapes between their members, a standard Zen device. One of the pairs is composed of a long, vertical rock set like an up-turned blade in the sand, with a companion that is hardly more than a negligible lump, a token foil. The other pair has one sharp-sided vertical stone with a flat plateau as a top, accom-

panied by a larger round rock which spreads at the base. As
has been noted, the Ashikaga gardeners prized flat-topped
stones highly because of their resemblance to the angular
brushstrokes of certain Zen ink painters. Life, in this case, was
made to imitate art, or rather sculptural art was made to imitate
the pictorial. Both pairs of stones are situated slightly off the
lengthwise axis of the garden, maintaining the asymmetry considered so essential.

In the two groups of three stones, the intent is to establish
the visual pre-eminence of the largest member and to flank it
with two comparatively insignificant smaller stones—usually
differentiated in shape and attitude—thereby forming a vertical
triangle with the peak of the largest stone representing the
apex. This particular arrangement was so common in Ashikaga
gardens that it became known as the "three-deity" stone setting,
supposedly a pious reference to a Buddhist legend but probably
merely a convenient tag for a standardized artistic device. The
last grouping is five stones, since arrangements of four were
considered too symmetrical by Zen gardeners. In this case, the
group is dominated by one large central boulder with four
ancillary rocks spread about its base like the feet of a granite
beast.

Such, in physical terms, is the arrangement of the garden,
and when so described it seems undeserving of all the acclaim.
Its subjective qualities tell a bit more of the story. It seems
clear that the inclination of the stones is intended to evoke
a sense of motion, for they have all been placed with their
longer axis corresponding to that of the garden. This quality is
further enhanced by the practice of raking the sand lengthwise,
which makes the observer's eye sweep from left to right or
right to left. And although the overall purpose of the garden
is to induce mental repose, it has a dynamic tension, such as
a high-speed photograph of surging rapids in a mountain
stream might catch. But the sand, like the blank spaces in a
Chinese ink drawing, is as important as the placement of the
stones. The empty areas both emphasize the stones and invite
the mind to expand in the cosmological infinity they suggest.

This interaction between form and space is one of the keys to Ryōan-ji's compelling suggestiveness. Evoking a sense of infinity in a strictly confined space, it is a living lesson in the Zen concept of nothingness and nonattachment. It expresses a timelessness unknown in earlier landscape gardens, particularly those of the Heian era, which, with their fading blossoms and falling leaves, were attuned to the poignant transience of life. In the Ryōan-ji garden, the Heian aesthetic concept of *aware*, the thought that beauty must die, has been replaced by the Zen idea of *yūgen*, which means, among other things, profound suggestiveness, a reduction to only those elements in a creative work that move the spirit, without the slightest concession to prettiness or ornament. The number and placement of stones seem arbitrary, but they are intuitively perfect—like a phrase from Beethoven that, with the alteration of a single note, could be transformed into a comic tune. Like all masterpieces, Ryōan-ji has simplicity, strength, inevitability.

Between them, the gardens at Daisen-in and at Ryōan-ji encompass the range of *kare sansui* gardening in Ashikaga Japan. The first is a symbolic landscape of parched waterfalls and simulated streams drawn in monochromatic granite; the second, a totally nonrepresentative abstraction of stone arrangements in the sand-covered "flat-garden" style. The *kare sansui* flat-garden style, in particular, has no real counterpart in world art. Imagine the Egyptians, Greeks, or Florentines collecting rocks, strewing them about a bed of sand in a courtyard, and calling it religious art. Ryōan-ji seems strikingly modern today and in fact it was only after a critical following for abstract art developed in the West that the Zen *kare sansui* was "discovered." As recently as the 1930s Ryōan-ji was ignored, an unkempt sandpile the monks rarely bothered to rake; and only in 1961 was the garden at Daisen-in restored to what is believed to be its original condition. Ryōan-ji is now the most celebrated site in Japan and so internationally appreciated that a full-sized replica has been constructed in the Brooklyn Botanic Gardens, New York.

Zen gardeners were sophisticated aestheticians, and one can

recognize in their work at least two artistic techniques that the West did not discover until this century. The first is the Surrealist principle, derived from the earlier Dadaist idea, of *objets trouvés,* that is, the use of aesthetically interesting natural or accidental materials as part of an artistic composition. The stones of Ryōan-ji and other Ashikaga gardens were left in the condition in which they were discovered and used in the gardens as stones, yet they were also symbols for something larger than themselves. The second "modern" artistic principle found in Zen gardens is the reliance on abstract expressionism. Flat gardens like Ryōan-ji are not meant to depict a natural scene; they are exercises in the symbolic arrangement of mass and space. The Zen gardeners actually created a new mode of artistic expression, anticipating the West by several centuries.

Perhaps Ryōan-ji went unnoticed for so long because it was not explicitly intended as a work of art, but rather as a statement in physical terms of the essence of mystical truth. One's reaction upon first coming into the presence of Ryōan-ji is like the famous Western mystic Meister Eckhart's description of the realization of Oneness, called *satori* in Zen: "Then at once, God comes into your being and faculties, for you are like a desert, despoiled of all that was particularly your own. . . ." Ryōan-ji presents this desert in physical terms, a place of no attachments and no antagonistic polarities. This is Zen art at its most noble; beauty and aesthetics are present, but they are secondary to a realm of the spiritual.

CHAPTER 9

Zen and the Ink Landscape

Heard melodies are sweet, but those unheard
Are sweeter; therefore, ye soft pipes, play on;
Not to the sensual ear, but, more endeared,
Pipe to the spirit ditties of no tone.

John Keats

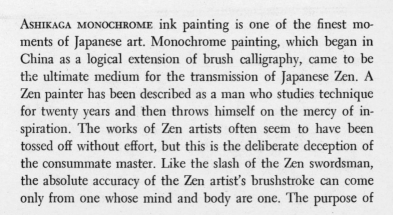

ASHIKAGA MONOCHROME ink painting is one of the finest moments of Japanese art. Monochrome painting, which began in China as a logical extension of brush calligraphy, came to be the ultimate medium for the transmission of Japanese Zen. A Zen painter has been described as a man who studies technique for twenty years and then throws himself on the mercy of inspiration. The works of Zen artists often seem to have been tossed off without effort, but this is the deliberate deception of the consummate master. Like the slash of the Zen swordsman, the absolute accuracy of the Zen artist's brushstroke can come only from one whose mind and body are one. The purpose of

Zen painting is to penetrate beyond the perceptions of the rational mind and its supporting senses, to show not nature's surface but its very essence. The artist paints the enlightenment of a moment, and there is therefore no time to labor over each stroke; the technique must flow thoughtlessly, from deep within, capturing the fleeting images of the inner sense, beyond mind and beyond thought.

To watch a Zen painter is to receive a lesson in the discipline of Zen. As he sets out to create a work, he first brings to hand the essential artistic materials: brush, inkstone, ink, paper. Kneeling on the floor, he spreads the paper out before him, and as he grinds and mixes the ink, begins to envision the outline and scope of his work. Like a *samurai* warrior before a battle, he banishes thoughts of the world and in a state of contemplation organizes his energies for a burst of action. When the ink is ready, the paper smoothed, an appropriate brush tested for point and feel, and his spirits composed, he strikes.

The ink is absorbed almost immediately by the fibrous rice paper preferred by Zen artists, allowing no alteration of a line once it has been set down. If the artist is dissatisfied with a stroke, he attempts no corrections but tears up the work and begins another. In contrast to conventional Western oil painting, which allows for retouching, an ink brushstroke on paper (or silk, which is sometimes used) becomes dull and lifeless if it is painted over, and corrections are always obvious when the painting dries. The work must flow out of the Zen discipline of no-mind. The artist never pauses to evaluate his work; the ink flows in an unending flurry of strokes—heavy or sparing, light or dark, as required—producing a sense of rhythm, movement, form, and the artist's vision of life's inner music.

The discipline of ink painting was only one of the qualities that endeared it to Zen painters. Equally important was the understated, suggestive art it made possible. Learning from the Chinese, Ashikaga Japanese discovered that black ink, carefully applied to suggest all the tones of light and shade, could be more expressive and profound than a rainbow of colors. (A similar lesson has been learned by modern photographers, who often find black and white a medium more penerating than color.) The Chinese painters of the T'ang and Sung dynasties were the first to discover that black ink could be made to abstract all pigments and thereby suggest, more believably than actual color paintings, the real tones found in nature. Whereas the medium of ink has been used in the West primarily for line drawings and lithographs, the Eastern artists use ink to produce the illusion of color—an illusion so perfect that viewers must at times remind themselves that a scene is not in full polychrome. And just as the seemingly unfinished artistic statement nudges the viewer into participating in a work, the suggestive medium of monochrome with its implied rather than explicit hues tricks the viewer into unwittingly supplying his own colors.

The Zen insight that the palette of the mind is richer than that of the brush has been best described by a Japanese artist and critic, who explained the rich suggestiveness of black ink, called *sumi* by the Japanese:

> At first glance, this bit of ink on a sheet of white paper seems dull and plain, but as one gazes at it, it transforms itself into an image of nature—a small part of nature, to be sure, seen dimly, as though through a mist, but a part that may guide one's spirit to the magnificent whole. Armed with pigments by the dozen, artists have tried for centuries to reproduce the true colors of nature, but at best theirs has been a limited success. The *sumi-e* [ink painting], by reducing all colors to shades of black, is able, paradoxically, to make one feel their genuine nuances. . . . By recognizing that the real colors of nature cannot be reproduced exactly, the *sumi-e* artist has grasped one of the most fundamental truths of nature. He is, therefore, more in tune with her than the painter who tries to encage her in oils and water colors.[1]

Zen painting seems to have been created, like the religion itself, by antischolastic thinkers of the latter T'ang dynasty. The eccentric monks who invented *kōan* paradoxes also seem to have been fond of calligraphy and monochrome painting.

These monks, together with non-Buddhist painters at odds with academic styles, loved to outrage their conservative colleagues by flinging ink at the paper and smearing it about with their hands, their hair, or sometimes the body of an assistant. Even those who restricted themselves to the brush delighted in caricature and unconventional styles. The school of painting represented by disaffected T'ang literati and Ch'an monks came to be well respected (much like the abstract expressionist school of today) and was given the name of "untrammeled class." During the Sung dynasty, Ch'an monks became respectable members of Chinese society, and gradually three distinct types of Ch'an-influenced painting were established. One, known in Japanese as *zenkiga,* featured didactic figure paintings (*zenki-zu*) illustrating Ch'an parables, depicting Bodhidharma in some legendary situation, recording the critical moment of a *kōan,* or simply illustrating a Zen adept practicing self-discipline through some humble task.

The second type was portraiture, known as *chinzō.* These solemn, reverential studies of well-known teachers, sometimes executed in muted pastels as well as in ink, clearly were intended to represent the physical likeness of the sitter as closely as possible. They must be ranked among the world's finest portraits. The insight into character in the *chinzō* is not so harsh as that of Rembrandt nor so formal as that of the Renaissance Florentines, but as sympathetic psychological studies they have rarely been surpassed.

The third type of painting associated with Ch'an is the monochrome landscape. Landscape was not originally a major Ch'an subject, but Ch'an monks experimented with the traditional Chinese treatment of such scenes and so influenced Chinese landscape painting that even academic paintings during the Sung dynasty reflected the spontaneous insights of Ch'an philosophy. Landscapes represent Chinese painting at its finest, and the Japanese Zen painters who embraced the form made it the great art of Zen.

The technical mastery of landscape painting had been achieved late in the T'ang dynasty when the problems of perspective, placement, and vantage point were solved. The classic rules for the genre which were formalized during the early Sung dynasty were respected for several hundred years thereafter in both China and Japan. One must appreciate these rules if one is to understand the Far Eastern landscape. To begin with, the objective is not photographic accuracy, but a representation of an emotional response to nature, capturing the essentials of a landscape rather than the particular elements that happen to be present in a single locale. (In fact, Japanese Zen landscapists frequently painted Chinese scenes they had never seen.) Nature is glorified as a source of meditative insight, and the artist's spontaneity is expressed within a rigid framework.

Certain specific items are expected to appear in every painting: mountains, trees, rocks, flowing water, roads, bridges, wildlife, houses (or at least thatched huts). The mountainsides vary with the seasons, being lush and sensuous in spring, verdant and moist in summer, crisp and ripe in autumn, and austerely bare in winter. The tiny human figures show the dignity of retired Sung officials at a hermitage; there are no genuine farmers or fishermen. The paintings have no vanishing point; receding lines remain parallel and do not converge. The position of the viewer is that of someone suspended in space, looking down on a panorama that curves up and around his range of sight.

To depict distances extending from the immediate foreground to distant mountain ranges, a painting is divided into three distinct tiers, each representing a scene at a particular distance from the viewer. These include a near tableau close enough to show the individual leaves on the trees and ripples on the water, a middle section where only the branches of the trees are delineated and water is usually depicted as a waterfall, and a far section containing mountain peaks. Since these three levels represent quantum jumps in distance, fog or mist is often introduced to assist in slicing the painting into three planes.

These landscape conventions were the subject of volumes of

analysis and interpretation during the Sung dynasty. According to the painter Han Cho in a work dated 1121:

> In paintings of panoramic landscapes, mountains are placed in ranges one above the other; even in one foot's space they are deeply layered; . . . and proper order is adhered to by first arranging the venerable mountains followed by the subservient ones. It is essential that . . . forests cover the mountain. For the forests of a mountain are its clothes, the vegetation its hair, the vapor and mists its facial expressions, the scenic elements its ornaments, the waters its blood vessels, the fog and mists its expressions of mood.[2]

Two characteristics of Sung landscape paintings that were later to become important elements in the canon of Zen aesthetic theory were the use of empty space as a form of symbolism, later to be found in all of Zen art from rock gardens to the Nō theater, and the specific treatment of rocks and trees, elements that the Zen school would one day take as metaphors for life itself. These characteristics have been eloquently described by the Western critics Osvald Sirén and Ernest Fenollosa, respectively:

> We hardly need dwell on the well-known fact that the Chinese painters, and particularly those who worked in Indian ink, utilized space as a most important means of artistic expression, but it may be pointed out that their ideas of space and their methods of rendering it were far from the same as in European art. Space was not to them a cubic volume that could be geometrically constructed, it was something illimitable and incalculable which might be, to some extent, suggested by the relation of forms and tonal values but which always ex-

---

A Japanese monochrome ink landscape, showing the prescribed separation of the vista into three tiers, each a complete world: the first on a human scale, the second on an architectural scale, and the third on a geologic scale.

tended beyond every material indication and carried a suggestion of the infinite.[3]

The wonderful twisted trees, mighty mountain pines and cedars, loved by these early Chinese and later Japanese, which our Western superficial view first ascribed to some barbarian taste for monstrosities, really exhibit the deep Zen thinker in their great knots and scaly limbs that have wrestled with storms and frosts and earthquakes—an almost identical process through which a man's life-struggles with enemies, misfortunes, and pains have stamped themselves into the wrinkles and strong muscular planes of his fine old face. Thus nature becomes a vast and picturesque world for the profound study of character; and this fails to lead to didactic overweighting and literary conceit, as it would do with us, because character, in its two senses of human individuality and nature individuality, are seen to become one.[4]

During the early years of the Sung dynasty, two distinct styles of landscape painting developed, which today are known as "Northern" and "Southern," reflecting their geographical locations. Although it is extremely dangerous to venture generalizations about painting schools, it might be said that the Northern school produced comparatively formal, symmetrical works done in sharp, angular, axlike brushstrokes which distinguished clearly between ink line and ink wash and in which the distant mountains were generally portrayed as crisply as the foreground. In contrast, the Southern school as a rule preferred a more romantic treatment of landscape elements, with rounded hills and misty valleys. Distant mountains were portrayed in graded washes of ink, suggesting mysterious recesses bathed in fog, while the middle ground was filled with rolling hills mellowed by a sense of diffuse lighting. A Chinese critic of the period described a Northern artist's work as all brush and no ink, and a Southern artist's as all ink and no brush—a simplified but basically accurate characterization of the two schools.

The Northern style was originally centered around the northern capital of Kaifêng and the Southern around Nanking in the Yangtze valley, but when the Sung court fled to the South after the fall of the northern capital in 1127, the styles of the two schools were merged to some degree in a new academy that was established in the lovely southern city of Hangchow. Painters of the Southern Sung dynasty, as this later era came to be known, often were masters of both styles, sometimes producing jagged Northern landscapes, sometimes misty Southern vistas, or sometimes combining the two in a single painting. In time, however, as the mood of the age grew increasingly romantic and Ch'an Buddhism became more influential in academic circles, the jagged brushstrokes of the Northern painters retreated farther and farther into the mist, leaving the landscapes increasingly metaphorical, with contorted trees and rugged, textured rocks.

This new lyrical style, which predominated in the last century of the Sung painting academy, was primarily the creation of two artists, Ma Yüan (active ca. 1190–1224) and Hsia Kuei (active ca. 1180–1230), whose works were to become the models for Ashikaga Zen landscapes. They both experimented with asymmetry and the deliberate juxtaposition of traditional landscape elements. Space became an element in its own right, particularly in the works of Ma Yüan, whose "one-corner" compositions were often virtually blank save for a bottom corner. An eclectic stylist, he frequently depicted the foreground in the ax-cut brushstrokes and sharp diagonals of the North, while distant mountains in the same painting were treated by the soft, graded washes of the South. Hsia Kuei did much the same, except that he took a marked interest in line and often painted foreground trees and rocks in sharp silhouette. In later years, after the Ming dynasty came to power, Chinese tastes reverted to a preference for the Northern style, but in Japan the so-called Ma-Hsia lyric school was revered and copied by Zen artists who found the subjective treatment of nature a perfect expression of Zen doctrines concerning intuitive insight.

The Southern Sung academy did not deliberately produce

Ch'an art; it was the Japanese who identified the Ma-Hsia style explicitly with Zen. However, during the early years of the thirteenth century, an expressionist, Ch'an school of art—the heir of the earlier T'ang eccentrics—arose and produced a spontaneous style of painting as unpredictable as Zen itself. The center for this protest school of landscape art was not the Sung academy but rather a Ch'an monastery near Hangchow, and its leader was a monk named Mu-ch'i (ca. 1210–ca. 1280), who painted all subjects—landscapes, Ch'an *kōan*, and expressionistic still-lifes—with brushstrokes at once skillfully controlled and deceptively casual. His was a disciplined spontaneity. A master of technique, he deliberately disregarded all the conventions. As time passed, various staid painters of the Sung academy heard his siren call of ecstasy and abandoned their formal styles, ending their days drinking with the Ch'an monks in monasteries around Hangchow, lost in the sheer exhilaration of ink and brush.

When Japanese monks began traveling to China, their first encounter with landscape painting was in these monasteries. Consequently, the styles and the paintings of the Ch'an Mu-ch'i school were the first to be sent to Japan. In later years, after the Northern school of painting was again in vogue in China, Ming Chinese were only too happy to unload outdated Southern Sung monochromes on the eager Japanese. The emissaries of Yoshi-mitsu (as well as earlier traveling monks) had their pick of these works, with the result that the very best examples of the spontaneous Mu-ch'i and the lyric Ma-Hsia styles of Sung painting are today in Japan.

The paintings of Mu-ch'i, the first Chinese monochrome art to be seen in Japan, were an instant success, and Zen monks rapidly took up the style. The most successful imitator was a Japanese priest-painter named Minchō (1351–1431), who before long was producing landscapes virtually indistinguishable from Mu-ch'i's. It was almost as though Mu-ch'i had risen from the dead and begun a new career in Japan a century later. Subsequently, the landscapes of the Ma-Hsia school found their way to Japan, and before long a second "Sung dynasty" was in full swing under the Ashikaga. Japanese Zen had found its art, and soon Yoshimitsu had established a painting academy at the temple of Shōkoku-ji, where painter-monks gathered to study each new boatload of Sung works and to vie with one another in imitating Chinese brush styles.

The head of the Zen academy was the priest Josetsu (active ca. 1400–1413), who took full control after Yoshimitsu's death in 1408. Josetsu's famous "Man Catching a Catfish with a Gourd," a parable of the elusiveness of true knowledge, is a perfect example of Japanese mastery of Sung styles, with its sharp foreground brushwork and misty distant mountains. The Zen academy dominated Japanese art until well after the Ōnin War, exploring and copying the great Sung works, both those in the lyric academic style and those in the spontaneous Ch'an style. Josetsu was succeeded by his pupil Shūbun (flourishing 1423–d. ca. 1460), whose vast (attributed) output of hanging scrolls and sixfold screens was a precise re-creation of the Sung lyric style. He was not a mere imitator, but rather a legitimate member of a school long vanished, with a genuine understanding of the ideals that had motivated the Southern Sung artists. Shūbun was a perfect master, a Zen Raphael, who so disciplined his style that it seemed effortless. His paintings are things of beauty in which the personality of the artist has disappeared, as was the intention of the Sung masters, resulting in works so perfectly of a type that they stand as a foundation on which others might legitimately begin to innovate.

However, under Shūbun's successor Sōtan (1414–1481), the academy continued to copy the techniques of dead Sung artists (as so often happens when art is institutionalized), producing works that showed no glimmer of originality. Zen art had reached maturity and was ready to become its own master; but it needed an artist who would place more trust in his own genius than in the dictates of the academy.

The individual who responded to this need is today looked upon as the finest Japanese artist of all time. Sesshū Tōyō (1420–1506) was a pupil of Shūbun and very nearly the contemporary of Sōtan. Painting out of a profound sense of the

"Catching a Catfish with a Gourd," by the Japanese priest Josetsu (active ca. 1400–1413), thought to be a parable on the difficulty of grasping enlightenment. The angular river rocks are of the type later sought for stone gardens, and the treatment of the figure and the distant mountains reveals a sense of spatial depth heralding the new age of Zen landscape art.

spirit of Zen, Sesshū was able to dismantle the components of Sung landscapes and reassemble them into an individual statement of Zen philosophy. It is thought that he became a Zen priest early in life and spent his formative years in an obscure

rural village on the Inland Sea. However, records show that at
the age of thirty-seven he was a priest in a reasonably high
position at Shōkoku-ji, under the patronage of Yoshimasa, and
a member of the academy presided over by Shūbun. He apparently studied under Shūbun until shortly before the Ōnin War,
when he left Kyōto for a city on the southwestern coast
and soon was on his way to China aboard a trading vessel.

Traveling as a Zen priest and a painter of some reputation,
Sesshū was immediately welcomed by the Ch'an centers of
painting on the mainland and by the Ming court in Peking.
Although he was able to see and study many Sung paintings
not available in the Kyōto Ashikaga collection, he was disap-
pointed in the Ming artists he encountered and returned to
Japan declaring he had found no worthy teacher in China except
her streams and mountains. He also pronounced Josetsu and
Shūbun the equals of any Chinese painters he had met—probably the first time in history such a statement could have gone
unchallenged. He never again returned to Kyōto, but established
a studio in a western seaside village, where he received the
mighty and passed his years in painting, Zen meditation, and
pilgrimages to temples and monasteries. According to the traditional account, he declined an opportunity to become Sōtan's
successor as head of the Kyōto academy, recommending that
the post be given to Kanō Masanobu (1434–1530), who did in
fact assume a position as official painter to the shōgun in the
1480s. It later passed to Masanobu's son Kanō Motonobu
(1476–1559). This launched the decorative Kanō school of
painting which dominated Japanese art for centuries thereafter.

Sesshū was a renegade stylist who mastered the Sung formulas
of Shūbun early in his career and then developed striking new
dimensions in ink painting. Despite his scornful assessments of
Ming art, he learned a great deal in China which he later used,
including an earthy realism that freed him from Shūbun's sublime perfection, a sense of design that allowed him to produce
large decorative sixfold screens which still retained the Zen
spirit, and, perhaps most importantly, the Ch'an-inspired
"flung ink" technique which took him into the realm of semi-

abstraction. In his later years he became famous for two distinct styles which, though not without Chinese precedents, were strongly individualistic.

In the first of these, known as *shin*, the polished formulas of Shūbun were supplanted by a controlled boldness, with rocks and mountains outlined in dark, angular brushstrokes seemingly hewn with a chisel. The landscapes were not so much sublimely unattainable as caught and worked to his will. The reverence for nature remained, but under his hand the depiction was almost cubist; the essence of a vista was extracted in an intricate, dense design of angular planes framed in powerful lines. Delicacy was replaced by dominance. Precursors of this style can be found in the works of Ma Yüan and Hsia Kuei, both of whom experimented in the hard, Northern-influenced techniques of brushstroke, but it was Sesshū who was the true master of the technique. Writing in 1912, the American critic Ernest Fenollosa declared him to be the greatest master of the straight line and angle in the history of the world's art.

Sesshū's second major style was *sō*, an abstraction in wash combining the tonal mastery of the Southern Sung school with the "flung ink," or *haboku*, of the Ch'an school—a style in which line is almost entirely ignored, with the elements of the landscape being suggested by carefully varied tones of wash. A viewer familiar with the traditional elements of the Sung landscape can identify all the required components, although most are acknowledged only by blurred streaks and seeming dabs of ink which appear to have been applied with a sponge rather than a brush. In contrast to the cubist treatment of the *shin* style, the *sō* defines no planes but allows elements of the landscape to blend into one another through carefully controlled

---

Sesshū (1420–1506) landscape in the angular shin *style, with a tiny figure in the foreground leaving his boat at the lower right to enter a world of slashing, jagged lines, while over his head the traditional separation of landscape tiers has been realized through a simple, bold discontinuity.*

variations in tonality. As effortless as the style appears to be, it is in fact a supreme example of mastery of the brush, an instrument intended for carving lines rather than subtle shading and blending of wash.

Because Sesshū chose to live in the secluded provinces, he did not perpetuate a school, but artists in Kyōto and elsewhere drew on his genius to invigorate Zen painting. One artist inspired by him was Sō'ami, a member of the Ami family which flourished during the academy's heyday. The earlier members of the family had produced acceptable works in the standard Sung style, but Sō'ami distinguished himself in a number of styles, including the *sō*. The other artist directly influenced by Sesshū was the provincial Sesson (ca. 1502–ca. 1589), who took part of the earlier master's name as his own and became adept in both *shin* and *sō* techniques. Although he, too, avoided strife-ridden Kyōto, he became famous throughout Japan, and his works suggest what the academy might have produced had Sesshū chosen to remain part of the Zen establishment. Yet even in Sesson's work one can detect a polished, effortless elegance that seems to transform Sesshū's hard-earned power into an easy grace, a certain sign that the creative phase of Zen art had ended.

The Ashikaga era of Japanese monochrome landscape is really the story of a few inspired individuals, artists whose works spanned a period of something more than one hundred and fifty years. As men of Zen, they found the landscape an ideal expression of reverence for the divine essence they perceived in nature. To contemplate nature was to contemplate the universal god, and to contemplate a painting of nature, or better still to paint nature itself, was to perform a sacrament. The

---

Sesshū (1420–1506) landscape in the misty sō style: the first level of landscape is represented by the houses, boat, and towering tree in the foreground; the middle level by the inkwork at left of the treetop; and the third level by the draped wash at top center.

landscape painting was their version of the Buddhist icon, and its monochrome abstraction was a profound expression of Zen aesthetics. Like the artists of the Renaissance, the Ashikaga artists worshiped through painting. The result is an art form showing no gods but resonant with spirituality.

CHAPTER 10

The Zen Aesthetics of Japanese Architecture

Architecturally [the Zen-inspired Silver Pavilion's] chief interest lies in the compromise which it exhibits between religious and domestic types, and a new style of living apartments (called shoin) which specialists regard as the true forerunner of the Japanese dwelling.

George B. Sansom, *Japan: A Short Cultural History*

ASK ANY JAPANESE why the traditional Japanese house is bitterly cold in winter and uncomfortably hot in summer, and he will unfailingly tell you that the design is historically adapted to the climate. Inquire about his purpose in rejecting furniture, thus to kneel daylong on a straw floor mat, and he will explain that the mat is more comfortable. Question his preference for sleeping on a wadded cotton floor pallet instead of a conventional mattress and springs, and he will reply that the floor provides surer rest. What he will not say, since he assumes a Westerner cannot comprehend it, is that through these seeming physical privations he finds shelter for the inner man.

The exquisite traditional Japanese house has been compared to an outsized umbrella erected over the landscape, not dominating its surroundings but providing a shaded space for living amid nature. The outside resembles a tropical hut, while the inside is an interworking of Mondrian geometrics. Together they represent the culmination of a long tradition of defining and handling interior space, using natural materials, and integrating architecture and setting. The Japanese house is one of those all too rare earthly creations that transcend the merely utilitarian, that attend as closely to man's interior needs as to his physical comfort.

The classic house evolved over two millennia through the adaptation and blending of two dissimilar architectural traditions—the tropical nature shrine, which was part of the Shintō religion of the early immigrants to Japan, and the Chinese model, beginning with the palace architecture of the T'ang dynasty and culminating in the designs used in the monasteries of Chinese Ch'an Buddhism. The early immigrants, the Yayoi, today are believed to have arrived from points somewhere to the South, bringing a theology that defied the earth, the sun, and all the processes of nature. Their shrines to these gods were like conventional Oceanic huts. Thanks to a peculiar quirk of Shintō, which dictates that certain of these wood-and-thatch shrines be dismantled and built anew every two decades, it is still possible to see these lovely structures essentially as they were two millennia ago. Spartan and elegant in their simplicity, they were lyrically described by the nineteenth-century Western Japanophile, Lafcadio Hearn:

The typical shrine is a windowless oblong building of unpainted timber with a very steep overhanging roof; the front is a gable end; and the upper part of the perpetually closed doors is a wooden lattice work—usually a grating of bars closely set and crossing each other at right angles. In most cases the structure is raised slightly above the ground on wooden pillars; and the queer peaked facade, with its visor-

A *prehistoric style of Shintō shrine at Ise, the prototype of later Japanese architecture, set in a graveled yard and showing the natural cypress woods, elevated floor, thatch roof, and encircling veranda later to appear in the traditional Japanese house.*

like apertures and the fantastic projections of beamwork above its gable-angle, might remind the European traveler of old gothic forms of dormer. There is no artificial color. The plain wood soon turns, under the action of rain and sun, to a natural gray varying according to surface exposure from a silvery tone of birch bark to a somber gray of basalt.[1]

Although the early immigrants lived first in caves and later in roofed pits dug into the earth, by the beginning of the Christian Era the aristocracy was building elevated dwellings on posts, with roofs supported not by the walls but by a central horizontal ridge pole suspended between two large columns at either end of the structure.[2] It was, in fact, identical to the Shintō shrine design described by Hearn. As a home for the Shintō gods, this tropical design may well have been adequate, since nature spirits are presumably adapted to the rigors of a Japanese winter, but the Yayoi must have found that it enforced an unwelcome communion with the seasons. Even so, Hearn's description could be applied almost without alteration to the external qualities of the traditional dwelling as it finally evolved. One still finds the thatch roof, the use of pillars to suspend the floor above the ground, unfinished natural wood, and the virtual absence of nails.

During the fifth and sixth centuries A.D. the early Japanese became aware of the complex Chinese culture on the Asian mainland, and by the beginning of the eighth century they had forsworn the primitive tropical architecture of Shintō and begun to surround themselves with palaces and temples modeled on the Chinese. During the Heian era, a Chinese-inspired aristocrat dwelling developed which represented a compromise between Japanese requirements and Chinese models. Although influenced by T'ang Chinese palaces, it was the first indigenous Japanese architectural style and is known as *shinden*.

The *shinden* mansion was a sprawling complex dominated by a main building facing a pond, around which were flanked ancillary structures connected to it by open galleries protected only by a roof. These open galleries, being very much the fashion, were also built around the outside of all the larger rooms and served as passageways. There were no solid walls inside the buildings; privacy was obtained by curtains and two-part horizontal doors hinged at the top and attached to the ceiling. Adopting Chinese construction methods, Japanese began roofing the buildings with dark clay tiles instead of native thatch, and walls were frequently surfaced with clay rather than wood planks or woven straw. Exterior woods were painted Chinese vermilion instead of being left to age naturally.

Furnishings were meager, and rooms were not identified according to usage; the building was one large area temporarily divided according to the needs of the moment. Instead of chairs there were movable floor mats of woven straw, while around the exterior of the rooms there were heavy shutters; these could be removed in summer or replaced by light bamboo blinds, which rolled down like window shades. Lighting was not a prominent feature of *shinden* mansions, and in winter the aristocracy huddled around a smoky fire in almost total darkness, the price of seeing being to open the blinds and freeze.

The *shinden* style suppressed for a time the indigenous affection for simplicity and unadorned natural materials revealed in the earlier, pre-Heian dwellings. However, it was never really naturalized, and it was eventually to be remembered in Japan's architectural history largely as an aberrant interlude, whose major legacy was the sense of openness or fluid space in the classic Zen house.

When the *samurai* warriors of the Kamakura era (1185–1333) assumed power, they did not immediately disown the architectural styles of the Heian nobles, but merely added (or, in some cases, removed) features in response to their martial needs and their new Zen outlook. As the country was at war, there was no logic in detached rooms and open galleries, and the *samurai* immediately tightened up the design, putting the entire house under one roof. They eliminated the pond and added a surrounding board fence for protection, even as interior curtains and hinged doors were replaced by sliding doors of paper over a wooden frame. And as rooms became more clearly identified, they were defined in terms of function. The early influence of Zen was seen most noticeably in the gradual disappearance of the ornamental aspects of *shinden* design as the *samurai* came to prize austerity and frugality.

During the Ashikaga era (1333–1573) which followed, when Zen monks assumed the role of advisers and scribes for the illiterate military rulers, a special writing desk, called a *shoin*, appeared in the houses of the more influential *samurai*. The *shoin* was a window alcove with a raised sill, which overlooked a private garden and was used by the monks for reading and writing. Next to this was a *chigai-dana*, a wall cabinet recessed in a niche and used for storing papers and writing utensils. (These new domestic appointments had been lifted by the Zen monks directly from the chief abbot's study in Chinese Ch'an monasteries.) The *shoin* study room immediately became a focus of fashion among the *samurai*, even those who could neither read nor write, and before long it was the finest room in a house. Guests began to be received there and another feature from Zen monasteries was added: the art-display alcove, or *tokonoma*. (In Chinese Ch'an monasteries the *tokonoma* was a special shrine before which monks burned incense, drank ceremonial tea, and contemplated religious artwork. That such a shrine should appear in a reception room of a social-climbing *samurai*'s house is vivid testimony to the pervasive influence of the Zen monk advisers.) The *samurai* also added an entry vestibule called a *genkan*, still another feature drawn from Zen temples. As a result of all these additions and modifications, *shinden* architecture was completely transformed into a functional *samurai* house whose style became known as *shoin*. Forgotten were the Chinese tile roofs and vermilion paint; thatch and unfinished woods reappeared. Paradoxically, the supplanting of *shinden* design by *shoin* was in many ways merely the ousting of a T'ang Chinese style by a Sung Chinese style. However, the T'ang architecture had been that of the Chinese court, whereas the Sung was drawn from Ch'an monasteries and coincidentally contained many of the aesthetic ideals of the earlier native Japanese dwellings and shrines.

By the waning years of the Ashikaga era, the *shoin* design had influenced virtually every aspect of Japanese architecture, bringing into being almost all the qualities of what is now thought of as the traditional Japanese house. The movable floor mats were replaced by wall-to-wall *tatami*, woven straw mats bound with a dark fabric band at either end and standardized to a size of approximately three by six feet. Soon rooms were being defined in terms of the number of *tatami* required for the floor—and modular architecture had been invented. Sliding, but removable paper partitions called *fusuma* became the standard room dividers, and the *tokonoma* became less a religious shrine than a secular display case where vertical monochrome scrolls and flower arrangements were put on view. Oddly enough, one of the few Chinese innovations the Japanese persistently chose to ignore was the chair. As a result, a Japanese residence has always maintained an entry vestibule where footwear is removed, something unnecessary for the Chinese, who had no reason to consider the floor a couch and could keep their shoes on. One important side effect of this choice is that eye level in the Japanese room—that is, the level from which the room, its art, and its appointments are viewed —has remained significantly lower than in houses with furniture, a characteristic that influences the placement of art as well as the layout of the accompanying garden.

The culminating style of Japanese architecture was the *sukiya* house, essentially a free-hand rendering of the formal *samurai shoin*. The *sukiya* style reflected a number of aesthetic and architectural ideas embodied in the Zen-inspired Japanese teahouse, and it allowed for considerable experimentation with materials and design. Less powerful and more delicate than the *shoin*, it was in many ways the ultimate extension of Zen austerity, even to the point where walls were often left unplastered. The *shoin* had been the house of warriors; the *sukiya* was a style for the common man and as such has contributed significantly to the overall tradition of Japanese architecture. *Shoin* and *sukiya* houses, heirs to the legacy of medieval Zen monks and later Zen aesthetes, are the reference point for what is now understood to be the traditional Japanese dwelling.

The deceptively fragile appearance of the house makes it appear at first an impractical invention for a land faced with recurrent earthquakes. Yet its lightness and flexibility, like those of a judo expert, actually contribute to its safety. Part of the reason is its foundation, which "floats" with the earth rather than being anchored rigidly. The traditional house is not held

The traditional Japanese architectural style, emphasizing the Zen ideals of simplicity, natural materials, and an openness to nature.

up by walls but by stout columns, almost a half-foot in diameter, embedded at their base in niches sunk into large, individually placed stones which are only partially buried. These columns reach through the house to the ceiling, whose weight secures them in their precarious foundation. In ordinary houses, the roof is a steeply sloping, four-sided pyramid whose light underframe is covered with multiple layers of shingles made from the tough bark of the *hinoki* tree.

A second set of shorter posts, similarly supported by partially buried stones, holds up the platform that is the floor, a wooden deck of closely fitted planks set about two feet above the earth. The outer perimeter of the flooring becomes a veranda or walkway, called the *engawa*, and the inner space is partitioned into rooms by light walls of paper, plaster, and wooden grillwork. The outer walls of the house, which serve no structural purpose, are sliding latticework panels called *shōji*, which are covered with translucent white rice paper, bathing the exterior rooms in a soft daytime light. The *shōji*, ordinarily installed in pairs approximately six feet high and three feet wide, unite rather than divide the interior and exterior; during the summer they slide open to provide fresh air and direct communication with the outdoors. If greater insulation or safety is required, a second set of sliding panels, or *amado*, similar in appearance to Western doors, may be installed outside the *shōji*. Between columns too narrow to accommodate a pair of *shōji* there may be a solid wall consisting of a two-inch-thick layer of clay pressed into a bamboo and rice-straw framework and finished inside and out with a thin veneer of smooth white plaster. Similar walls may be built inside the house where appropriate, and they and the columns are the house's only solid surfaces. The dull white color and silken texture of the plaster walls contrast pleasantly with the exposed natural grain of the supporting columns.

Interior rooms are separated by partitions consisting of light wooden frames covered in heavy opaque paper, often decorated with unobtrusive designs. These paper walls, called *fusuma*, are suspended from tracks attached to overhead crossbeams. They slide to form instant doorways, or when removed entirely, convert two smaller rooms into one large apartment. *Fusuma* provide little privacy between rooms except a visual screen, and it is rumored that this undesired communication increasingly inhibits lovemaking by modern parents.

The overhead crossbeams, installed between the columns at a

height of slightly over six feet, are similar to the columns in diameter and appearance. The ceiling of the rooms is roughly two feet above the crossbeams, or *kamoi*, with the intervening space usually filled either by a vertical open wooden latticework, the *ramma*, or a plaster-and-board combination, the *nageshi*. On exterior walls of the *ramma* is ordinarily a solid extension of the *shōji* which inhibits air flow from the outside. The *kamoi*, *nageshi*, and *ramma* have a structural as well as aesthetic obligation; they are the only solid lateral supports between the upright columns. The ceiling itself is a light wood latticework over which has been laid a platform of thin boards still in their natural state, as is all the woodwork.

Visitors enter through the genkan portico, where street shoes are replaced by soft-soled slippers, to prevent scratches on the exposed wooden veranda and hallways. At the entrance to a *tatami*-carpeted room, the slippers too are relinquished, and host and guests are both in stocking feet, a state that encourages familiarity. The reception room is empty as a cell, and as it basks in the diffuse light of the *shōji*, it seems suspended in time—heedless of the season. The only furniture may be a small central table around which guests and host seat themselves on square cushions. Or perhaps there are lamps with rice-paper shades, one or two knee-high chests of drawers, and if the weather requires it, one or more charcoal braziers, either a small moveable *hibachi* for hand warming or a larger heater sunk into a center recess in the flooring, often beneath the table, or both. The purpose of these is apparently more symbolic than functional, for they do little to influence the temperature in the paper-walled rooms. Arrangements for summer cooling are equally metaphysical; the *shōji* are simply thrown open in hopes of snaring wayward breezes, whose meager cooling is enhanced psychologically by the tinkle of wind bells hung in the verandas.

The aesthetic focus of the room is the *tokonoma*, or picture recess, set into one of the plaster walls, with a raised dais for its floor and an artificial, lowered ceiling. The *tokonoma* has a small *shōji*-covered window at one side which illuminates a

A *modern version of a classic architectural interior, displaying austere elegance in simple wood, straw, and clay, with the* tokonoma *art alcove and* kakemono *hanging scroll at the left rear, a small* chigai-dana *shelf and cabinet system at the right rear,* shōji *rice-paper windows at the left, removable* fusuma *sliding paper doors at the right, and a carpet of modular* tatami *woven straw mats.*

hanging scroll, and there is usually an incense burner (in recognition of its original monastic function) or a simple flower arrangement on its floor. Adjacent to the *tokonoma* is the *chigai-dana*, a shelved storage area hidden by sliding panels, which may be used to store kimonos or bedding rather than the writing implements of Zen monks as in the past. The *tokonoma* and *chigai-dana* are separated by a thin dividing wall whose outer edge is fronted by a single polished post, the *toko-bashira*, a natural tree trunk stripped of its bark to reveal its gnarled surface texture. The *toko-bashira* has the quality of polished driftwood, intended to bring a touch of raw nature to the otherwise austere and monastic ambience of the room.

As the guest kneels on the cushions and sips green tea, the host may slide aside a rear *shōji* to reveal the roofless garden of the inner courtyard, his private abstraction of the natural landscape. Flowers are purposely absent, but in their place may be tiny shaped pines, a pond, and receding, rocky pathways. The mossy stones glisten with dew (or with water from a recent dousing by the host in preparation for his guests), and the air is fresh with the scent of greenery. Only upon careful inspection does the deception evaporate and the garden reveal itself to be a tiny plot surrounded by a bamboo and plaster fence; the natural world has been extracted and encapsulated into a single view, at once as authentic as the forest and as artfully detailed as a Flemish miniature. This view—a heritage of Zen *shoin* design—is vital to the aesthetic magic of the house, for it brings the works of man and nature together in a way that blurs their distinction. Exterior space is united with interior space just as Zen philosophy identifies the external world as an extension of man's inner life.

Indeed, all the subjective aspects of the Japanese house are Zen-inspired. The most apparent design feature is the clean lines that mark the boundaries of space, from the geometrical delineation of floor areas, brought out by the dark bindings of the *tatami*, to the exposed skeletal framework of columns and horizontal beams. By deliberately excluding curved lines (whose implied sensuality would be at odds with Zen ideals of austerity) in the partitioning of space, the house achieves a geometrical formality both elegant and pure. This sense of free space is further realized by the rigorous exclusion of extraneous ornamentation (again a Zen aesthetic precept) and by placing all essential furnishings in the center of the room rather than around the sides, as in the West. Design aesthetics are also served by the emphasis on the natural texture of materials and the contrast realized when different materials (such as clay walls and exposed wood) are placed side by side. Finally, the indirect lighting provided by the *shōji* gives daytime rooms a subjective sense of perpetual afternoon, mellowing the visual properties of the materials, softening harsh colors to pastels, and enhancing the overall feeling of naturalness in the exposed woods.

The removable partitions, both internal and external, create a sense of interdependent yet fluid space so startling to Westerners that it is often the first thing they notice in a Japanese house. The concept is, of course, derived from a basic philosophical presumption inherent in all Zen art, from ink paintings to ceramics, that freedom is most keenly perceived when it is exercised within a rigorous framework of constraints and discipline. More important, and more difficult to define, is the Zen concept of *shibui*, the studied restraint that might be described as knowing when to stop. *Shibui*, perhaps more than any other aesthetic principle, typifies the influence of Zen on Japanese ideals. It means many things, including the absence of all that is not essential; a sense of disciplined strength deliberately held in check to make what *is* done seem effortless; the absence of the ornate and the explicit in favor of the sober and the suggestive; and the elegance that can be realized when the purest of natural materials are integrated in a formal, balanced orchestration.[3]

In addition to the aesthetic aspects, there is also a quality of psychological suggestion stemming from Zen in the Japanese house. Zen monks early realized that the cell-like austerity of a room could be used to manipulate the consciousness of those caught in its precincts. The impact of this was well described by the early-twentieth-century traveler Ralph Adams Cram:

> There is something about the great spacious apartments, airy and full of mellow light, that is curiously satisfying, and one feels the absence of furniture only with a sense of relief. Free from the rivalry of crowded furnishings, men and women take on a quite singular quality of dignity and importance.[4]

The "singular quality of dignity and importance" is one of the most fundamental discoveries of Zen interior designers. In the absence of decorative distractions, one must concentrate on his own mind and on the minds of others present. Host and guest find their focus on one another has been deliberately enhanced, breaking down the barriers of separateness and individual identity. Each word, each gesture is rendered richer, more significant. Heinrich Engel, who understood the source of the mysterious effects which Ralph Adams Cram could only describe in bewilderment, has explained this phenomenon:

> [The individual interior room] provides an environment that requires man's presence and participation to fill the void. Room in the Western residence is human without man's presence, for man's memory lingers in the multiple devices of decoration, furniture, and utility. Room in the Japanese residence becomes human only through man's presence. Without him, there is no human trace. Thus, the empty room provides the very space where man's spirit can move freely and where his thoughts can reach the very limits of their potential.[5]

Stated differently, the Japanese room forces introspection on those who enter it alone—a function completely in keeping with the interests of Zen. Souls who have felt the weight of too much liberty (and undeserved decorator's license) will find here a solemn retreat and a heightened sense of internal awareness. Here as never before one's mind is one's own, undistracted by the prosaic implements of living with which Westerners ordinarily engulf themselves. One should be warned, however, that this liberation of the consciousness is powerful stuff. The Japanese Zen room is a concentration cell which, although it can unite the minds of those who share it, can often tell those who enter it alone more than they want to know about their own interior lives.

The restraining discipline taught by Zen has both made the traditional Japanese house possible and reconciled its inhabitants to the practical difficulties of living in it. Although few Westerners would accept the inconvenience and sometime discomfort of these houses, many of the early Zen designers' ideals have begun to be seen in architecture and design in the West. It is well known that the Japanese integration of house and environment influenced Frank Lloyd Wright and that a purging of ornamentation was the credo of the Bauhaus. The medieval Japanese principle of modular design is now influential in the West, and we have finally discovered the possibilities for multiple uses of space, with modern "efficiency" apartments that combine all living functions, from dining to entertaining to sleeping, in a single room. Interest has grown recently in the texture of interior materials, which it is now realized provide a necessary visual warmth, and there is increasing integration of living areas with gardens, patios, and the outdoors, and a blessed reduction in superfluous decoration, with the re-establishment of emphasis on clean lines, open space, and the quality of light. Perhaps most important of all, we in the West are finally taking to heart what the Japanese Zen monks knew in medieval times: that domestic architecture and interiors can and should fulfill a requirement in our lives that is ordinarily served by art.

CHAPTER 11
The Nō Theater

It is not, like our theatre, a place where every fineness and subtlety must give way; where every fineness of word or of word-cadence is sacrificed to the "broad effect"; where the paint must be put on with a broom. It is a stage where every subsidiary art is bent precisely upon upholding the faintest shade of difference; where the poet may be silent while the gestures consecrated by four centuries of usage show meaning.

Ezra Pound and Ernest Fenollosa,
The Classic Noh Theatre of Japan

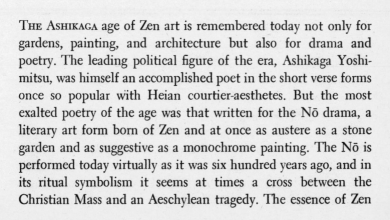

THE ASHIKAGA age of Zen art is remembered today not only for gardens, painting, and architecture but also for drama and poetry. The leading political figure of the era, Ashikaga Yoshimitsu, was himself an accomplished poet in the short verse forms once so popular with Heian courtier-aesthetes. But the most exalted poetry of the age was that written for the Nō drama, a literary art form born of Zen and at once as austere as a stone garden and as suggestive as a monochrome painting. The Nō is performed today virtually as it was six hundred years ago, and in its ritual symbolism it seems at times a cross between the Christian Mass and an Aeschylean tragedy. The essence of Zen aesthetic theory is evoked throughout its haunting poetry, its understated but intense style of acting, its delicately carved masks, and its mournful music and songs.

Like other Zen arts, the Nō was fashioned out of materials from distant times and places. The first Japanese dramatic arts were derived from various forms of Chinese farces and court dances. The farces, or *gigaku*, were popular with the Nara aristocracy, while the dances, or *bugaku*, came into favor with the more refined Heian court. Although the *bugaku* form undoubtedly influenced Japanese ideas on the blending of drama and dance, by the end of the Heian era it had become a lifeless ceremony for the emperor and his court—a role it still enjoys on occasions when performances are staged for the imperial family.

The real origins of the Nō are traceable to a somewhat lustier Chinese import, a circus-type entertainment called by the Japanese *sarugaku*. In addition to the display of various physical feats of daring, the *sarugaku* included farcical playlets and suggestive, sometimes indecent dances. A common theme seems to have been the lampooning of clergy, both Buddhist and Shintō. (In this respect, the development of native drama in Japan ran parallel with the resurgence of dramatic art in Europe after the Middle Ages, as citizens on both sides of the globe taunted the theological enslavement of feudal society by burlesques and dances ridiculing hypocritical authority figures.)

The studied indecency of early *sarugaku* was undoubtedly intended to parody the pomposity of Shintō rituals. But as time went by, the rustic dance-stories evolved into a more structured drama, the *sarugaku-no-nō*, which was the thirteenth-century Japanese equivalent of the European morality play. The earlier farces were transformed into comedies known as *kyōgen* (in which wily servants repeatedly tricked their masters), which today serve as interlude pieces to relieve the gravity of a program of Nō plays, just as the early Greek satyr plays were performed after a trilogy of tragedies in the Athenian theater.

In the early versions of the *sarugaku-no-nō*, the performers sang and danced, but as the form matured a chorus was added to supply the verses during certain segments of the dance. By the middle of the fourteenth century, about the time of Chaucer's birth, Japanese Nō was already an established dramatic form, containing all the major elements it has today. It was, however, merely village drama, and so it might have remained except for a chance occurrence in the year 1374.

In that year Ashikaga Yoshimitsu, already shōgun at age seventeen, attended a performance of the *sarugaku-no-nō* for the first time. The entertainment was a great favorite with his subjects, and he was trying to establish himself as a man of the people. A particularly well-known actor was scheduled to perform in Kyōto, and Yoshimitsu went to see him. The actor was Kannami (1333–1384), today famous as the father of the Nō. Yoshimitsu was excited by Kannami, but he was even more enthralled by the actor's handsome eleven-year-old son Zeami (1363–1444), who also appeared in the play. Yoshimitsu became Kannami's patron, but young Zeami he took to his couch (a common enough occurrence in *samurai* circles of the age). Zeami was devoted to the Nō, even as Yoshimitsu became devoted to Zeami, and thus began the long marriage of Zen culture and the Nō theater.

Through Yoshimitsu the *sarugaku-no-nō* came under the influence of the circle of Zen aesthetes surrounding him, and what had once been a broad popular entertainment became an aristocratic art. Supported by Yoshimitsu's patronage, Zeami became the Shakespeare of the Nō, writing the finest plays in the repertoire as well as several volumes of essays on aesthetic theories and acting technique. Although Zeami claimed to have learned everything from his father, the austere and poetic Nō that came to perfection during the Ashikaga was largely his own creation. His poetry has never been equaled, and his handbook of technique has remained the Nō actor's bible. Yet he might never have been heard of had it not been for Yoshimitsu, who, in the words of Donald Keene, found the Nō brick and left it marble.

The classic Nō stage is a splendid example of Zen-influenced architecture. The stage is a platform of golden, polished wood covered by a heavy arched roof supported by stout pillars at each of the four corners. The entire structure projects out into the audience, almost as though a wooden shrine had been reconstructed in the middle of the auditorium. The actors approach the platform along a wide entry ramp that leads off stage right to a curtained entranceway at the rear of the auditorium. The ramp has three small pine trees spaced evenly along its length, while on the backdrop of the stage proper there is a painting of a massive gnarled pine. As though to suggest Shintō origins for the drama, the stage and entrance ramp are symbolically separated from the audience by an encircling expanse of white sand, spanned at the very front of the stage by a small symbolic wooden stair. The acting platform is square, approximately twenty feet by twenty, with an additional rear area to accommodate the musicians and another area at stage left where the chorus kneels. Underneath the stage, unseen by the audience, are a number of large clay pots, a traditional acoustic device to amplify the resonance of the actors' voices. The few properties used in the plays are introduced and removed through an auxiliary entrance at the rear of the stage.

The beginning of the play is signaled offstage by the high-pitched wail of a bamboo flute. Two attendants with bamboo poles lift back the variegated brocade curtain covering the doorway to the ramp, and the musicians, either three or four in number, enter single file and position themselves in the prescribed order along the rear of the stage—the flautist sitting on the floor Japanese style, and the two major drummers on stools they carry with them. (If a bass drum is required, its player must join the flautist on the floor.) The Nō flute is not particularly unusual, except for an exceptionally strident tone, but the two primary Nō drums are unlike anything in the West. Although they are of different sizes, both resemble a large hourglass with an ox hide drawn over either end and held taut by heavy leather cords. The smaller drum, whose hide surface the players must periodically soften with his breath, is held on the player's right shoulder and struck with the right hand. Its sound is a muffled, funereal boom, lower in pitch than that of the other, larger drum. The larger drum is held on the player's left knee and struck with the fingers of the left hand, which may be protected by thimbles of leather or ivory. It produces a sharp, urgent click, used to punctuate the cadence of the performance. The bass drum used in certain dramas is played with drumsticks in the Western manner. The drummers also sometimes provide rhythm by interjecting monosyllabic shouts between drumbeats.

As the musicians enter, so does the chorus, eight or ten men dressed in formal Japanese "black tie" kimonos. They seat themselves Japanese style in two rows along stage left, where they must remain immobile for the duration of the play (which may be well over an hour). Since younger Japanese are less resigned to the persistent ache accompanying the traditional seating posture than their elders, the chorus usually tends to be well on in years. The chorus fills in dialogue for the actors during dance sequences; it makes no commentary on the action as does the chorus in Greek tragedy, nor does it have any special identity as part of the cast. Its members merely take up the voice of the actors from time to time like a dispassionate, heavenly choir.

With chorus and orchestra present, the overture begins. The first sounds are the piercing lament of the flute and the insistent crack of the drums, against which the drummers emit deep-throated, strangled cries. This stunning eruption of sound signals the entrance of the dramatis personae as the brocade curtain is again drawn aside for the first cast member, usually a *waki*, or supporting actor, who enters with measured, deliberate pace onto the entrance ramp, where he advances with a sliding, mechanical tread toward the stage.

The *waki*, often representing an itinerant monk dressed in subdued black robes, begins telling the story, either in his own voice or aided by the chorus, establishing the locale and circumstances of the scene about to unfold, after which he retires to a corner of the stage and seats himself to await the entrance of the protagonist, or *shite*. The brocade curtain parts again to reveal the *shite*, richly costumed and frequently masked, who

The performing ensemble at a dramatic moment in a Nō play, with the masked central character at center stage, the chorus kneeling at right, and the drum and flute "orchestra" at the rear, backed by a symbolic pine tree painted as a backdrop on the otherwise bare wood.

approaches to sing and dance out his story before the waiting *waki*. The *shite*'s splendid costume contrasts strikingly with the austerity of the stage and the other costumes.

On first appearance the *shite* ordinarily is intended to be a human form, albeit often a troubled one, but as his tale unfolds he becomes not so much an actual being as the personification of a soul. If the play is in two parts, in the second part he may assume his real identity, often only hinted in the first, of a spirit from the dead. Prefiguring the Shakespearean soliloquy, the confessional song of the *shite* speaks for the universal consciousness as he pours out his tortured inner emotions. As the *shite* sings, the knowing *waki* serves as confessor and provides a foil for any dialogue. The play climaxes with the dance of the *shite*, a stiff, stylized, sculptural sequence of mannered postures and gestures which draw heavily upon traditional Shintō sacred dances. With this choreographic resolution the play closes, and all exeunt single file as they entered—to the restrained acknowledgment of the audience.

The Nō repertoire contains five primary categories of plays. There are "god plays," in which the *shite* is a supernatural spirit, frequently disguised, whose divinity is made manifest during the final dance. In "warrior plays," the *shite* may be a martial figure from the Kamakura era who speaks in universal terms about his own personal tragedy. "Woman plays" are lyric evocations of a beautiful woman, often a courtesan, who has been wronged in love. The fourth category includes a grab bag of dramas often focusing on an historical episode or on the *shite* being driven to madness by guilt or, in the case of a woman, jealousy. Finally, there are "demon plays," in which the *shite* is a vengeful ogre, often sporting a flowing red or white wig, who erupts into a frenzied dance to demonstrate his supernatural displeasure over some event.

Many of the classic plays are a study of the tortured mental world of the dead. Even in warrior plays and woman plays the central character is frequently a spirit from the nether world who returns to chronicle a grievance or to exact some form of retribution from a living individual. Plot is deliberately suppressed. Instead of a story, the play explores an emotional experience or a state of mind—hatred, love, longing, fear, grief, and occasionally happiness. The traditional components of Western drama—confrontation, conflict, characterization, self-realization, development, resolution—are almost entirely absent. In their place is the ritualized reading of an emotional state that rarely grows or resolves during the play; it is simply described.

The artistic content of the Nō is embodied in the masks, dances, and poetry, all of which deserve to be examined. The masks carved for the Nō drama are the only representative sculptured art form of Zen; indeed, Zen was basically responsible for the disappearance of a several-hundred-year-old tradition of Buddhist sculpture in Japan. During the late Kamakura era, Japanese wood sculpture went through a phase of startling realism; but the Zen monks had no use for icons or statues of Buddhist saints, and by the beginning of the Ashikaga era Japanese statuary was essentially a thing of the past. However, the Japanese genius for wood carving had a second life in the Nō masks. Nō plays required masks for elderly men, demons, and sublime women of all ages. (The Nō rigidly excluded women from the stage, as did the Kabuki until recent times.)

Nō masks, especially the female, have a quality unique in the history of theater: they are capable of more than one expression. Nō masks were carved in such a way that the play of light, which could be changed by the tilt of the actor's head, brought out different expressions. It was a brilliant idea, completely in keeping with the Zen concept of suggestiveness. Nō companies today treasure their ancient masks, which frequently have been handed down within the troupe for centuries, and certain old masks are as famous as the actors who use them.

For reasons lost to history, the masks are somewhat smaller than the human face, with the unhappy result that a heavy actor's jowls are visible around the sides and bottom. They also cup over the face, muffling to some extent the actor's delivery. The guttural Nō songs, which are delivered from deep in the chest and sound like a curious form of tenor gargling, are rendered even more unintelligible by the mask. This specialized Nō diction, which entered the form after it had passed from popular entertainment to courtly art, is extremely difficult to understand; today even cognoscenti resort to libretti to follow the poetry.

The slow-motion movement around the stage, which goes by the name of "dance" in the Nō, is one of its more enigmatic aspects for Western viewers. As R. H. Blyth has described it, "the stillness is not immobility but is a perfect balance of opposed forces."[1] Such movements as do transpire are subtle, reserved, and suggestive. They are to Western ballet what the guarded strokes of a *haboku* ink landscape are to an eighteenth-century oil canvas. They are, in fact, a perfect distillation of human movement, extracting all that is significant—much as a precious metal is taken from the impure earth. The feeling is formal, pure, and intense. As described in a volume by William Theodore de Bary:

> When a Nō actor slowly raises his hand in a play, it corresponds not only to the text he is performing, but must also suggest something behind the mere representation, something eternal—in T. S. Eliot's words, a "moment in and out of time." The gesture of an actor is beautiful in itself, as a piece of music is beautiful, but at the same time it is the gateway to something else, the hand that points to a region as profound and remote as the viewer's powers of reception will permit. It is a symbol, not of any one thing, but of an eternal region, of an eternal silence.[2]

The evocation of an emotion beyond expression—of "thoughts that do often lie too deep for tears"—is the special Zen aesthetic realm of *yūgen*. The quality, heightened to almost unendurable levels by poetry, is that of a Zen landscape: sparse, monochromatic, suggestive. Universal human emotions are cloaked in obscurity rather than set forth explicitly. The passion is open-ended, a foreboding sonnet with the last line left for the listener to complete. Zeami and other Nō poets believed that the deepest sentiments cannot be conveyed by language; the poetry merely sets the stage and then sends the listener's imagination spinning into the realm of pure emotion, there to discover an understanding too profound for speech. In Western terms, if King Lear were a *shite*, he would speak in understated terms of the darkness of the heath rather than chronicle his own anguish.

The concept of *yūgen*, the incompleteness that triggers poetic emotions in the listener's mind is, as has been previously noted, an extension of the Heian concept of *aware*. Like *yūgen*, *aware* describes not only the properties of some external phenomenon but also the internal response to that phenomenon. *Aware* originally meant the emotional lift and sense of poignance experienced in contemplating a thing of beauty and reflecting on its transience. *Yūgen* extends this into the realm

of eternal verities; not only beauty but all life fades, happiness always dissolves, the soul passes alone and desolate. In an art form that transmits *yūgen*, none of this is stated; one is forced to *feel* these truths through suggestion, the degree of feeling depending, of course, upon the sensitivity of the individual. One can find excellent examples of *yūgen* in almost any Nō drama of the fifteenth century, like the following from "The Banana Tree" (*Bashō*), by Komparu-Zenchiku:

> Already the evening sun is setting in the west,
> Shadows deepen in the valleys,
> The cries of homing birds grow faint.[3]

Here the sense of universal loneliness at nightfall, the emptiness one feels in a desolate locale, the Gothic coldness that penetrates from the physical senses into one's interior emotions, are all much more fully realized through the simple evocation of the scene than would be possible by detailing them explicitly. The mournful call of evening birds in the bleak, empty, windswept fields cuts, like the Nō flute, to the very core of one's feelings.

The Nō is perhaps the most difficult Zen art for Westerners to enjoy. The restrained action transmits virtually nothing of what is occurring onstage, and the poetry does not translate well. (As Robert Frost once observed, in translations of poetry, it is the poetry that is lost.) The music is harsh to the Western ear; the chorus interrupts at intervals that seem puzzling; the strange cries and dances befog the mind. Most important of all, the concept of *yūgen* is not a natural part of Western aesthetics. The measured cadences of the Nō have, for the Westerner, all the mystery of a religious ceremony wrought by a race of pious but phlegmatic Martians. Yet we can admire the taut surface

---

The Nō drama's principal actor, whose rich brocade robes and elaborate headpiece contrast strikingly with the suggestive austerity of his mask.

beauty and the strangely twentieth-century atonality of the form.

Its enigmatic remoteness notwithstanding, the Nō remains one of the greatest expressions of Ashikaga Zen art. Some of Zeami's texts are ranked among the most complex and subtle of all Japanese poetry. For six hundred years the Nō has been a secular Zen Mass, in which some of man's deepest aesthetic responses are explored.

Part III

THE RISE OF POPULAR ZEN CULTURE: 1573 TO THE PRESENT

CHAPTER 12

Bourgeois Society and Later Zen

God has given us the Papacy; let us enjoy it.

Pope Leo X, 1513

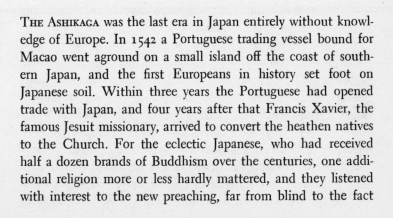

THE ASHIKAGA was the last era in Japan entirely without knowledge of Europe. In 1542 a Portuguese trading vessel bound for Macao went aground on a small island off the coast of southern Japan, and the first Europeans in history set foot on Japanese soil. Within three years the Portuguese had opened trade with Japan, and four years after that Francis Xavier, the famous Jesuit missionary, arrived to convert the heathen natives to the Church. For the eclectic Japanese, who had received half a dozen brands of Buddhism over the centuries, one additional religion more or less hardly mattered, and they listened with interest to the new preaching, far from blind to the fact that the towns with the most new Christians received the most new trade. Indeed, the Japanese appear to have first interpreted Christianity as an exotic form of Buddhism, whose priests borrowed the ancient Buddhist idea of prayer beads and venerated a goddess of mercy remarkably like the Buddhist Kannon. In addition to bringing a new faith, the Portuguese, whose armed merchant ships were capable of discouraging pirates, were soon in full command of the trade betwen China and Japan—a mercantile enterprise once controlled by Zen monks.

Still, the direct influence of Europe was not pronounced. Although there was a brief passion for European costume among Japanese dandies (similar to the Heian passion for T'ang Chinese dress), the Japanese by and large had little use for European goods or European ideas. However, one European invention won Japanese hearts forever: the smoothbore musket. The Japanese, sensing immediately that the West had finally found a practical use for the ancient Chinese idea of gunpowder, soon made the musket their foremost instrument of social change. Overnight a thousand years of classical military tactics were swept aside, while the Japanese genius for metalworking turned to muskets rather than swords. Musket factories sprang up across the land, copying and often improving on European designs, and before long Japanese warlords were using the musket with greater effect than any European ever had. The well-meaning Jesuits, who had arrived with the mission of rescuing Japanese souls, had succeeded only in revolutionizing Japanese capacity for combat.

The musket was to be an important ingredient in the final unification of Japan, the dream of so many shōguns and emperors in ages past. The process, which required several bloody decades, was presided over by three military men of unquestioned genius: Oda Nobunaga (1534–1582), Toyotomi Hideyoshi (1536–1598), and Tokugawa Ieyasu (1542–1616). The character of these three men is portrayed in a Japanese allegory describing their respective attitudes toward a bird reluctant to sing. Nobunaga, the initiator of the unification movement and one of the cruelest men who ever lived, ordered bluntly, "Sing or I'll wring your neck." Hideyoshi, possibly the most skillful diplomat in Japanese history, told the bird, "If you don't want to sing, I'll make you." Ieyasu, who eventually inherited the fruits of the others' labor, patiently advised the bird, "If you won't sing now, I'll wait until you will." Today the years dominated by Nobunaga and Hideyoshi are known as the Momoyama era, and the following two centuries of peace presided over by Ieyasu and his descendants are referred to as the Tokugawa.

After the Ōnin War, which had destroyed the power of the Ashikaga shōgunate and the aristocratic Zen culture of Kyōto, Japan had become a collection of feudal fiefdoms. The emperor and Ashikaga shōguns in Kyōto were titular rulers of a land they in no way governed. Into this regional balance of power came Nobunaga, who began his military career by killing his brother in a family dispute and taking control of his home province. Shortly thereafter he defeated a powerful regional warlord who had invaded the province with an army far outnumbering his own. The victory made him a national figure overnight and destroyed the balance of dynamic tension that had preserved the system of autonomous *daimyō* fiefs. Rival *daimyō*, covetous of their neighbors' lands, rushed to enlist his aid until, in 1568, he marched into Kyōto and installed a shōgun of his own choosing.

When the Buddhists on Mt. Hiei objected to Nobunaga's practices of land confiscation, he marched up the hill and sacked the premises, burning the buildings to the ground and killing every last man, woman, and child. This style of ecumenicity had been practiced often enough among the Buddhists themselves as one sect warred against the other, but never before had a secular ruler dared such a feat. This act and the program of systematic persecution that followed marked the end of genuine Buddhist influence in Japan.

Nobunaga's armies of musket-wielding foot soldiers were on the verge of consolidating his authority over all Japan when he was unexpectedly murdered by one of his generals. The clique responsible for the attempted coup was dispatched in short order by Nobunaga's leading general, the aforementioned diplomat Hideyoshi. Hideyoshi, who later became known as the Napoleon of Japan, was not of *samurai* blood and had in fact begun his military career as Nobunaga's sandal holder. He was soon providing the warlord with astute military advice, and it was only a matter of time until he was a trusted lieutenant. He was the first (and last) shōgun of peasant stock, and his sudden rise to power caused aristocratic eyebrows to be raised all across Japan. Physically unimposing, he was one of the seminal figures in world history, widely acknowledged to have been the best military strategist in the sixteenth-century world, and he completed the process of unification. The anecdotes surrounding his life are now cherished legends in Japan. For example, a favorite military stratagem was to bring a recalcitrant *daimyō* to the very brink of ruin and then fall back, offering an incredibly generous peace. However unwise such a tactic might be in the West, it had the effect in Japan of converting a desperate enemy into an indebted subordinate.

With the country at peace, foreign trade flourishing, and a rigorous system of taxation in force, Hideyoshi found himself with an excess of time and money. His response was to launch the Momoyama age of Japanese art. With more power than any ruler since Ashikaga Yoshimitsu, he was in a position to direct taste, if not to dictate it. This time there were few Zen monks in attendance to advise him on expeditures (Hideyoshi continued to keep the Buddhists under close guard, a practice as pleasing to the Jesuits as his harem was displeasing), and his flamboyant taste had full reign. Momoyama art became, in many ways, the antithesis of Zen aesthetics. Hideyoshi ordered huge screens to be covered in gold leaf and decorated with explicit still-lifes painted in vibrant primary colors. Yet he was no stranger to Zen ideals; he kept a famous tea-ceremony aesthete as adviser and lavished huge sums on the special ceramics required for this ritual. In many ways, the Zen tea ceremony and tea ceramics became for Hideyoshi what Zen gardens, painting, and the Nō were for the Ashikaga. His patronage not only inspired a flourishing of ceramic art; the tea ceremony now became the vehicle through which Zen canons of taste and aesthetics were transmitted to the common man. The patronage of the Ashikaga had furthered Zen art among the *samurai* and the aristocracy; Hideyoshi's patronage opened it to the people at large.

Ironically, the Zen arts profited from Hideyoshi's military blunders as well as from his patronage. At one point in his career he decided to invade China, but his armies, predictably, never got past Korea. The enterprise was unworthy of his military genius, and puzzled historians have speculated that it may actually have been merely a diversion for his unemployed *samurai*, intended to remove them temporarily to foreign soil. The most significant booty brought back from this disastrous venture (now sometimes known as the "pottery campaign") was a group of Korean potters, whose rugged folk ceramics added new dimensions to the equipment of the tea ceremony.

Having maneuvered the shōgunate away from Nobunaga's heirs, Hideyoshi became increasingly nervous about succession as his health began to fail, fearing that his heirs might be similarly deprived of their birthright. The problem was particularly acute, since his only son, Hideyori, was five years old and scarcely able to defend the family interests. In 1598, as the end approached, Hideyoshi formed a council of *daimyō* headed by Tokugawa Ieyasu to rule until his son came of age, and on his deathbed he forced them to swear they would hand over the shōgunate when the time came. Needless to say, nothing of the sort happened.

Tokugawa Ieyasu was no stranger to the brutal politics of the age, having once ordered his own wife's execution when Nobunaga suspected her of treason, and he spent the first five years after Hideyoshi's death consolidating his power and destroying rival *daimyō*. When Hideyoshi's son came of age, Ieyasu was ready to move. Hideyori was living in the family citadel at Ōsaka defended by an army of disenfranchised *samurai* and disaffected Christians, but Ieyasu held the power. In the ensuing bloodbath Hideyoshi's line was erased from the earth, and the Christians' faulty political judgment caused their faith eventually to be forbidden to all Japanese under threat of death. Christianity continued to be practiced on a surreptitious basis, however, as the Christians found shelter in, of all places, the Zen monasteries.

With the passing of Hideyoshi's line, the Tokugawa family became the only power in Japan, a land at last unified and with an imposed peace. Viewing foreign influences as a source of domestic unrest, the Tokugawa moved to bring down a curtain of isolationism around their shores: Christian Europeans were expelled and Japanese were forbidden to travel abroad. Ieyasu established a new capital at Edo (now Tokyo) and required the local *daimyō* to spend a large amount of time and money in attendance. Thus he craftily legitimatized his own position while simultaneously weakening that of the *daimyō*—a technique used with equal effect almost a century later by Louis XIV, when he moved his court from Paris to Versailles to contain the French aristocracy.

Content with the status quo, members of the Tokugawa family felt it could best be preserved by extreme conservatism, so they sent forth a volley of decrees formalizing all social relationships. Time was brought to a stop, permitting the Tokugawa to rule unhindered until the middle of the nineteenth century, when the country was again opened to foreign trade under the guns of American warships.

During the Tokugawa regime another Chinese "religion" assumed the place in the hearts of the shōguns that Buddhism had enjoyed in centuries past. This was Confucianism, more a philosophy than a religion, which in its original form had taught a respect for learning, the ready acceptance of a structured hierarchy, and unquestioning obedience to authority (that of both elders and superiors). The Tokugawa perverted Confucianism to establish a caste system among their subjects, separating them into the *samurai* class, the peasant class, and the merchant and artisan classes—the order given here denoting their supposed status. However, as the Japanese social system began to evolve, the idea backfired, causing great difficulties for the government. The reasons for this are interesting, for they bear directly upon the eventual role of Zen culture in Japanese life.

For centuries, Japan's major source of income had been agriculture. The *samurai* were local landholders who employed peasants to grow their rice and who were beholden to a local *daimyō* for protection. Money played no large part in the economy, since most daily needs could be obtained by barter. But the sudden wealth brought into being by the European traders had nothing to do with the amount of rice a *samurai*'s peasants could produce; it accrued instead to the merchants in port cities. Furthermore, the accommodations required to keep the *daimyō* and their families in the capital city of Edo called for artisans and merchants in great number. Thus the Tokugawa government had mistakenly decreed the agricultural *samurai* and peasants the backbone of the economy at the very moment in history when Japan was finally developing an urban, currency-based culture. Predictably, the urban merchants, who were at the bottom of the Confucianist social system, soon had their supposed social betters, the *samurai*, completely in hock.

The Tokugawa struggled hard to keep the townspeople, now the controllers of the economy, in their place. Merchants were forbidden to build elaborate houses or wear elaborate clothes, and they were expected to defer to the penurious *samurai* in all things. Japan had never before had a bourgeoisie—the traditional divisions were aristocracy, warriors, and peasants— and consequently popular taste had never really been reflected in the arts. Much to the dismay of the Tokugawa (and to the detriment of classical Zen culture), this was changing. While the aristocrats and warrior families in Kyōto preserved the older arts of Zen, in the bourgeois city of Edo there were new popular art forms like the Kabuki theater and the woodblock print, both eons removed from the Nō and the monochrome landscape. Classical Zen culture was largely confined to aristocratic Kyōto, while in boisterous Edo the townspeople turned to explicit, exciting arts full of color and drama.

In spite of this democratic turn of events, the Zen aesthetics of Kyōto continued to be felt, largely through the tea ceremony, which had been officially encouraged in the Momoyama age of Hideyoshi. Later in the Tokugawa era the poetic form of Haiku developed, and it too was highly influenced by the Zen idea of suggestiveness. Domestic architecture also maintained the ideals of Zen, as did Ikebana, or flower arranging, and the Japanese cuisine, which employed Zen ceramics. Thus Zen aesthetics seeped into middle-class culture in many forms, tempering taste and providing rigid rules for much of what are today thought of as the traditional arts and crafts of the Japanese.

Traditional Buddhism did not fare well during the Momoyama and Tokugawa ages: the militaristic Buddhist strongholds were either put to rout or destroyed entirely during the Momoyama, and Confucianism had considerably more influence under the Tokugawa than did Buddhism. The great medieval upsurge of Buddhism with its fiery teachers and believing shōguns was over, as the faith settled into empty ritual and a decidedly secondary station in a basically secular state. The only Buddhist sect demonstrating any vigor at all was Zen.

The brief flourishing of Zen during the Tokugawa era was actually a revival, for the faith had become static and uninspired during the years of Nobunaga and Hideyoshi. The formalized practice of Zen at the end of the seventeenth century was described by a visiting Jesuit Father:

> The solitary philosophers of the Zenshu sect, who dwell in their retreats in the wilderness, [do not] philosophize with the help of books and treatises written by illustrious masters and philosophers as do the members of the other sects of the Indian gymnosophists. Instead they give themselves up to contemplating the things of nature, despising and abandoning worldly things; they mortify their passions by certain enigmatic and figurative meditations and considerations [*kōan*] which guide them on their way at the beginning. . . . [s]o the vocation of these philosophers is not to contend or dispute with another with arguments, but they leave everything to the

contemplation of each one so that by himself he may attain
the goal by using these principles, and thus they do not teach
disciples.[1]

The good Father was describing a Zen faith that had become a
set piece, devoid of controversy but also devoid of life.

The man who brought Zen out of its slumber and restored
its vigor was the mystic Hakuin (1685–1768), who revived the
kōan school of Rinzai and produced the most famous *kōan* of
all times: "You know the sound of two hands clapping; what
is the sound of one hand clapping?" Hakuin gave a new, mystical dimension to the Rinzai school of Zen, even as Hui-nêng
created nonintellectual Chinese Ch'an Buddhism out of the
founding ideas of Bodhidharma. Hakuin was also a poet, a
painter, and the author of many commentaries on the *sūtras.*
Yet even when he enjoyed national fame, he never lost his
modesty or his desire for enlightenment.

Hakuin lived the greater part of his life in the small rural
village of his birth. A sensitive, impressionable child, he was
early tormented by an irrational fear of the fires of the Buddhist hell as dwelt upon by the priests of his mother's sect,
the Nichiren. For relief he turned to the Lotus Sūtra, but
nothing he read seemed to ease his mind. Finally he became a
wandering Zen monk, searching from temple to temple for a
master who could give him enlightenment. He studied under
various famous teachers and gradually achieved higher and
higher levels of awareness. At the age of thirty-two he returned
to his home village and assumed control of the ramshackle
local Zen temple, which he eventually made the center of
Rinzai Zen in Japan. Word of his spiritual intensity spread and
soon novices were flocking to him. His humility and humanity
were a shining light in the spiritual dark age of the Tokugawa,
and he breathed life and understanding back into Zen.

Despite Hakuin, official Zen never regained its influence in
Japan. Someday perhaps the twentieth-century Western interest
in Zen will give it new life somewhere outside Japan, but this
life will almost certainly be largely secular. Indeed, the influence

of Zen in the Momoyama and Tokugawa ages was already more pronounced in the secular world than in the spiritual. The bourgeois arts of these later years were notably less profound than those of the Ashikaga, but the spirit of Zen spread to become infused into the very essence of Japanese life, making the everyday business of living an expression of popular Zen culture.

CHAPTER 13
The Tea Ceremony

Chazen ichimi (Zen and tea are one.)

Traditional Japanese expression

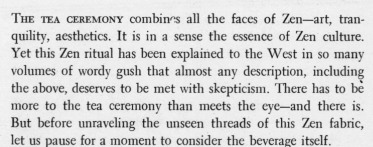

THE TEA CEREMONY combines all the faces of Zen—art, tranquility, aesthetics. It is in a sense the essence of Zen culture. Yet this Zen ritual has been explained to the West in so many volumes of wordy gush that almost any description, including the above, deserves to be met with skepticism. There has to be more to the tea ceremony than meets the eye—and there is. But before unraveling the unseen threads of this Zen fabric, let us pause for a moment to consider the beverage itself.

The drinking of tea seems almost to have been the world's second oldest profession. One legend claims that tea was discovered in the year 2737 B.C., when leaves from a tea bush accidentally dropped into the campfire cauldron of a Chinese emperor-aesthete. Early Chinese texts are sometimes vague about the identity of medicinal plants, but it is clear that by the time of Confucius (around 500 B.C.) tea was a well-known drink. During the T'ang dynasty (618–907), tea leaves were treated with smoke and compressed into a semimoist cake, slices of which would subsequently be boiled to produce a beverage—a method that was perpetuated for many centuries in Russia. The Chinese spiced this boiled tea with salt, a holdover from even earlier times when a variety of unexpected condiments were added, including orange peel, ginger, and onions.

The refined courtiers of the Sung dynasty (960–1279) apparently found brick tea out of keeping with their delicate tastes, for they replaced it with a drink in which finely ground tea leaves were blended with boiling water directly in the cup. Whipped with a bamboo whisk, this mixture superficially resembled shaving lather in texture, although the color could be a fine jade green if fresh leaves were used. (This green powdered tea was the drink one day to become enshrined in the Zen tea ceremony.) The Chinese chronicle of tea ends with the Ming dynasty (1368–1644), which saw the rise of the familiar steeping process, now the commonly accepted practice worldwide. Our ignorance of the earlier methods of tea preparation may be attributed to the West's discovery of China after the older methods had been discarded.

Unlike its misty origins in China, the use of tea in Japan is well authenticated. In the year 792 the Japenese emperor surprised the court by holding a large tea party at which Buddhist monks and other notables were invited to sample a curious beverage discovered by his emissaries to the T'ang court. Tea drinking soon became a fashionable pastime, occupying a position comparable to taking coffee in eighteenth-century Europe, but tea remained an expensive import and little thought was given to cultivation in Japan. This changed early in the ninth century when tea drinking came to be associated with the new Buddhist sects of Tendai and Shingon. Under the supervision of the court, tea growing was begun near Kyōto, where the emperor blessed the bushes with a special *sūtra* in the spring and autumn. Tea remained an aristocratic habit for several centuries thereafter and did not become really popular until the late twelfth century, when the famous Zen teacher Eisai "reintroduced" the beverage upon his return from China. Eisai also brought back new seeds for planting, the progeny of which are still growing.

Chinese Ch'an monks had long been devoted to tea. In fact, a famous but apocryphal legend attributes the tea bush to Bodhidharma, relating that during his nine years of meditation outside Shao-lin monastery he found himself nodding and in anger tore off his eyelids and flung them to the ground, whereupon tea plants sprang forth. There was a reason for the legend. Tea had long been used to forestall drowsiness during long periods of meditation. (A cup of modern steeped tea contains an average three-quarters of a grain of caffeine, about half the amount in a cup of coffee.) The drinking of tea became ritualized in Ch'an monasteries, where the monks would congregate before an image of Bodhidharma and take a sacrament of tea from a single shared bowl in his memory. This ritual was gradually adopted by Japanese Zen monasteries, providing the forerunner of the solemn moment of shared tea which became the basis of the tea ceremony.

The Japanese aristocracy and the warrior class also took up tea, and borrowing a custom from the Sung court, gave tea-tasting parties, similar to modern wine-tasting affairs. From the time of Ashikaga Takauji to Ashikaga Yoshimasa, these parties were an accompaniment to many of the courtly evenings spent admiring Sung ceramics and discussing Sung art theories. Although Zen monks played a prominent role in these aesthetic gatherings, the drinking of tea in monasteries seems to have been a separate activity. Thus the ceremonial drinking of tea developed in two parallel schools: the aristocracy used it in refined entertainments while the Zen monks drank tea as a pious celebration of their faith.

These two schools were eventually merged into the Zen-inspired gathering known simply as the tea ceremony, *cha-no-yu*. But first there was the period when each influenced the other. Zen aesthetic theory gradually crept into the aristocratic tea parties, as taste turned away from the polished Sung ceramic cups toward ordinary pottery. This was the beginning of the tradition of deliberate understatement later to be so important in the tea ceremony. Zen ideals took over the warrior tea parties. During his reign, Yoshimasa was persuaded by a famous Zen monk-aesthetician to construct a small room for drinking tea monastery-style. The mood in this room was all Zen, from the calligraphic scroll hanging in the *tokonoma* art alcove to the ceremonial flower arrangements and the single cup shared in a sober ritual. After this, those who would serve tea had first to study the tea rituals of the Zen monastery. Furthermore, warriors came to believe that the Zen tea ritual would help their fighting discipline.

By the sixteenth century the discipline and tranquility of the ceremony had become fixed, but the full development of *cha-no-yu* as a vehicle for preserving Zen aesthetic theory was yet to come. Gradually, one by one, the ornate aspects of the earlier Sung tea parties were purged. The idea took hold that tea should be drunk not in a room partitioned off from the rest of the house, but in a special thatch-roofed hut constructed specifically for the purpose, giving tea drinking an air of conspicuous poverty. The elaborate vessels and interior appointments favored in the fifteenth century were supplanted in the sixteenth by rugged, folk-style pottery and an interior décor as restrained as a monastery. By stressing an artificial poverty, the ceremony became a living embodiment of Zen with its distaste for materialism and the world of getting and spending.

It remained for a sixteenth-century Zen teacher to bring all the aesthetic ideas in the tea ceremony together in a rigid system. He was Sen no Rikyū (1521–1591), who began as the tea instructor of Nobunaga and continued to play the same role for Hideyoshi. Hideyoshi was devoted to the tea ceremony, and under his patronage Rikyū formalized the classic rules under which *cha-no-yu* is practiced today.

The most famous anecdote from Rikyū's life is the incident remembered as the "tea party of the morning glory." As the son of a merchant in a port city, Rikyū developed a taste for the new and exotic. At one time he began the cultivation of imported European morning glories, a novel flower to the Japanese, which he sometimes used for the floral display accompanying the tea ceremony. Hideyoshi, learning of these new flowers, informed Rikyū that he wished to take morning tea with him in order to see the blossoms at their finest. On the selected date, Hideyoshi arrived to find that all the flowers in the garden had been plucked; not a single petal was to be seen. Understandably out of temper, he proceeded to the tea hut—there to discover a single morning glory, still wet with the dews of dawn, standing in the *tokonoma* alcove, a perfect illustration of the Zen precept of sufficiency in restraint.

Tea ceremonies today are held in special backyard gardens, equipped for the purpose with a waiting shelter at the entrance and a tiny teahouse at the far end. When one arrives at the appointed time, one joins the two or three other guests in the garden shed for a waiting period designed to encourage a relaxed state of mind and the requisite Zen tranquility. The tea garden, known as the *roji*, or "dewy path," differs from conventional Japanese temple gardens in that it is merely a passageway between the waiting shelter and the teahouse. Since the feeling is meant to be that of a mountain path, there are no ponds or elaborate stone arrangements. The only natural rocks in evidence are the stepping stones themselves, but along the path are a carved stone in the shape of a water basin and a bamboo dipper, so that one can rinse one's mouth before taking tea, and a stone lantern to provide illumination for evening gatherings. The unpretentious stones of the walkway, set deep in natural mossy beds, divide the garden into two parts, winding through it like a curving, natural path. Dotted about the garden are carefully pruned pine trees, azalea bushes clipped into huge globes, or perhaps a towering cryptomeria whose arching branches protect guests against the afternoon sun. Although the garden floor is swept clean, it may still have a vagrant leaf

The stepping stones of the roji, *the "dewy path" leading to the tea room, whose open entranceway reveals the interior mats where guests will kneel for tea.*

or pine needle strewn here and there. As one waits for the host's appearance, the garden slowly begins to impose a kind of magic, drawing one away from the outside world.

When all the guests have arrived, they sound a wooden gong,

and the host silently appears to beckon them to the tea room. Each guest in turn stops at the water basin for a sip. At closer range, the teahouse turns out to be a rustic thatch-roofed hut with gray plaster walls and an asymmetrical supporting framework of hand-hewn woods. The floor is pitched above the ground as in the traditional house, but instead of a doorway there is a small square hole through which one must climb on his knees—a psychological design feature intended to ensure that all worldly dignity is left outside. Only the humble can enter here, for each must kneel in the sight of the others present.

The interior of the tea room may feel cramped at first. Although the room is virtually bare, there seems little space left after the other guests have knelt about the central hearth. The room is in the *sukiya* style favored by Rikyū, with the walls a patchwork of dull plaster, raw wood, a few *shōji* rice-paper windows, and a small *tokonoma* art alcove. The only decoration is a single object on the *tokonoma* dais and the hanging scroll against the back wall. This impression of simple rusticity is deliberately deceptive, however, for the tea room is actually fashioned from the finest available woods and costs considerably more per unit area than the host's home. It is ironic that the sense of poverty and antimaterialism pervading the tea room can be achieved only at enormous expense, yet this deceit is one of the outstanding creations of Zen culture. The room and its psychological impact have been eloquently analyzed by the Zen scholar D. T. Suzuki.

As I look around, in spite of its obvious simplicity the room betrays every mark of thoughtful designing: the windows are irregularly inserted; the ceiling is not of one pattern; the materials used, simple and unornamental . . . the floor has a small square opening where hot water is boiling in an artistically-shaped iron kettle.

The papered *shōji* covering the windows admit only soft light, shutting out direct sunshine. . . . As I sit here quietly before the fireplace, I become conscious of the burning of incense. The odor is singularly nerve soothing. . . . Thus composed in mind, I hear a soft breeze passing through the needle leaves of the pine tree; the sound mingles with the trickling of water from a bamboo pipe into the stone basin.[1]

The tea ceremony is intended to engage all the senses, soothing each in turn. As described by Suzuki, the organs of sight, hearing, and smell are all embraced even before the ceremony begins. The purpose, of course, is to create a feeling of harmony and tranquility conducive to the reverential spirit of the Zen sacrament. The surroundings massage your mind and adjust your attitude. This point is particularly stressed by Suzuki.

Where [tranquility] is lacking, the art will lose its significance altogether. . . . The massing of rocks, the trickling of water, the thatched hut, the old pine trees sheltering it, the moss-covered stone lantern, the sizzling of the kettle water, and the light softly filtering through the paper screens—all these are meant uniformly to create a meditative frame of mind.[2]

If a multicourse ceremony is in store, a light meal of hors d'oeuvres and saké is served first. If the dinner hour is near, it may in fact be a substantial repast, all of which is eaten from lacquer or porcelain bowls set on a tray on the floor. After the food is consumed, the guests file out of the teahouse and wait for the host to announce the beginning of the actual tea ceremony. When they return, the ambience of the tea room has been subtly changed: the hanging scroll has vanished from the *tokonoma* to be replaced by a simple vase containing one or two partially opened buds; and a cheerful charcoal fire, seasoned with pine needles and a touch of incense, glows from the sunken hearth in the center of the room there. Water is boiling in a kettle, emitting a sound that suggests wind in a pine forest, a subtle aural effect caused by small bits of iron attached to the bottom of the vessel.

Beside the seated host are the implements of the ceremony: a lacquer or ceramic tea caddy with the powdered green tea (*koicha*), a jar of cold water for replenishing the kettle, a bamboo dipper, a new bamboo whisk, a receptacle for waste water, a linen napkin for the bowl, and, finally, the tea bowl itself, best described as a Zen loving cup or chalice. All the utensils have been selected for their special aesthetic qualities, but the bowl is always the unchallenged *pièce de résistance* and may well be an heirloom from the hand of a seventeenth-century potter. Each guest is also provided with tiny sweet cakes, to salve his mouth against the bitter tea.

With everything at hand, the host begins to prepare the whipped green tea. It is a seated dance, an orchestrated ritual, as deliberate, paced, and formal as the elevation of the host in a Catholic Mass. All the gestures have been practiced for years, until they fit together in a fluid motion. First the bowl is rinsed with hot water from the kettle and wiped with a napkin. Next the bamboo scoop is used to transport the powdered *koicha* from the caddy into the bowl, after which boiling water is added from the bamboo dipper. The host then proceeds, with measured motions, to blend the tea with the bamboo whisk, gradually transforming the dry powder and boiling water into a jade blend as exquisitely beautiful as it is harshly bitter.

The guest of honor has the first taste. Taking the bowl, he salutes the host and then samples the preparation, complimenting the host on its quality. After two more precise sips, he wipes the lip with a napkin he has brought for that purpose, rotates the bowl, and passes it to the next guest, who repeats the ritual. The last to drink must empty the bowl. Curiously enough, only the host is denied a taste of his handiwork. After the formal drinking of *koicha*, the bowl is rinsed and a second batch of tea is made—this time a thinner variety known as *usucha*. Although it is also whipped Sung-style, it is considerably lighter in consistency and taste.

After the second cup of tea, the formal part of the ceremony is completed, and the guests are at liberty to relax, enjoy sweets, and discuss Zen aesthetics. The focus of conversation is usually the tea bowl, which is passed around for all to admire in detail. Comments on the flower arrangement are also in order, as is a

bit of poetry appropriate to the season. What is not discussed —indeed, what no one wants to discuss—is the world outside the garden gate. Each guest is at one with himself, his place, and the natural setting. Values have been subtly guided into perspective, spirits purified, appreciation of beauty rewarded; for a fleeting moment the material world of dualities has become as insubstantial as a dream.

The tea ceremony is the great parable of Zen culture, which teaches by example that the material world is a thief depriving us of our most valuable possessions—naturalness, simplicity, self-knowledge. But it is also much more; its underlying aesthetic principles are the foundation of latter-day Zen culture. It is a perfect blending of the three faces of Zen. First there are the physical art forms themselves: the tea ceremony deeply influenced architectural tastes, bringing into being the informal *sukiya* style to replace the rigid *shoin* formulas of the *samurai* house; the art of flower arrangement, or Ikebana, owes much to the floral arrangements required for the ceremony; painting and calligraphy were influenced by the understated decorative requirements of the *tokonoma* hanging scroll; lacquer ware developed in directions designed to complement the artistic principles of the ceremony utensils; and, finally, the growth of Japanese ceramic art from the fifteenth century onward was largely due to the particular aesthetic and practical needs of the tea ceremony.

The second face of Zen, tranquility in a troubled world, found its finest expression in *cha-no-yu*, which demonstrates as no sermon ever could the Zen approach to life.

The third face of Zen is that of aesthetics. By becoming a vehicle for the transmission of Zen aesthetic principles, *cha-no-yu* has preserved Zen culture for all times. It has given the

---

The solemn ritual of whipping powdered tea with boiling water in preparation for the tea ceremony; the central focus is on the drinking bowl while the tea caddy rests at the right and the water cauldron with dipper at the left.

people at large a standard of taste, guaranteeing that certain basic ideals of beauty will always be preserved against the ravages of mechanical civilization. And it is in this connection that we must examine the special features of the tea ceremony introduced by Hideyoshi's tea master, Sen no Rikyū. To the ancient Zen ideas of *yūgen* and *sabi* he brought the new concept of *wabi*.

Yūgen, the realization of profundity through open-ended suggestion, found its finest expression in Nō poetry. *Sabi* grew out of the Heian admiration for lovely things on the verge of extinction. By the medieval period this curious attitude was extended to things already old, and so entered the idea of *sabi*, a term denoting objects agreeably mellowed with age. *Sabi* also brought melancholy overtones of loneliness, of age left behind by time. New objects are assertive and striving for attention; old, worn objects have the quiet, peaceful air that exudes tranquility, dignity, and character. Although there is no word in a Western language precisely equivalent to *sabi*, the ideal is well understood. For example, we say that the sunburned face of a fisherman has more character than that of a beardless youth. But to the Japanese *sabi* is first and foremost the essence of beauty, whether in a weathered house or temple, the frayed golden threads of fabric binding a Zen scroll, a withered bough placed in the *tokonoma* alcove, or an ancient kettle rusty with time. The ideal of *sabi*, which became part of the Zen aesthetic canon of beauty, was perfectly at home in the tea ceremony, where even the utensils were deliberately chosen for their weathered look.

Sabi, however, seemed an incomplete ideal to Sen no Rikyū. The fact that rich objects are old does not make them less rich. *Sabi* can still encompass snobbery. As tea master for both Nobunaga and Hideyoshi, Rikyū was so pained by their ostentation that he eventually revolutionized the tea ceremony and created a new aesthetic standard: *wabi*, a deliberate restraint, which is exemplified in his tea party of the single morning glory. *Wabi*, now a cornerstone of Zen aesthetic theory, is well described in a poem by Rikyū, which includes the lines:

How much does a person lack himself,
Who feels the need to have so many things.

In a sense, *wabi* is the glorification of artificial poverty, artificial because there must be the element of forced restraint and in genuine poverty there is nothing to restrain. The *wabi* tea ceremony permits no hint of wealth to be in evidence; those who enter the tea garden must leave their worldly status at the gate. Similarly, the *sukiya*-style teahouse must look like a rustic hut—not made out of something new, for that would destroy *sabi*, but not out of expensive antique woods, either. This ideal extends even to the floral arrangement, one or at most two buds; the clothes one wears, simple not dressy; the pots and cups, plain and undecorated.

Wabi purged the tea ceremony of all its lingering aristocratic qualities, bringing into being *cha-no-yu* as it is practiced today. Today many Japanese, even those who practice neither tea drinking nor Zen, know and appreciate the ideals preserved in the ceremony. In recent years the concept of *wabi* has become the rallying point for those who regret the intrusions of the modern West into traditional Japanese culture, and *cha-no-yu* is valued as never before as a lesson in life's true values.

CHAPTER 14
Zen Ceramic Art

Thou, silent form, dost tease us out of thought
As doth eternity.

John Keats, *Ode on a Grecian Urn*

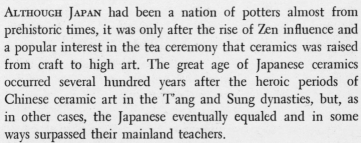

ALTHOUGH JAPAN had been a nation of potters almost from prehistoric times, it was only after the rise of Zen influence and a popular interest in the tea ceremony that ceramics was raised from craft to high art. The great age of Japanese ceramics occurred several hundred years after the heroic periods of Chinese ceramic art in the T'ang and Sung dynasties, but, as in other cases, the Japanese eventually equaled and in some ways surpassed their mainland teachers.

The Stone Age Jōmon tribes in Japan created some of the richest figurine art of any of the world's prehistoric peoples. These Jōmon figurines, fired at low temperatures and rarely

over six or eight inches in height, are a classic puzzle to anthro-
pologists and art historians, for they sometimes seem Polynesian,
sometimes pre-Columbian, and sometimes pure abstraction in
the modern sense of the term. Indeed, certain Jōmon figurines
could pass as works of Picasso or Miró. At times the features of
the body were rendered recognizably, but usually they were
totally stylized and integrated into the figure as part of some
larger interest in material and pure form. It was a noble beginning for what would be a permanent Japanese interest in the
look and feel of natural clay.

When the Jōmon were displaced around the third century
B.C. by the Yayoi, their beautiful figurine art disappeared, and
for several centuries Japan produced mainly pedestrian crocks
and drinking vessels. The few figurines created retained little
of the sophisticated Jōmon abstraction. Around the turn of the
fourth century A.D., however, Yayoi potters found their métier,
and began the famous *haniwa* figurines, hollow-eyed statuettes
in soft brown clay which were used to decorate aristocratic
tombs, and simple but elegant vases and water pots in low-fired
brown clay, which often were dyed with cinnabar and which
give evidence of being thrown on some form of primitive wheel.

This domestic ware was in such demand that a class of pro-
fessional potters came into being—inevitably leading to a gradual
falling off of the individualistic character of the pots, as craftsmen began to mass-produce what had previously been a
personal art form. The Korean Buddhist culture which reached
Japan in the fifth and sixth centuries brought the Japanese new
techniques for high-firing their stoneware pots, introducing a
process whereby ashes from the kiln were allowed to adhere
to the surface of a piece to produce a natural glaze. These new
high-temperature pots had a hard surface texture and an ashen-
gray color, while the existing native wares of low-fired porous
clays retained their natural brown hues.

Typically the average Japanese preferred the natural-colored,
soft clay vessels, and so the two types of pottery continued to
be produced side by side for several hundred years, with the
aristocracy choosing the hard-surfaced mainland-style gray works

and the common people continuing to use the simpler, un-decorated brown vessels, which were often fashioned by hand. The importance of this instinctive Japanese reaction for the later acceptance of Zen-inspired ceramic art cannot be over-stressed. Not only did the Japanese love of natural clay make them reject glazes for centuries after they had learned the necessary techniques, they also seem to have had little spon-taneous interest in decorating their pots or using high-firing or mechanized techniques for their production, perhaps because the technology came between man and object, distancing the potter too far from his handiwork. Japanese potters cherished their regional individuality, and they continued to express their personal sensibilities in their work, so there were a multiplicity of rural kilns and a wide variety of styles.

The passion for Chinese culture during the Nara period of the eighth century led to a brief fling with T'ang Chinese-style three-color glazed wares among the imitative Japanese aristoc-racy; but these seem to have been too much at odds with na-tive instincts, for they were soon forgotten. After the govern-ment moved to Kyōto and launched the Heian era, both the indigenous pottery techniques—the low-fired, brown, porous pots for the common people and the high-fired, gray, polished bowls for the aristocracy—continued to thrive side by side. However, technical advances in the high-firing kilns brought about subtle changes in the mock-glazes of the aristocratic wares. It was discovered that if they were fired in an atmosphere where there was abundant oxygen, the fused particles of fueled ash on the surface would turn amber, whereas if oxygen was excluded from the kiln, the surface ash would fuse to a pastel green. Thus by varying the baking process, Heian potters could produce a variety of light colors, creating a pottery considerably more delicate than had been possible before. Aside from this refined technique for firing, however, the Japanese steadfastly refused to change their traditional methods of making pots.

For this reason, Japanese ceramics were deliberately kept at a technically primitive stage until the early part of the thir-teenth century while the Chinese were making considerable advances in the art. During the years from the ninth to the thirteenth century, while the Japanese isolated themselves from the mainland, the Sung Chinese were learning of new glazes far more subtle and refined than those employed during the T'ang. In the early years of the thirteenth century, when Japanese monks journeyed to China to study the new faith of Zen, they were dazzled by the sophisticated new Chinese wares they encountered. Through the offices of Zen a second revolution in Japanese ceramics occurred.

The instrument for this second revolution (according to tradition) was the priest Dōgen, founder of Japanese Sōtō Zen, who on one of his trips to China was accompanied by a Japanese potter known as Toshiro. Toshiro stayed in China for six years, studying the Sung techniques of glazing, and on his return he opened a kiln at Seto, where he began copying Sung glazed wares. Although he has been called the father of modern Japanese ceramics, his attempts to duplicate the highly praised Sung products were not entirely successful. Furthermore, the wares he did produce, decorative and thick-glazed, found no acceptance except among the aristocracy and priesthood, both of whom favored Seto wares for the new pastime of drinking Chinese tea. But while the Zen aesthetes and tea drinkers amused themselves with Seto's fake Sung celadons, the commoners continued to use unglazed stoneware.

All this changed dramatically around the middle of the sixteenth century with the rise of an urban middle class and the sudden popularity of the Zen tea ceremony among this new bourgeoisie. Zen, which had brought Chinese glazes to Japan in the thirteenth century, sparked the emergence of a brilliant era of glazed ceramic art in the sixteenth. No longer content with primitive stoneware or reproductions of Chinese vessels, the potters of Japan finally developed native styles at once uniquely Japanese and as sophisticated as any the world has seen. It was another triumph for Zen culture. Rural kilns with long traditions of stoneware water vessels converted to the production of tea-ceremony wares, and throughout the land the search was on for colored glazes. The craze reached such heights that the shōgun generals Nobunaga and Hideyoshi rewarded their successful military commanders not with decorations but with some particularly coveted tea-ceremony utensils.

Although ceramic tea caddies and water jars were required for the ceremony, the real emphasis was on the drinking bowl, for this was the piece that was handled and admired at close range. A proper bowl, in addition to being beautiful, had to be large enough and deep enough to allow sufficient tea for three of four drinkers to be whisked; it had no handle and consequently had to be of a light, porous, nonconducting clay with a thick, rough glaze to act as a further insulator and to permit safe handling between drinkers; the rim had to be thick and tilted slightly inward, to provide the participants with a pleasant sensation while drinking and to minimize dripping. In other words, these bowls were as functionally specialized in their own way as a brandy snifter or a champagne glass of today.

A number of styles of tea bowl developed during the sixteenth century, reflecting the artistic visions of various regional potters and the different clays available. What these bowls had in common, beyond their essential functional characteristics, was an adherence to the specialized dictates of Zen aesthetic theory. Equally important, they were a tribute to the historic Japanese reverence for natural clay. Even though they were glazed, portions of the underlying clay texture were often allowed to show through, and the overall impression was that the glaze was used to emphasize the texture of the underlying clay, not disguise it. The colors of the glazes were natural and organic, not hard and artificial.

The social unrest preceding the rise of Nobunaga caused a number of potters to leave the Seto area, site of the fake Ṣung production, and resettle in the province of Mino, where three basic styles of tea bowl eventually came to prominence. First there was the Chinese-style tea vessel, which had been the mainstay of the older Seto kilns. Yellow glazes, once the monopoly of Seto, were also used at Mino, but different clays, combined with advancing technical competence and a new willingness to experiment, produced a new "Seto" ware that was

A Shino bowl (Momoyama) whose deliberately imperfect shape, glaze, and decoration are all a device to lead the mind past any impulse toward easy categorization to a direct experiencing of its surface texture, material, and process of creation.

a rich yellow and considerably more Japanese than Chinese. Second there was a new, thoroughly Zen-style bowl developed by the Mino potters. It was broader-based than the Chinese style, with virtually straight sides, and it was covered with a thick, creamy off-white glaze. Warm and endearing in appearance, with a flowing sensuous texture inviting to the touch, it became known as Shino.

Some say Shino bowls were named after a celebrated master of the tea ceremony, while others maintain the term was taken from the Japanese word for white, *shiro*. Whatever the case, this was the first glazed ware of truly native origins; and it marked the beginning of a new Japanese attitude toward pottery. No longer inhibited by reverence for Chinese prototypes, the makers of Shino let their spontaneity run wild. The new white glaze was deliberately applied in a haphazard manner, often covering only part of the bowl or being allowed to drip and run. Sometimes part of the glaze was wiped off after it had been applied, leaving thin spots where the brown under-clay could show through after the firing. Or bubbles, burns, and soot were allowed to remain in the glaze as it was fired. Sometimes the white glaze was bathed in a darker coating in which incisions were made to allow the white to show through. At other times, sketchy designs, seemingly thrown down with a half-dry brush, were scribbled on the white bowls so that they appeared to be covered with Zen graffiti. Throughout all these innovations, the potters seemed to want to produce works as rough, coarse, and unsophisticated as possible. Before long they had a gray glaze as well, and finally they produced a shiny black glaze whose precise formulation remains one of the unsolved mysteries of Momoyama art.

The next color to enter the Mino repertory, after yellow, white, gray, and black, was a stunning green. This was the third style of Mino tea bowl, and it was invented by a disciple of Rikyū whose name, Oribe, has been given to an incredible variety of wares—tea bowls, tea caddies, water jars, incense burners, and a host of dishes for serving food. Sometimes the wares were solid green, but Oribe also had a habit of splashing the green over one section of a piece, or allowing it to run into one corner of a plate and freeze there in a limpid puddle. The portions of Oribe wares not covered with the splash of green were dull shades, ranging from gray to reddish brown, and on this background artists began to paint decorative designs— flowers, geometrical figures, even small sketches or still-lifes— something new and revolutionary for Japanese ceramics, but the forerunner of the profusion of decorative wares that appeared after the Momoyama. Shino had broken the bonds of the centuries of unglazed stoneware and proper copies of Chinese pots by introducing a native style of glazing and a new aesthetic freedom; Oribe led the way into a new world

*Oribe tray from Momoyama era, brown and white with touches of
dark green glaze spilling over two of the sides—a device to draw the
viewer into the creation and make him share the potter's involve-
ment.*

of anything-goes pottery, with half-glazes, painted decorative
motifs, and experimentation in new, hitherto unknown shapes
and types of vessels.

While the native Japanese potters at Mino were expanding
their craft, another important development with far-reaching
consequences for the Zen arts was taking place in the far south
of the Japanese archipelago near the Korean peninsula. The
ceramic arts of Korea were quite advanced at the beginning of
the sixteenth century, with high-fired glazed wares as heavy and
sturdy as the peasant stock from which they sprang. But the
pots were made by building up coils of clay and beating them
into a solid walled vessel rather than throwing them on a
wheel. This combination of high and low seems to have appealed to the Japanese clans living near the Korean mainland,

for they brought a number of Korean potters to the southern city of Karatsu and started an industry.

The staple product of the Korean craftsman was a crude medium-sized bowl with sloping sides, used in their homeland for individual servings of rice. The primitive quality of these bowls perfectly suited the growing inverse snobbery of the tea ceremony, and soon Japanese aesthetes were drinking tea and admiring the Zen beauty in the Korean rice bowl. While the Mino potters were deliberately making the Sung tea bowl rougher and rougher (that is, adding *wabi*), those in Karatsu found themselves with a foreign bowl ready-made for tea.

When Hideyoshi invaded Korea during the last decade of the sixteenth century, he and his generals were careful to kidnap as many Korean potters as possible, whom they settled over a large part of Japan. No longer restricted to a small area in the south, the Koreans injected a vigorous transfusion of peasant taste into all of Japanese ceramic art, extinguishing the last remnants of the refined Sung ideals. The Momoyama tea masters were given a new but still foreign standard of rustic chic perfectly in accord with *wabi* tea.

Not surprisingly, it was Sen no Rikyū who synthesized the new native freedom and the fresh influx of mainland technology to create the undisputed glory of Japanese ceramics—the famous *raku*. Unquestionably Japan's most original contribution to the history of ceramics, *raku* is produced in a manner entirely different from earlier techniques, and it is impossible to speak of *raku* without speaking of Zen. As might be expected, *raku* was invented in the Zen center of Kyōto, a city with no previous history of ceramic production, and it came into being when Rikyū happened to take a fancy to the roof tiles being produced by a Korean workman named Chōjirō. Rikyū hit upon the notion that the texture and feel of these tiles would be perfect for *wabi*-style tea, and he encouraged Chōjirō in the making of a few tea bowls with the materials and firing techniques used for tiles.

The bowls Chōjirō made were neither thrown on a wheel nor built up from coils, but molded and carved like sculpture.

A mixture of clays was first blended to gain the desired consistency of lightness and plasticity, after which a spatula and knife were used to shape a rough-sided, textured bowl whose sense of process was flaunted rather than obscured—an overt tactile quality perhaps first seen in the West in the rough-hewn sculptures of Rodin. These bowls were fired in a most unconventional manner: rather than being placed cold in a woodburning kiln and gradually heated, baked, and cooled over a period of days, they, like the tiles, were thrust directly into a torrid charcoal kiln for a blistering thermal shock, which gave them an instant look of the ravaged face of ancient *sabi*. *Raku* wares were first made in black with an ironlike glaze that is almost like frozen lava, but the later repertory included glazes that were partly or wholly red or off-white. Unlike the Shino and Oribe bowls, *raku* pieces were not decorated with designs or spots of color; they were *wabi* and *sabi* with unpretentious, weathered grace. The last term you think of when seeing *raku* is ornate.

Rikyū found *raku* bowls perfect for the tea ceremony; they were austere, powerful, seemingly wrenched from melted rock. In shape they were broad-based with gently rounded, one might almost say organically rounded, sides leading to an undulating lip, wrapping in slightly over the tea, thereby holding the heat and preventing drips. Not only were they light and porous, allowing for minimal heat conduction and comfortable handling, their center of gravity was so low they were almost impossible to tip over, permitting easy whisking of the powdered tea as they rested on the *tatami*-matted floor of the tea room. (It should be noted that special bowls for summer usage deemphasized certain of these characteristics: they were thinnerwalled and shallower, since the object in hot months was to dissipate heat rather than conserve it.) But the most appealing qualities of the *raku* were its sculptural sense of natural plastic form and its soft, bubbly, almost liquid glaze, which virtually invites one to hold it in his lips. Also, the colors of the glazes just happen to contrast beautifully with the pale sea-green of the powdered tea.

This was the end of the search for the perfect Zen tea bowl, and Hideyoshi was so pleased with Chōjirō's handiwork that he gave the potter's family a seal bearing the word that would give the form its name: *raku*, meaning pleasure or comfort. Chōjirō's descendants became the *raku* dynasty, as generation after generation they set the standards for others to follow.

Hideyoshi's act of official recognition meant that Japanese potters were no longer merely craftsmen, but fully accredited artists. In later years, Japanese ceramics became distinguished in many areas—from the traditional wares produced at a multiplicity of local kilns to a vast new nationwide porcelain industry producing decorative works for both export and home consumption. Tea-ceremony vessels were created in great profusion as well, but, unfortunately, genuine art cannot be mass-produced. By the eighteenth century, the great age of Zen ceramic art was over, never to be recovered. Today the early wares of the Zen Momoyama artists command their weight in gold, perhaps platinum. This is the great irony of the *wabi* tea vessels, if not of all Zen culture.

Tea bowls, the major expression of Zen art, seem at once both primitive and strikingly modern. To begin to understand this contradiction we must go back to our own nineteenth century in the West, when tastes ran to decoration for its own sake and the rule of perfect, symmetrical, polished form was the aesthetic ideal. Into this smug, serene sea of aesthetic sureties, which in some ways reached back to the ancient Greeks, the English critic John Ruskin threw a boulder when he wrote:

Never demand an exact finish for its own sake, but only for some practical or noble end. . . . [t]he demand for perfection is always a sign of a misunderstanding of the ends of art. . . . Imperfection is in some sort essential to all we know of life. It is the sign of life in a mortal body. . . . To banish imperfection is to destroy expression, to check exertion, to paralyze vitality. All things are literally better, lovelier, and more beloved for the imperfections which have been divinely appointed.[1]

A *black* raku *tea bowl, attributed to Chōjirō (1516–1592), in the classic rounded style, which suggests the feel of molten lava. (Mitsui Collection, Tokyo)*

Ruskin was rediscovering a large piece of Zen aesthetic theory while laying the groundwork for many of our modern ideals of beauty.

To see the similarity, let us examine for a moment a few of the finer points of Zen aesthetic theory as exemplified in the classic tea bowls. In form the bowls are frequently asymmetrical and imperfect; the glaze seems to be a species of moss still in the process of spreading over portions of the sides it somehow never managed to reach, and it is uneven, marred by cracks, lumps, scratches, and foreign contaminants. If imperfection is the goal, these bowls extend well beyond Ruskin's original standards. But not only are they imperfect, they also seem old and weathered, with the natural patina of a dried-up riverbed. They show absolutely no evidence that any conscious attempt

Tea bowl attributed to Dōnyū (1599–1656), the third raku *potter, with a brilliant blue-black luster surface revealing a glaze overflow and a T-shaped scar.*

was made to create a work of art; they appear to be completely functional.

It is all a deception. Master potters spend literally decades perfecting the Zen art of the controlled haphazard. One of the first principles they honor is *wabi*, which deplores nonfunctional decorative objects, polished surfaces, artificiality in shape or color, and anything unnatural to the materials used. Works of art without *wabi* may have superficial external beauty, but they forfeit inner warmth. Bowls out of shape, with cracks, blobs, and ashes in the glaze, invite us to partake of the process of creation through their asymmetry and imperfection. They also lead us past the surface by virtue of its being deliberately marred.

Making a bowl with *wabi* is considerably more difficult than making a smooth, symmetrical, perfectly glazed piece. The creation of contrived "accidents," on which much of the illusion of artlessness depends, is particularly difficult. Everywhere there are scars, contaminants, spotty glaze—all as deliberate as the decoration on a Dresden plate; connoisseurship consists in admiring how the artist managed to make it seem so natural and unavoidable.

The same skill goes to make a piece look old, the essential quality of *sabi*. By suggesting long years of use, the bowls acquire humility and richness. There is no need to "wear the new off" in order to give them character; they are already mellow and unpretentious. The potter's genius has gone to create the *sense* of wear, a quality considerably more difficult to realize than an aura of newness.

The potter wants the Zen connoisseur to understand what he has done: to see the clay, to feel and admire its texture, to appreciate the reasons for the type and color of the glaze. The pieces are carefully contrived to draw attention to both their original elements and the process by which these elements were blended. For example, a bowl whose glaze only partially covers its clay provides a link with the natural world from which it came. Its texture springs out, like that of a piece of natural driftwood. At the same time, the bald clay, the streaks of glaze, the hand-formed sculpture, allow one to recognize the materials and the process of formation. When the potter keeps no secrets, one enters into the exhilaration of his moment of creation. Once again, this is a deliberate aesthetic device, reminding one that the potter is an individual artist, not a faceless craftsman. The look and feel of Zen ceramics make them seem forerunners of the modern craft-pottery movement, but few modern potters are blessed with the rich legacy of Zen aesthetic ideals that made these ceramics possible. The secret lies deep in ancient Zen culture, which taught the Momoyama masters how the difficult could be made to seem effortless.

CHAPTER 15
Zen and Haiku

Music, when soft voices die,
Vibrates in the memory—

Percy Bysshe Shelley

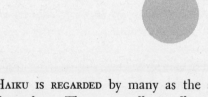

HAIKU IS REGARDED by many as the supreme achievement of Zen culture. The supposedly wordless doctrine of Zen has been accompanied throughout its history by volumes of *kōan* riddles, *sūtras*, and commentaries, but until Haiku was invented it had never enjoyed its own poetic form, nor might it ever have if the rise of popular Zen culture had not happily coincided with a particularly receptive stage in the evolution of traditional Japanese poetry—an accident seized upon by a great lyric poet of the early Edo period to create an exciting new Zen form. Haiku today is a worldwide cult, with California poets striving to capture in English the spareness and fleeting images that seem so effortless in the Japanese of the early Zen masters.

On first acquaintance Japanese seems an unlikely language for poetry. It is a syllabic tongue with each syllable ending in a vowel or the nasal *n*; consequently there are only five true rhymes in the entire language. Italian poets overcame a somewhat similar handicap, but their language is stressed, which Japanese is not. With no usable rhymes and no stress, how can the music of poetry be created? Over the centuries, the Japanese solved this problem by replacing meter with a system of fixed syllables—either five or seven—for each line. (This means that some lines of Japanese poetry may have only one word, but the system seems to work.) In place of rhyme, Japanese poets learned to orchestrate the pitch of individual vowels within a single line to give a sense of music. This device was illustrated by the American poet Kenneth Rexroth using a poem from the classical era. (The vowels are pronounced as in Italian.)

> Fu-ta-ri yu-ke-do
> Yu-ki su-gi ga-ta-ki
> A-ki ya-ma wo
> I-ka-de ka ki-mi ga
> Hi-to-ri ko-ge na-mu

In his analysis of this particular poem, Rexroth has pointed out that the first and last lines contain all five vowels in the language, whereas the middle lines contain various combinations and repetitions, which produce a pronounced musical effect.[1] The ability to create such music without rhyme, one of the finer achievements of Japanese poetry, is far more difficult than might at first be imagined and leads naturally to assonance, or the close repetition of vowel sounds, and alliteration, the repetition of similar consonant sounds. Some of the vowels have psychological overtones, at least to the sensitive Japanese ear: *u* is soft, *a* is sharp and resonant, *o* connotes vagueness tinged with profundity.[2] Various consonants also convey an emotional sense in a similar manner.

Another clever device of the early Japanese versifiers was the use of words with double meanings. One example of this is the so-called pivot word, which occurs approximately halfway through a poem such as the above and serves both to complete the sense of the first part of the poem with one meaning and to begin a new sense and direction with its second meaning. This can at times produce a childish effect, and it does not always elevate the overall dignity of the verse. Another use of double meaning is far more demanding. Since the Japanese *kana* script is entirely phonetic and allows for no distinction in spelling between homonyms, words which sound alike but have different meanings, it is possible to carry two or more ideas through a poem. (A somewhat labored example in English might be, "My tonights hold thee more," "My two knights hold the moor." If these were written alike and pronounced alike, then the poem could mean either or both.) The first meaning may be a concrete example of a lover pining for his love, and the second a metaphor. Ideally, the two meanings support each other, producing a resonance said to be truly remarkable.

The early Japanese poets overcame the limitations of the Japanese language both by attuning their ears to the music of the words and by capitalizing on the large incidence of homonyms. They settled the matter of meter, as noted, by prescribing the number of syllables per line, with the principal form being five lines with syllable counts of 5,7,5,7, and 7. This thirty-one-syllable poem, known as the *waka*, became the Japanese "sonnet" and by far the most popular poetic form during the Heian era. Almost all a poet can do in five lines, however, is to record a single emotion or observation. The medium governed the message, causing Japanese poets early on to explore their hearts more than their minds. The *waka* became a cry of passion; a gentle confirmation of love; a lament for the brevity of blossoms, colored leaves, the seasons, life itself. A sampling of *waka* from the early classical era shows the aesthetic sense of the seasons and lyric charm of these verses.

Tsuki ya aranu	Can it be that the moon has changed?
Haru ya mukashi no	Can it be that the spring
Haru naranu	Is not the spring of old times?
Waga mi hitotsu wa	Is it my body alone
Moto no mi nishite	That is just the same?[3]

Judged on its concentrated power alone, for this is virtually all an English reader can evaluate, this poem is a masterpiece. Its content can be condensed into five lines because much of its impact lies in its suggestiveness. It is, however, closed-ended, with no philosophical implications other than a wry look at human perceptions. Haiku added new dimensions to Japanese poetry.

The early aristocratic era gave Japanese poetry its form, the five-line *waka*, and its subject matter, nature and the emotions. Later the familiar Japanese idea that life is but a fleeting moment and all things must blossom and fade was added. One critic has noted that as this idea took hold, poems gradually changed from praise of the plum blossom, which lasts for weeks, to praise of the cherry blossom, which fades in a matter of days.

Hisakata no	On a day in spring
Hikari nodokeki	When the light throughout the sky
Haru no hi ni	Warms with tranquility,
Shizugokoro naku	Why is it with unsettled heart
Hana no chiru ran	That the cherry flowers fall?[4]

Japanese poetry of the pre-Zen period has been handed to us primarily in a few famous collections. The first great anthology of Japanese poetry is the *Manyōshū*, a volume of verses from the middle of the eighth century. A glance through the *Manyōshū* shows that the earliest poets did not confine themselves to five-line verses, but indulged in longer verses on heroic subjects, known as *chōka*. The tone, as Donald Keene has observed, is often more masculine than feminine, that is, more vigorous than refined. As sensibilities softened in the early part of the Heian era and native verse became the prerogative of women, while men struggled with the more "important" language of China, the feminine tone prevailed to such an extent that male writers posed as women when using the native script. The next great collection of verse, the *Kokinshū*, published in the tenth century, was virtually all five-line *waka* concerned with seasons, birds, flowers, and fading love, and embracing the aesthetic ideals of *aware*, *miyabi*, and *yūgen*.

As the aristocratic culture gradually lost control in the twelfth and thirteenth centuries, a new verse form, derived from the *waka*, came into being: *renga*. This form consisted of a string of verses in the repeated sequence of 5,7,5 and 7,7 syllables per line—in reality a related series of *waka* but with the difference that no two consecutive two- or three-line verse sequences could be composed by the same individual. At first this new form seemed to offer hope of freeing poets from the increasingly confining range of subject matter prescribed for the *waka*. Unfortunately, the opposite happened. Before long the *renga* was saddled with a set of rules covering which verse should mention what season; at what point the moon, cherry blossoms, and the like should be noted; and so forth. Little creativity was possible under such restrictions. Versifying became, in fact, a party game much in favor with provincial *samurai* and peasants alike in medieval times. While the remaining Kyōto aristocrats tried to keep their *renga* in the spirit of the classical *waka*, with allusions to Chinese poems and delicate melancholy, the provincials threw *renga* parties whose only aesthetic concern was adherence to the rules of the game. During the Ashikaga age, *renga* and saké parties were the most popular forms of entertainment, but *renga*'s only genuine contribution to Japanese poetry was the use of the vernacular by provincial poets, which finally broke the stranglehold of Heian feminine aesthetics.

By the beginning of the Momoyama era, linked verse had

run its course and the time was ripe for a new form. The new form was Haiku, which was nothing more than the first three lines of a *renga*. The *waka* had been aristocratic, and the best *renga* provincial, but the Haiku was the creation of the new merchant class. (To be rigorously correct, the form was at first called *haikai*, after the first verse of the *renga*, which was called the *hokku*. The term "Haiku" actually came into use in the nineteenth century.) Although the Haiku was a response to the demands of the merchant class, its composers almost immediately split into two opposing groups, superficially similar in outlook to the older classical and provincial schools. One group established a fixed set of rules specifying a more or less artificial language, while the other turned to epigrams in the speech of the people. The form was on the way to becoming yet another party game when a disenchanted follower of the second school broke away and created a personal revolution in Japanese verse. This was the man now considered Japan's finest poet, who finally brought Zen to Japanese poetry: the famous Haiku master Bashō (1644–1694).

Bashō was born a *samurai* in an age when it was little more than an empty title, retained by decree of the Edo (Tokyo) government. He was fortunate to be in the service of a prosperous *daimyō* who transmitted his interest in Haiku to Bashō at an early age. This idyllic life ended abruptly when Bashō was twenty-two: the lord died, and he was left to shift for himself. His first response was to enter a monastery, but after a time went to Kyōto to study Haiku. By the time he was thirty he had moved on to Edo to teach and write. At this point he was merely an adequate versifier, but his technical competence attracted many to what became the Bashō "school," as well as making him a welcome guest at *renga* gatherings. His poems in the Haiku style seem to have relied heavily on striking similes or metaphors:

> Red pepper pods!
> Add wings to them,
> and they are dragonflies![5]

This verse is certainly "open-ended" insofar as it creates a reverberation of images in the mind, and, what is more, the effect is achieved by the comparison of two concrete images. There is no comment; the images are simply thrown out to give the mind a starting point. But the overall impact remains merely decorative art. It reflects the concept of *aware*, or a pleasing recognition of beauty, rather than *yūgen*, the extension of awareness into a region beyond words.

When he was about thirty-five, Bashō created a Haiku that began to touch the deeper regions of the mind. This is the famous

> Kare-eda ni   On a withered branch
> karasu-no tomari-keri   a crow has settled—
> aki-no-kure   autumn nightfall.[6]

As a simple juxtaposition of images the poem is striking enough, but it also evokes a comparison of the images, each of which enriches the other. The mind is struck as with a hammer, bringing the senses up short and releasing a flood of associations. Its only shortcoming is that the scene is static; it is a painting, not a happening of the sort that can sometimes trigger the sudden sense of Zen enlightenment.

Perhaps Bashō realized that his art had not yet drunk deeply enough at the well of Zen, for a few years after this poem was written he became a serious Zen student and began to travel around Japan soaking up images. His travel diaries of the last years are a kind of Haiku "poetics," in which he extends the idea of *sabi* to include the aura of loneliness that can surround common objects. Zen detachment entered his verses; all personal emotion was drained away, leaving images objective and devoid of any commentary, even implied.

More important, the Zen idea of transience appeared. Not the transience of falling cherry blossoms but the fleeting instant of Zen enlightenment. Whereas the antilogic *kōan* anecdotes were intended to lead up to this moment, Bashō's Haiku were the moment of enlightenment itself, as in his best-known poem:

Furu-ike ya   An ancient pond
kawazu tobi-komu A frog jumps in
mizu-no-oto   The sound of water.

These deceptively simple lines capture an intersection of the timeless and the ephemeral. The poem is said to have described an actual occurrence, an evening broken by a splash. The poet immediately spoke the last two lines of the poem, the ephemeral portion, and much time was then devoted to creating the remaining static and timeless part. This was as it should be, for the inspiration of a Haiku must be genuine and suggest its own lines at the moment it occurs. Zen eschews deliberation and rational analysis; nothing must come between object and perception at the critical moment.

With this poem Bashō invented a new form of Zen literary art, and Haiku was never the same afterward. To write this kind of poem, the artist must completely disengage—if only for an instant—all his interpretive faculties. His mind becomes one with the world around him, allowing his craft to operate instinctively in recording the image he perceives. For a moment he is privy to the inexpressible truth of Zen—that the transient is merely part of the eternal—and this instantaneous perception moves directly from his senses to his innermost understanding, without having to travel through his interpretive faculties. Earlier Zen writings in both Japan and China had described this process, but none had captured the phenomenon itself. By catching the momentary at the very instant of its collision with the eternal, Bashō could produce a high-speed snapshot of the trigger mechanism of Zen enlightenment. In a modern metaphor, the Haiku became a Zen hologram, in which all the information necessary to re-create a large three-dimensional phenomenon was coded into a minuscule key. Any interpretation of the phenomenon would be redundant to a Zen adept, since the philosophical significance would re-create itself spontaneously from the critical images recorded in the poem. Thus a perfect Haiku is not *about* the moment of Zen enlightenment;

it *is* that moment frozen in time and ready to be released in the listener's mind.

Haiku is the most dehumanized of all poetry. Instead of the artist's sensations and feelings, we get simply the names of things. By Western standards they are hardly poems at all, merely a rather abbreviated list. As the critic-poet Kenneth Yasuda has pointed out, a Haiku poet does not give us meaning, he gives us objects that have meaning; he does not describe, he presents.[7] And unlike the poetry of the Nō, Haiku seems a form strangely devoid of symbolism. The tone seems matter-of-fact, even when touching upon the most potentially emotional of subjects. Take, for example, Bashō's poem composed at the grave of one of his beloved pupils.

Tsuka mo ugoke	Grave mound, shake too!
waga naku koe wa	My wailing voice—
aki-no-kaze	the autumn wind.[8]

No betrayal of emotion here, simply a comparison of his grief-ridden voice, a transient thing, with the eternal autumn wind. It is a Zen moment of recognition, devoid of emotion or self-pity, and yet somehow our sympathies spring alive, touching us in a way that the early classical poems on the passage of time never could.

Love in Haiku is directed toward nature as much as toward man or woman. Part of the reason may be the stylistic requirement that every Haiku tell the reader the season. This is done by the so-called season word, which can either be an outright naming of the season (such as the "autumn" wind above) or some mention of a season-dependent natural phenomenon, such as a blossom, a colored leaf (green or brown), a summer bird or insect, snow, and so on. The tone is always loving, never accusatory (a tribute to the nature reverence of ancient Japan), and it can be either light or solemn. Chirps of insects, songs of birds, scents of blossoms, usually serve as the transient element in a Haiku, whereas water, wind, sunshine, and the season itself are the eternal elements.

> Ume-ga-ka ni   With the scent of plums
> notto hi-no deru on the mountain road—suddenly,
> yama-ji kana   sunrise comes![9]

This is nature poetry at its finest, full of all the detached reverence and affection of Zen. It is also impassive and accepting: nature is there to be enjoyed and to teach the lessons of Zen. Bashō's Haiku discover an instant of heightened awareness and pass it on unaltered and without comment. The poem is as uncolored with emotion as is the world it so dispassionately describes. It is up to the reader to know the proper response.

It hardly needs to be said that Bashō's poems must be interpreted on several levels: not only do they describe a moment in the life of the world, they are also symbols or metaphors for deeper truths, which cannot be stated explicitly. Underneath a vivid image of a physical phenomenon is a Zen code pointing toward the nonphysical. Not only was Bashō Japan's finest lyric poet, he was also among the finest interpreters of Zen.

Bashō left a large following. The Haiku was established as Japan's foremost poetic form, and to touch upon every Haiku poet would require an encyclopedia. However, three other Haiku masters were outstanding. The first is Buson (1715–1783), also a well-known painter, whose blithe if somewhat mannered style reflected the gradual dissolution of severe Zen ideals in favor of the lighter touch preferred by the prosperous merchant class.

Buson was also master of the classical double entendre so beloved by the aristocratic poets of the classical era. The first example given here is a subtle reference to the theme of transience, set in the context of an exchange of love poems, while the second is a somewhat ribald jest about the one-night stand.

> Hen-ka naki   No poem you send
> ao-nyōbo yo   in answer—Oh, young lady!
> kure-no haru   Springtime nears its end.[10]

Mijika yo ya	The short night is through:
kemushi-no ue ni	on the hairy caterpillar,
tsuyu-no-tama	little beads of dew.[11]

Buson could also be serious and moving when he tried, as with the following, one of his most admired works.

Mi-ni-shimu ya	The piercing chill I feel:
bō-sai-no kushi	my dead wife's comb, in our bedroom,
neya ni fumu	under my heel . . .[12]

Buson clearly had less Zen about him than Bashō, but his verses suited the temper of his age, and he strongly influenced both students and contemporaries, although not the next great Haiku master, Issa (1762–1826), who was a romantic provincial through and through, immune to the fancy phrasing of the sophisticated Buson school.

Issa is the sentimental favorite in the canons of Japanese Haiku. He used simple, even colloquial language, and he brought heartfelt love to all things he touched, great and small. Although he was not immersed in the heavier aspects of Zen, his lighthearted approach to life was well in accord with the latter days of the Zen revival. His Haiku style seems the literary equivalent of the comic Zen drawings of Hakuin (1685–1768) or Sengai (1751–1837). There is also a Zen quality to his rejection of the literary conventions of the time. Yet Issa was not consciously a rebel; rather, he was a simple, sincere man who wrote sincerely of simple things. His approach to nature was as honest in its own way as Bashō's, but Issa was happy to let his own personality and response shine through, while Bashō deliberately circumvented his own emotions.

Orphaned at an early age and seeing to the grave all the children born during his lifetime (as well as two of his three wives), Issa seems to have known little but hardship. Much of his life was spent as an itinerant poet-priest, an occupation that allowed him to learn the life of the people while also keeping him close to the earth. A compendium of his life's experiences and a fine sampling of his Haiku were recorded in his famous book *The Year of My Life*, which seems to have been his answer to Bashō's travel diaries. However, his humanity was far distant from Bashō's lonely *sabi*. For condensed effect, compare the following with Wordsworth's "Solitary Reaper."

> Yabu-kage ya   In the thicket's shade,
> tatta hitori-no   and all alone, she's singing—
> ta-ue-uta   the rice-planting maid.[13]

Perhaps his most touching poem, which shames into oblivion all the "transient dew" posturing of a thousand years of classical Japanese verse, is the famous Haiku written on the death of one of his children.

> Tsuyu-no-yo wa   The world of dew
> tsuyu-no-yo nagara   Is the world of dew,
> sari nagara   And yet . . .
>   And yet . . .[14]

Issa's rustic, personal voice was not a style to be copied, even if the city poets had wished to do so, and Haiku seems to have fallen into the hands of formula versifiers during the mid-nineteenth century. In the waning years of the century, the last of the four great Haiku masters rose to prominence: Shiki (1867–1902), whose life of constantly failing health was as adversity-plagued as Issa's, but who actively took up the fight against the insincere parlor versifiers then ruling Haiku. No wandering poet-priest, Shiki was a newspaperman, critic, and editor of various Haiku "little magazines." The Zen influence that ruled Bashō's later poetry is missing in Shiki, but the objective imagery is there—only in a tough, modern guise. Shiki's verse is an interesting example of how similar in external appearance the godless austerity of Zen is to the existential atheism of our own century. (This superficial similarity is undoubtedly the reason so much of Zen art seems "modern" to us today—

it is at odds with both classical and romantic ideals.) Thus a completely secular poet like Shiki could revolutionize Haiku as a form of art-for-art's-sake without having to acknowledge openly his debt to Zen.

> Hira-hira to   A single butterfly
> Kaze ni nigarete   Fluttering and drifting
> Chō hitotsu   ⌐   In the wind.[15]

With the poems of Shiki, the influence of Zen had so permeated Haiku that it was taken for granted. Much the same had occurred with all the Zen arts; as the dynamic aspects of the faith faded away, all that was left were the art forms and aesthetic ideals of Zen culture. The rules of the ancient Zen masters were there as a theme for the modern arts, but mainly as a theme on which there could be variations. Zen culture as an entity was slowly dissolving, becoming in modern times merely a part of a larger cultural heritage.

CHAPTER 16
Private Zen:
Flowers and Food

European food—
Every wretched plate
Is round.

Traditional Japanese poem

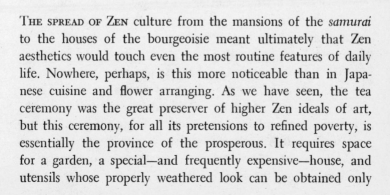

THE SPREAD OF ZEN culture from the mansions of the *samurai* to the houses of the bourgeoisie meant ultimately that Zen aesthetics would touch even the most routine features of daily life. Nowhere, perhaps, is this more noticeable than in Japanese cuisine and flower arranging. As we have seen, the tea ceremony was the great preserver of higher Zen ideals of art, but this ceremony, for all its pretensions to refined poverty, is essentially the province of the prosperous. It requires space for a garden, a special—and frequently expensive—house, and utensils whose properly weathered look can be obtained only at a price. Even a simple Zen garden is hardly available to a modern Japanese living in a cinderblock apartment building.

Everyone, however, can practice the classical art of arranging flowers in a manner reflecting the precepts of Zen. A flower arrangement is to a large garden what a Haiku is to an epic poem—a symbolic, abbreviated form whose condensed suggestiveness can encapsulate the larger world. Similarly, the Zen ideals of *wabi*, or deliberate understatement, and *sabi*, the patina of time, can be captured almost as well in the display of food—in both its artistic arrangement on a plate and the tasteful ceramics employed—as in the arts and ceramics of the tea ceremony. Thus a properly conceived serving of seasonal and subtly flavored foods accompanied by a Zen-inspired flower arrangement can be an everyday version of the tea ceremony and its garden, embodying the same aesthetic principles in a surrogate form just as demanding of Zen taste and sensibility.

It will be recalled that Zen itself is said to have originated when the Buddha silently turned a blossom in his hand before a gathering on Vulture Peak. The lotus blossom was one of the foremost symbols of classical Buddhism for many centuries; indeed the earliest Japanese flower arrangements may have been merely a lotus floating in a water-filled vessel set before a Buddhist altar. To the ancient Buddhists, the flower was a symbol of nature, a momentary explosion of beauty and fragrance embodying all the mysteries of life's cycle of birth and death. The early Japanese, who saw in nature the expression of life's spirit, naturally found the flower a congenial symbol for an abstract philosophy like Buddhism. In the years preceding Zen's arrival in Japan, a parallel but essentially secular taste for flowers permeated the aristocratic court civilization of the Heian, where lovers attached sprays of blossoms to letters and eulogized the plum and cherry as symbols of life's transient happiness. Indeed, it is hardly an exaggeration to describe blossoms as *the* foremost symbol of Japan's great age of love poetry.

Exactly when the Japanese began the practice of arranging

flowers in pots for decorative purposes has never been satis-
factorily determined. Perhaps not surprisingly, the first well-
known exponent of floral art seems to have been the famous
Zen aesthete Ashikaga Yoshimasa (1435–1490), builder of the
Silver Pavilion. However, Yoshimasa merely popularized an art
that was considerably more ancient. Ikebana, or flower arranging, had for some time been transmitted as a kind of secret
cult by a line of priests who had called themselves Ikenobo.
Just what role Zen and Zen art theory played in this priestly
art is questionable, for early styles were florid and decorative.
At first glance, it may seem strange that the flower arrangements
of the Ikenobo priests should have captured the interest of
Yoshimasa and his circle of Zen aesthetes during the high age
of Zen culture, since the Ikebana of this period, far from showing the spareness characteristic of Zen garden arts, was an
exuberant symbol of the world at large, rather like a complex
mandala diagram of some esoteric sect wherein all components
of the universe are represented in a structured spatial relationship.

This early style of formal flower arranging, now known as
Rikka, was later codified into seven specific elements, each
symbolizing some aspect of nature—the sun, the shade, and so
forth. There were three main branches in an arrangement and
four supporting branches, each with a special name and a special aesthetic-symbolic function. As with most art forms preceding the modern age, the distinction between religious symbolism
and purely aesthetic principles was not well defined, and artists
often preferred to use philosophical explanations as a means of
transmitting those rules of form they instinctively recognized
to be most satisfying. Not surprisingly, given the Zen ideals
of the age, Rikka-style flower arrangements were asymmetrical
and intended to suggest naturalness as far as possible. Although
complex, they were by no means artificial, seeming instead a
happy accident of nature. As with Zen gardens, great artifice
was used to give the impression of naturalness.

Since the elaborate Rikka style was supported by an equally

elaborate theory and required total discipline, flower arranging acquired many of the qualities of a high art. Certainly the arrangement of flowers in the West never approached anything like the formality and rules of technique surrounding Japanese floral displays, and for this reason we sometimes have difficulty in accepting the idea that it can be considered a genuine art form. But then we have never seriously considered the flower a primary religious symbol—a role that, to the Eastern mind, automatically makes it a candidate for artistic expression. The religion of Zen, with no particular god to deify, turned to flowers and gardens as symbols of the spirit of life.

The influence of Zen on the Rikka arrangement was more implicit than direct, and a wholly Zen flower style had to await the coming of the famous tea-ceremony master, Sen no Rikyū. Rikyū predictably found the Rikka style entirely too lavish for understated *wabi* aesthetics and introduced a new style known as Nageire, which was informal and spontaneous in appearance. Since it was for display at the tea ceremony, it was called *chabana*, or tea flowers. Instead of an elaborate seven-point design, the teahouse Nageire-style consisted of one or two blossoms stuck in a pot without any hint of artificiality. The Nagiere was not, of course, an undisciplined art—it was merely intended to seem so. Great care was taken to position the bud and its few surrounding sprigs into a perfect artistic composition that would seem natural and spontaneous. The *chabana* version of the Nageire style is the ultimate Zen statement in living materials. Pared down from the Rikka style, it became a powerful, direct expression of Zen ideals. The difference has been well expressed by Shozo Sato:

Rikka arrangements grew ultimately from a philosophic attempt to conceive of an organized universe, whereas Nageire arrangements represent an antiphilosophic attempt to achieve immediate oneness with the universe. The Rikka arrangement is an appropriate offering to be placed before one of the many icons of traditional Buddhism, but the Nageire arrangement is a direct link between man and his natural surroundings.

One style is conceptual and idealistic; the other, instinctive and naturalistic. The difference is similar to that between the arduous philosophic study associated with traditional Buddhism and the direct enlightenment of Zen Buddhism.[1]

Although the Nageire is still the preferred style for the tea-house, it is a bit too austere, not to mention demanding, for the average Japanese home. The rising middle class of the seventeenth and eighteenth centuries sought a compromise between the Rikka and Nageire, and finally developed a simplified Rikka style known as Seika, which made use of only the three main stems of the full Rikka arrangement.

Today various styles flourish, together with experimental modern schools which permit rocks, driftwood, and other natural materials in their compositions. Yet throughout all the schools—and they number in the thousands—the idea remains that flowers are a shorthand representation of man's connection with nature. Zen ideals are never far distant, even in the most abstract modern compositions.

If the Japanese attitude toward flowers differs from that of the West, their approach to dining differs even more. The almost universal Western attitude toward Japanese cuisine was voiced many centuries ago by the European visitor Bernardo do Avila Giron, who declared, "I will not praise Japanese food for it is not good, albeit it is pleasing to the eye, but instead I will describe the clean and peculiar way in which it is served."[2] Beauty counts as heavily as taste at a formal table, and to say Japanese food is "served" is like calling the members of a string quartet fiddlers. The Japanese devote more artistic resources to the rites of food than any other people on earth. Entire magazines are devoted to supplying housewives with the latest culinary creations: not new recipes but new ways to display dishes created according to well-known formulas. A new condiment is not sought so much as a new color, and a new sauce is of less interest than a new saucer. Indeed, a fine restaurant may prize its ceramics almost as much as its chef.

A chabana *flower arrangement for the tea ceremony, a design both elegant in itself and suggestive of a larger world.*

Yet for all its beauty, the food seems to be oddly deficient in pronounced flavors. This characteristic a Japanese will be the first to admit, but with pride rather than apology. Strong flavors are to a modern Japanese what bold colors were to the

Heian aesthetes—unrefined, obvious gratifications for those lacking in cultivated discernment. A connoisseur is one who can distinguish the subtle difference in taste among various species of raw mushrooms or different fermentations of bean curd. A cultivated Japanese can tell you not only what species of raw fish he is tasting, but the number of hours it has been away from the sea. A conscientious Japanese chef would no more think of serving a vegetable not scrupulously fresh than he would drown it in a heavy sauce. Furthermore, he would most prefer to serve it entirely raw, thereby preserving intact all its subtle natural flavor and texture.

Japanese cuisine, which is a water-based art as compared to the oil-based cooking of China or the butter-based dishes of France, is now known and appreciated worldwide. Dining in a Japanese restaurant in the far-flung corners of the globe can be as formal as a fine Continental meal or as expedient as a grilled-chicken-and-noodle emporium. However, whether formal or casual, it will lack the air of solicitude that a really discerning Japanese host can bring to a specially planned banquet. Since dining at his own home would do no honor to you, the guest, chances are he will entertain you at an inn or restaurant where he knows the chef, but he will still plan the meal, working out all the finer details with the cook. There will be few surprises on the menu, for the food is governed by the season. Only the freshest vegetables—preferably those ripening to their finest that week—and the primest sea fare will be permitted.

Upon entering the dining room you will know you have been selected as the guest of honor when you are requested to sit with your back to the art alcove, or *tokonoma*, a practice dating from rowdier days of the ambush when this represented the one location in a paper-walled room sure to be backed by a solid wall. After seating formalities are resolved, the host will call for tea. If the season is spring, the variety selected may be *shincha*, a dainty green brew steeped from the freshly plucked early leaves of the Japanese tea bush. When you realize that even your beverage has been brought fresh from the fields, you begin to understand the subtleties of seasonal tastes in store. Indeed, in late spring and summer the table will present delicacies only hours from the soil.

First to arrive may be a tray crowded with ceramic saucers, no two alike in shape or glaze, each offering a condiment or plant of the season. Slices of dark, pickled ginger, the traditional astringent, may be arranged on a diminutive round plate of blue and white porcelain, which stands adjacent to a rough-textured, gray square bowl heaped with slivers of fresh cucumber, its brilliant green contrasting with the splash of yellow from a bouquet of its own blossoms sprinkled across one corner of the dish. These may be joined by tender bamboo shoots from the hillside. (Slowly you begin to notice that the color and texture of each dish has been chosen to contrast and complement those of its contents.) Added to this fanciful course may be a pale brown dish of lotus-root slivers, each garnished with a mound of green horseradish. Next at hand might well be a pale yellow saucer holding sheets of dried seaweed alongside a thin slice of the porous white Japanese turnip, sliced so thin as to be transparent. If the season is fall instead of spring, there could be a thin rectangular dish with a crinkled black glaze containing a single maple leaf, on which might be displayed thinly sliced raw mushrooms skewered with pine needles and set in a display of gourd strands.

Next may come a cold omelet, whose fluffy strata of egg have been wrapped like a cinnamon roll around layers of dark seaweed. The omelet's exterior will have been glazed to an almost ceramic polish and garnished with a white radish sauce, light and piquant. After the omelet may come fish, raw *sashimi* in a plethora of varieties from freshwater carp to sea bream to the (sometimes lethal) *fugu*. The subtleties in taste and texture between the many species available are to the Japanese what fine wines are to the Western connoisseur. Yet the chef's real genius has gone into the careful cutting and display of the fish. The red back meat of the tuna must be cut into thick slices because of its tenderness, but the fatty pink meat from the belly can be cut into thin strips. The size of the slices governs how they are displayed. The display and garnishing of the *sashimi* is an important testing ground for the chef's artistic originality. After all, the fish are raw, and beyond making sure that they are fresh and of high quality, there is little to be done about the flavor. Therefore the chef must become an artist if the *sashimi* are to be memorable.

The banquet may continue with soup, often created from fish stock and fermented soybean paste called *miso*. The soup arrives in closed lacquer bowls, on the lids of which will be embellished a design of the season, perhaps a bamboo shoot or a chrysanthemum blossom. Beneath this lid is a tranquil sea of semitransparent marine broth, tinted amber and seasoned with delicate green scallion rings and cubes of bland white soybean curd. The bottom of the bowl may shelter a family of thumb-nail-sized baby clams, still nestled in their open shells. The soup hints of the field and the sea, but in delicate nuances, like an ink painting executed in a few suggestive strokes.

The parade of tiny dishes continues until the host's imagination falters or your appetite is conquered. Green beans, asparagus, lotus root, carrots, tree leaves, legumes . . . the varieties of plants will seem virtually endless. Each taste and texture will be slightly different, each color subtly orchestrated. Yet it all seems perfectly natural, as though the world of mountain and sea had somehow presented itself at your table to be sampled. You become acutely aware of the natural taste of the plants ripening in the fields outside at that very moment. But to enjoy this cuisine you must sharpen your senses; no flavor is allowed to be dominant, no spice overwhelming. You must reach out with your sensibilities and attune yourself to the world around you.

The *haute cuisine* of Japan is known as *kaiseki*, the name of the special meal served with the Zen tea ceremony. *Kaiseki* is the great preserver of cuisine aesthetics in Japan. The tea ceremony, the supreme transmitter of Zen culture, also happens to be the preserver of Japan's finest ideals in the realm of food. The governing principle of *kaiseki* is that the foods served should be natural, even as an unpainted traditional house reveals its fresh woods. Whereas artificiality would draw a diner's spirit away from the real world, naturalness brings him closer to it. The colors, of both the foods and the ceramics, are meant to suggest nature. The servings are simple, never elaborate or contrived, and the foods chosen must never be obviously expensive. A host is expected to display his skill and imagination in combining delicate flavors, not his wealth or extravagance in being able to buy the most expensive items he can find. Again it is the Zen idea of *wabi*, a deliberate turning away from the ostentatious.

But to speak of Zen dining in terms of flavor is to miss a good part of the pleasure. The display of glazed ceramic dishes on a Japanese table is carefully orchestrated by color and shape to form a unified, naturalistic, asymmetrical aesthetic whole. The sensitive Japanese regards the Western weakness for marshaled arrays of matched china as a demonstration of limited artistic vision. All the concepts of beauty developed in the tea ceremony have been transmitted to the Japanese formal dining experience, and a dimension has been added: in a formal meal the ceramics are decorated with foods; the various foods are positioned, down to the last bean, with care almost worthy of the stones in a Zen garden, and the color and texture of each is attuned to the color and texture of its dish. Thus dining becomes a display of art and design that tests the aesthetic discernment of both host and guest.

Perhaps in no other land is the serving of food so manifestly both a form of art and an expression of philosophy. But it seems less incredible if viewed merely as the last convolution of Zen culture. From medieval monks to modern housewives, Zen culture has touched every aspect of Japanese life. There are, of course, other voices and other rooms in the complex world of Japanese cultural history, but when you think of the finest moments in Japanese civilization, more often than not you find yourself thinking of Zen.

CHAPTER 17
The Lessons of Zen Culture

It is not surprising if the religious need, the believing mind, and the philosophical speculations of the educated European are attracted to the symbols of the East, just as once before the heart and mind of men of antiquity were gripped by Christian ideas.

Carl Gustav Jung, *Archetypes of the Collective Unconscious*

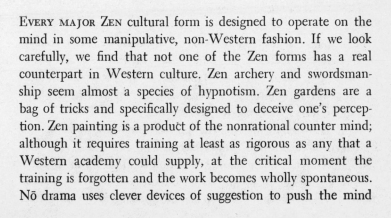

EVERY MAJOR ZEN cultural form is designed to operate on the mind in some manipulative, non-Western fashion. If we look carefully, we find that not one of the Zen forms has a real counterpart in Western culture. Zen archery and swordsmanship seem almost a species of hypnotism. Zen gardens are a bag of tricks and specifically designed to deceive one's perception. Zen painting is a product of the nonrational counter mind; although it requires training at least as rigorous as any that a Western academy could supply, at the critical moment the training is forgotten and the work becomes wholly spontaneous. Nō drama uses clever devices of suggestion to push the mind into areas of understanding too profound for words, while the open-ended Haiku is a spark igniting an explosion of imagery and nonrational perception in the listener's mind. The traditional Japanese house is a psychological chamber from floor to ceiling. Zen ceramics by subtle deceptions destroy our impulses to categorize, forcing us to experience directly materials, process, and form. The tea ceremony is still another exercise in deliberately altering one's state of mind, this time under the guise of a simple social occasion. It seems almost as if the Zen arts were intended to be an object lesson to us on the limitations of the senses in defining reality. Just as the *kōan* taunt the logical mind, the Zen arts, by toying with perception, remind us that there is a reality not subject to the five senses. In Eastern philosophy, although "seeing" involves the senses, it must ultimately transcend them.

Zen culture has been devised over the centuries to bring us in touch with a portion of ourselves we in the West scarcely know—our nonrational, nonverbal side. Whereas Ch'an masters of a thousand years ago were devising mind exercises to short-circuit and defeat the limiting characteristics of the rational side of the mind, the idea of the counter mind has only recently found experimental validation—and hence intellectual respectability—in the rationalist West. (As one example of many, recent experiments at Harvard University found that "questions demanding . . . verbal . . . processes result in the greatest left [brain] hemispherical activation . . . [while] emotional questions elicit the greatest right hemispheric activation."[1]) Apparently not only did the Ch'an masters intuitively realize the existence of the nonverbal half of the mind during the T'ang era (618–907), but they, and later the Japanese, used it to create a spectrum of art and cultural forms which exploits, strengthens, and sharpens these same nonverbal faculties.

Zen cultural forms are the perfect physical proof of the strength of the counter mind. Even those using language (the Nō and Haiku) rely more on suggestion than on words. Indeed, the very language of Japan was recently described by a Japanese scholar in terms that make it sound almost like an intuitive, counter-mind phenomenon: "English is a language intended strictly for communication. Japanese is primarily interested in feeling out the other person's mood, in order to work out one's own course of action based on one's impression."[2] This difference in approach to language, in which it is seen as a virtual barrier to communicating what is really significant (one's subjective response), appears to be a side effect of Zen culture. As a Japanese critic recently observed,

> A corollary to the Japanese attitude toward language might be called the "aesthetics of silence"—making a virtue of reticence and a vulgarity of verbalization or open expression of one's inner thoughts. This attitude can be traced to the Zen Buddhist idea that man is capable of arriving at the highest level of contemplative being only when he makes no attempt at verbalizations and discounts oral expression as the height of superficiality.[3]

Finally, Zen cultural forms use the nonverbal, nonrational powers of the mind to produce in the perceiver a complete sense of identification with the object. If a Zen art work is truly successful, the perceiver has no sense of "I" and "it." If reflection or analysis is required, the work is of no more use than a joke whose punch line needs explanation. One's mind must immediately experience something beyond the work. Even as the eye cannot see itself without a mirror, so it is with the mind. The inducing of introspection turns out to be a deliberate function of Zen art—the forcing of the mind past the surface form of an art work and into a direct experience of a greater truth.

The Zen arts are, we realize at last, completely internalized. They depend as much on the perception of the viewer or participants as they do on any of their own inherent qualities. For this reason they can be sparing and restrained. (They also happen to be perfectly suited to a land that, over the centuries, has been as physically impoverished as Japan.) By using small-scale, suggestive arts that depend to a large extent on the special perception of the audience for their impact, Zen artists were

able to provide immense satisfaction with only a minor investment of resources. It is rather like the relation of radio to
television drama. Given an audience with a good imagination, a
radio dramatist or a Zen artist can achieve the intended effect
through suggestion. This is what Sir George Sansom had in
mind when he remarked upon the

> important part played by aesthetic feeling in the enrichment
> of Japanese life. Among Japanese of all classes, an instinctive
> awareness of beauty seems to compensate for a standard of
> well-being which to Western judgement seems poor and bleak.
> Their habit of finding pleasure in common things, their quick
> appreciation of form and color, their feelings for simple ele-
> gance, are gifts which may well be envied by us who depend
> so much for our happiness upon quantity of possessions and
> complexity of apparatus. Such happy conditions, in which
> frugality is not the enemy of satisfaction, are perhaps the most
> distinctive features in the cultural history of Japan.[4]

Zen culture, working with the already highly developed
vocabulary and capacity for perception developed in the Heian
era, unlocked powerful new techniques that have made Japanese
culture a special case in the annals of world civilization. Perhaps the best case in point is the stone garden at Ryōan-ji,
which is a triumph of pure suggestiveness. It is clearly a symbol
—but a symbol of what? It is clearly an invitation to open
one's perception—but open it to what? The work gives no
hint. With Ryōan-ji Zen artists finally perfected the device of
suggestiveness to the point where it could stand on its own.
The garden seems almost to be a natural object, like a sunset
or a piece of driftwood. The impact of a traditional Zen room
is similar. It simply amplifies whatever powers of understanding
the viewer already possesses. Of itself it is a void.

By relying so strongly on perception, the Japanese have
created a strikingly original way of using and experiencing art.
Western critics for several hundred years have argued about
the function of art, the responsibilities of the audience vis-à-vis

a work of art, the varying types of perception, and so on, but they have never dealt with the peculiar phenomenon of Zen art, where the work can be merely a device to start the mind going. How do you write a critical analysis of a work of art that only takes shape after it gets inside your head? It is interesting to watch critic after critic struggling with Ryōan-ji, trying to explain its power, only to collapse at last in defeat.[5] Similarly, the most effective Haiku are those about which the least can be said. Ryōan-ji takes your breath away when you first see it; like a good Haiku it slams you against a moment of direct experience. Yet when you try to analyze it, you find there is nothing significant to say. Ryōan-ji may not even be a work of art by our Western definition; it may be some sort of mind device for which we have no word. Similarly, Haiku's relation to Western poetry may be limited to typography. The arts of the West—painting, poetry, drama, literature, sculpture—are all enhanced by critical analysis. When we speak of Milton, we really speak of Milton as seen through many layers of critical explanation and interpretation. The Zen arts have inspired no such body of critical analysis, perhaps because they do not have many of those qualities we normally think of as aesthetic. Does Ryōan-ji have beauty in any conventional sense? It merely exists. It is, if anything, anti-art.

If we in the West wish to borrow from the complex world of Zen culture, we must first begin to train and intensify our powers of perception. In this regard, one is tempted to speculate that the Japanese must have learned to turn these powers down as well as up. How else can one explain the Japanese ability to ignore so much of the blight of modern civilization while maintaining a national fetish for such purely aesthetic phenomena as cherry blossoms? As Donald Richie observed, "Japan is the most modern of all countries perhaps because, having a full and secure past, it can afford to live in the instantaneous present."[6] Alongside all the aesthetic indignities of the twentieth century, the ancient sense of taste appears to have survived undiminished. A concern for beauty is still very much a part of everyday life in Japan. Whereas the appreciation

The stone garden at Ryōan-ji.

of art is usually the pursuit of a privileged few in Western countries, in Japan the aesthetic quality of everyday objects is commonly acknowledged to be fully as important as their function. It is not uncommon to discover a rustic day laborer arranging flowers, practicing the tea ceremony, or fashioning a garden in his spare time. The peasant may be as sure a judge of tea bowls as the prince. Even the match boxes from the sleaziest bars are minor works of art, as are bundles and packages from even the most modern commercial establishments. A sense of beauty is not considered unmanly; indeed, it is regarded as essential to the good life, harking all the way back to the virile *samurai*.

Zen culture's primary lesson is that we should start trying to experience art and the world around us rather than analyzing them. When we do this, we find that everything suddenly comes alive. If we can take this power of direct perception, sharpened by the devices of Zen art, back to everyday activities, we will find a beauty in common objects that we previously ignored. Flowers—indeed individual petals—become objects of the most intense loveliness. When we see the world with a Zen-honed awareness, our sense of the beauty in objects supplants our desire to possess them. If we allow the ancient creators of Zen culture to touch our lives, we open wider the doors of perception.

References

CHAPTER 2 THE PRELUDE TO ZEN CULTURE

1. "The Diary of Murasaki Shikibu," from *Diaries of Court Ladies of Old Japan*, trans. Omori, Annie Shepley, and Kochi Doi (Tokyo, 1935; reprint ed., New York, AMS Press), p. 147.
2. *The Pillow Book of Sei Shōnagon*, trans. Ivan Morris (New York: Columbia University Press, 1967), p. 40.
3. Ibid., p. 214.
4. "The Diary of Murasaki Shikibu," p. 74.
5. *The Kokin Waka-shu*, trans. H. H. Honda (Tokyo: Hokuseido Press, 1970), p. 35.
6. See Wm. Theodore de Bary, ed., *Sources of Japanese Tradition*, vol. 1 (New York: Columbia University Press, 1958).
7. Earl Miner, *An Introduction to Japanese Court Poetry* (Stanford, Calif.: Stanford University Press, 1968), p. 9.

CHAPTER 4 THE CHRONICLES OF ZEN

1. *Essays in Zen Buddhism: First Series*, trans. D. T. Suzuki (London: Grove Press, 1949), p. 181.
2. Translated in *A Buddhist Bible*, ed. Dwight Goddard (Boston: Beacon Press, 1970), p. 315.
3. Ibid., p. 323.
4. *Chuang Tzŭ, Basic Writings*, trans. Burton Watson (New York: Columbia University Press, 1964), p. 94.

5. *The Sūtra of Hui Nêng*, trans. A. F. Price and Wong Mou-Lam (Berkeley: Shambala, 1969) p. 15.
6. Ibid., p. 18.
7. *The Diamond Sūtra*, trans. A. F. Price and Wong Mou-Lam (Berkeley: Shambala, 1969), p. 37.
8. de Bary, *Sources of Japanese Tradition*, 1: 236.
9. George Sansom, *A History of Japan to 1334* (Stanford, Calif.: Stanford University Press, 1958), p. 429.
10. Dōgen Zenji, *Selling Water by the River*, trans. Jiyu Kennett (New York: Pantheon, 1972), p. 115.

CHAPTER 5   ZEN ARCHERY AND SWORDSMANSHIP

1. D. T. Suzuki, *Zen and Japanese Culture* (Princeton, N.J.: Princeton University Press, 1959), p. 146.

CHAPTER 6   THE GREAT AGE OF ZEN

1. de Bary, *Sources of Japanese Tradition*, 1: 255.

CHAPTER 7   ZEN AND THE LANDSCAPE GARDEN

1. David H. Engel, *Japanese Gardens for Today* (Rutland, Vt.: Tuttle, 1959).

CHAPTER 9   ZEN AND THE INK LANDSCAPE

1. Seiroku Noma, *Artistry in Ink* (New York: Crown, 1957), p. 3.
2. *Two Twelfth-Century Texts on Chinese Painting*, trans. R. J. Maeda (Ann Arbor: University of Michigan Papers in Chinese Studies, No. 8, 1970), p. 17.
3. Osvald Sirén, *The Chinese on the Art of Painting* (New York: Schocken, 1963), p. 97.
4. Ernest F. Fenollosa, *Epochs of Chinese and Japanese Art* (New York: Dover, 1963), 2: 11. (Reprint.)

CHAPTER 10   THE ZEN AESTHETICS OF JAPANESE ARCHITECTURE

1. Lafcadio Hearn, *Gleanings in Buddha-Fields* (Rutland, Vt.: Tuttle, 1971), p. 1. (Reprint.)
2. For a fuller discussion of early Japanese architecture, see Arthur

Drexler, *The Architecture of Japan* (New York: Arno Press, 1955).

3. An excellent discussion of *shibui* may be found in Anthony West's essay, "What Japan Has That We May Profitably Borrow," *House Beautiful*, August 1960.

4. Ralph Adams Cram, *Impressions of Japanese Architecture* (New York: Dover, 1966) p. 127. (Reprint.)

5. Heinrich Engel, *The Japanese House* (Rutland, Vt.: Tuttle, 1964) pp. 373–374.

CHAPTER 11   THE NŌ THEATER

1. R. H. Blyth, *Eastern Culture* (Tokyo: Hokuseido, 1949), 1: 146.

2. de Bary, *Sources of Japanese Tradition*, 1: 278.

3. Charles E. Tuttle, *The Noh Drama* (Nippon: Gakujutsu Shinkōkai, 1955), p. 130.

CHAPTER 12   BOURGEOIS SOCIETY AND LATER ZEN

1. João Rodrigues, *This Island of Japan,* trans. Michael Cooper (Tokyo: Kodansha, 1973), pp. 272–273.

CHAPTER 13   THE TEA CEREMONY

1. Suzuki, *Zen and Japanese Culture*, p. 299.

2. Ibid., p. 305.

CHAPTER 14   ZEN CERAMIC ART

1. Ruskin, John, *The Stones of Venice, Volume II* (1853), from *Selected Prose of Ruskin*, Matthew Hodgart, ed. (New York: New American Library, 1970), pp. 119 and 124.

CHAPTER 15   ZEN AND HAIKU

1. See Kenneth Rexroth, *One Hundred Poems from the Japanese* (New York: New Directions, 1964).

2. See Geoffrey Bownas and Anthony Thwaite, eds., *The Penguin Book of Japanese Verse* (Baltimore: Penguin, 1964).

3. Ibid., p. 71.

4. Miner, *An Introduction to Japanese Court Poetry*, p. 91.

5. Harold G. Henderson, *An Introduction to Haiku* (Garden City, N.Y.: Doubleday Anchor, 1958), p. 18.
6. Ibid., p. 18.
7. See Kenneth Yasuda, *The Japanese Haiku* (Rutland, Vt.: Tuttle, 1957).
8. Henderson, *An Introduction to Haiku*, p. 39.
9. Ibid., p. 49.
10. Ibid., p. 94.
11. Ibid., p. 108.
12. Ibid., p. 113.
13. Ibid., p. 146.
14. Issa, *The Year of My Life*, trans. Nobuyuki Yuasa (Berkeley: University of California Press, 1960), p. 104.
15. R. H. Blyth, *A History of Haiku* (Tokyo: Hokuseido, 1964), 2: 82.

CHAPTER 16 PRIVATE ZEN: FLOWERS AND FOOD

1. Quoted in Michael Cooper, ed., *They Came to Japan* (University of California Press, 1965), p. 194.

CHAPTER 17 THE LESSONS OF ZEN CULTURE

1. Gary E. Schwartz, Richard J. Davidson, and Foster Maer, "Right Hemisphere Lateralization for Emotion in the Human Brain: Interactions with Cognition," *Science*, October 17, 1975, p. 287.
2. Frank Gibney, "The Japanese and Their Language," *Encounter*, March 1975, p. 35.
3. Masao Kunihiro, "Indigenous Barriers to Communication," *The Wheel Extended*, Spring 1974, p. 13.
4. George Sansom, *Japan: A Short Cultural History*, rev. ed. (New York: Appleton-Century-Crofts, 1962).
5. The best analysis to date is Eliot Deutsch, "An Invitation to Contemplation," *Studies in Comparative Aesthetics*, Monographs of the Society for Asian and Comparative Philosophy, No. 2, University of Hawaii Press, 1975.
6. Donald Richie, *The Inland Sea* (New York: Weatherhill, 1971), p. 60.

Bibliography

General History

de Bary, Wm. Theodore, ed. *Sources of Japanese Tradition*. 2 vols. New York: Columbia University Press, 1958.

Hall, John Whitney. *Japan, From Prehistory to Modern Times*. New York: Delacorte, 1970.

Hane, Mikiso. *Japan, A Historical Survey*. New York: Scribners, 1972.

Morris, Ivan. *The World of the Shining Prince: Court Life in Ancient Japan*. New York: Knopf, 1964.

Murdoch, James. *History of Japan*. 3 vols. New York: Ungar, 1964 (reissue).

Reischauer, Edwin O. *Japan: Past and Present*. 3rd ed. New York: Knopf, 1964.

Sansom, George B. *A History of Japan*. 3 vols. Stanford, Calif.: Stanford University Press, 1958–1963.

————. *Japan: A Short Cultural History*. Rev. ed. New York: Appleton-Century-Crofts, 1962.

Varley, H. Paul. *The Ōnin War*. New York: Columbia University Press, 1967.

————. *Japanese Culture: A Short History*. New York: Prager, 1973.

Wheeler, Post. *The Sacred Scriptures of the Japanese*. New York: Schuman, 1952.

GENERAL ARTS AND CULTURE

Benedict, Ruth. *The Chrysanthemum and the Sword*. Rutland, Vt.: Tuttle, 1954.

Boger, Batterson. *The Traditional Arts of Japan*. New York: Crown, 1964.

Boscaro, Adriana. *101 Letters of Hideyoshi*. Tokyo: Kawata Press, 1975.

Hall, John Whitney. *Twelve Doors to Japan*. New York: McGraw-Hill, 1965.

Hasegawa, Nyozekan. *The Japanese Character: A Cultural Profile*. Palo Alto, Calif.: Kodansha, 1966.

Hearn, Lafcadio. *Japan: An Interpretation*. Rutland, Vt.: Charles E. Tuttle, 1955 (reprint).

Hisamatsu, Shin'ichi. *Zen and the Fine Arts*. Palo Alto, Calif.: Kodansha, 1971.

Janeira, Armando Martins. *Japanese and Western Literature*. Rutland, Vt.: Tuttle, 1970.

Keene, Donald, trans. *Essays in Idleness*. New York: Columbia University Press, 1967.

Koestler, Arthur. *The Lotus and the Robot*. New York: Harper & Row, 1960.

Moore, Charles A., ed. *The Japanese Mind*. Honolulu: University of Hawaii Press, 1967.

Munsterberg, Hugo. *Zen and Oriental Art*. Rutland, Vt.: Tuttle, 1965.

————. *The Arts of Japan*, Rutland, Vt.: Tuttle, 1957.

Paine, Robert Treat, and Soper, Alexander. *The Art and Architecture of Japan*. Rev. ed. Baltimore: Penguin, 1960.

Rodrigues, João. *This Island of Japan*. Translated by Michael Cooper. Tokyo: Kodansha, 1973.

Sansom, George B. *An Historical Grammar of Japanese*. London: Oxford University Press, 1928.

Seckel, Dietrich. *The Art of Buddhism*. New York: Crown, 1963.

Suzuki, D. T. *Zen and Japanese Culture*. Princeton, N.J.: Princeton University Press, 1959.

Ueda, Makota. *Literary and Art Theories in Japan*. Cleveland: Press of Case Western Reserve University, 1967.

von Durckheim, Karlfried Graf. *The Japanese Cult of Tranquility*. London: Rider, 1960.

BUDDHISM AND JAPANESE BUDDHISM

Anesaki, Masaharu. *History of Japanese Religion*. London: Kegan Paul, Trench, Trubner, 1930 (reissue, Rutland, Vt.: Tuttle, 1963).

Bapat, P. V. *2500 Years of Buddhism*. New Delhi: Government of India, Ministry of Information, 1956.

Bunce, William K. *Religions in Japan*. Rutland, Vt.: Tuttle, 1955.

Ch'en, Kenneth. *Buddhism in China*. Princeton, N.J.: Princeton University Press, 1964.

Conze, Edward. *Buddhism, Its Essence and Development*. New York: Harper, 1959.

Cowell, E. B. *Buddhist Mahayana Texts*. New York: Dover, 1969 (originally published in 1894 as volume 49 of *The Sacred Books of the East*).

Eliot, Sir Charles. *Japanese Buddhism*. New York: Barnes & Noble, 1969.

Goddard, Dwight, ed. *A Buddhist Bible*. Boston: Beacon Press, 1970.

Hanayama, Shinsho. *A History of Japanese Buddhism*. Tokyo: Bukkyo Dendo Kyokai, 1966.

Katō, Bunnō, Tamura, Yoshirō, and Miyasaka, Kōjirō, trans. *The Threefold Lotus Sutra*. New York: Weatherhill/Kosei, 1975.

Kern, H. *Saddharma-pundarika or the Lotus of the True Law* (The Lotus Sūtra). New York: Dover, 1963 (originally published in 1884 as volume 21 of *The Sacred Books of the East*).

Ramanan, K. Venkata. *Nagarjuna's Philosophy*. New Delhi: Motilal Banarsidass, 1975.

Ross, Nancy Wilson. *Three Ways of Asian Wisdom*. New York: Simon & Schuster, 1966.

Saunders, E. Dale. *Buddhism in Japan*. Philadelphia: University of Pennsylvania Press, 1964.

Shoko, Watanabe. *Japanese Buddhism: A Critical Appraisal*. Tokyo: Japanese Cultural Society, 1970.

Suzuki, D. T. *Studies in the Lankavatara Sutra*. London: Routledge & Kegan Paul, 1952.

———. *Outlines of Mahayana Buddhism*. New York: Shocken, 1963.

ZEN

Benoit, Hubert. *The Supreme Doctrine: Psychological Studies in Zen Thought*. New York: Pantheon, 1955.

Blofield, John, trans. *The Zen Teaching of Huang Po*. New York: Grove Press, 1958.

―――. *The Zen Teaching of Hui Hai on Sudden Illumination*. New York: Samuel Weiser, 1972.

Blyth, R. H. *Zen in English Literature and Oriental Classics*. New York: Dutton, 1960.

―――. *Zen and Zen Classics*. 5 vols. Tokyo: Hokuseido Press, 1960–1970.

Chang, Chung-Yuan, trans. *Original Teachings of Ch'an Buddhism* (The Transmission of the Lamp). New York: Random House, 1969.

Chang, Garma C. C. *The Practice of Zen*. New York: Harper & Row, 1959.

Cleary, Thomas, and Cleary, J. C., trans. *The Blue Cliff Record*. Berkeley: Shambala Publications, Inc., 1977.

Dōgen Zenji. *Selling Water by the River*. Jiyu Kennett, trans. New York: Pantheon, 1972.

Dumoulin, Heinrich. *A History of Zen Buddhism*. New York: Random House, 1960.

Hirai, Tomio. *Zen Meditation Therapy*. Tokyo: Japan Publications, 1975.

Hoffman, Yoel. *The Sound of One Hand*. New York: Basic Books, 1975.

Humphreys, Christmas. *Zen Buddhism*. New York: Macmillan, 1949.

Hyers, Conrad. *Zen and the Comic Spirit*. Philadelphia: Westminster Press, 1973.

Kapleau, Philip, ed. *The Three Pillars of Zen*. New York: Weatherhill, 1965.

Kubose, Gyomay M. *Zen Koans*. Chicago: Regnery, 1973.

Luk, Charles. *Ch'an and Zen Teachings*. 3 vols. London: Rider, 1962.

―――. *The Transmission of the Mind Outside the Teaching*. New York: Grove Press, 1974.

Miura, Isshu, and Sasaki, Ruth Fuller. *The Zen Kōan*. New York: Harcourt, Brace and World, 1965.

————. *Zen Dust*. New York: Harcourt, Brace and World, 1966. (Contains *The Zen Kōan* plus additional material.)

Price, A. F., and Wong, Mou-Lam, trans. *The Diamond Sutra and the Sutra of Hui Nêng*. Berkeley, Calif.: Shambala, 1969.

Ross, Nancy Wilson, ed. *The World of Zen*. New York: Random House, 1960.

Sasaki, Ruth Fuller, Iriya, Yoshitaka, and Fraser, Dana R. *The Recorded Sayings of Layman P'ang: A Ninth-Century Zen Classic*. New York: Weatherhill, 1971.

Shibayame, Zenkei. *Zen Comments on the Mumonkan*. New York: Harper & Row, 1974.

Suzuki, D. T. *Essays in Zen Buddhism*. 3 vols. London: Luzak, 1927–1933, 1934.

————. *Manual of Zen Buddhism*. New York: Evergreen, 1960.

————. *Studies in Zen*. New York: Philosophical Library, 1955.

————. *Zen Buddhism*. Garden City, N.Y.: Doubleday, 1956.

————. *The Zen Doctrine of No Mind*. New York: Samuel Weiser, 1973.

Watts, Alan W. *The Spirit of Zen*. New York: Grove Press: 1958.

————. *The Way of Zen*. New York: Pantheon, 1957.

Wu, John C. H. *The Golden Age of Zen*. Committee on Compilation of the Chinese Library, Taipei, Taiwan: 1967.

Yampolsky, Philip B. *The Platform Sutra of the Sixth Patriarch*. New York: Columbia University Press, 1967.

————, trans. *The Zen Master Hakuin: Selected Writings*. New York: Columbia University Press, 1971.

Yokoi, Yūhō. *Zen Master Dōgen*. New York: Weatherhill, 1976.

Architecture

Cram, Ralph Adams. *Impressions of Japanese Architecture*. New York: Dover, 1966 (reprint).

Drexler, Arthur. *The Architecture of Japan*. New York: Museum of Modern Art, 1955.

Engel, Heinrich. *The Japanese House—A Tradition for Contemporary Architecture*. Rutland, Vt.: Tuttle, 1964.

Ishimoto, Kiyoko, and Ishimoto, Tatsuo. *The Japanese House*. New York: Crown, 1963.

Itoh, Teiji, and Futagawa, Yukio. *The Elegant Japanese House:*

Traditional Sukiya Architecture. New York: Walker/Weatherhill, 1969.

Morse, Edward S. *Japanese Homes and Their Surroundings.* New York: Dover, 1961 (reprint).

Sadler, A. L. *A Short History of Japanese Architecture.* Rutland, Vt.: Tuttle, 1963.

Tange, Kenzo, and Kawazoe, Noboru. *Ise: Prototype of Japanese Architecture.* Cambridge, Mass.: MIT Press, 1965.

Watanabe, Yasutada. *Shinto Art: Ise and Izumo Shrines.* New York: Weatherhill/Heibonsha, 1974.

GARDENS

Condor, Joseph. *Landscape Gardening in Japan.* New York: Dover, 1964 (reprint).

Engel, David H. *Japanese Gardens for Today.* Rutland, Vt.: Tuttle, 1959.

Graham, Dorothy. *Chinese Gardens.* New York: Dodd, Mead, 1937.

Inn, Henry. *Chinese Houses and Gardens.* New York: Crown, 1940.

Kuck, Loraine. *The World of the Japanese Garden.* New York: Walker/Weatherhill, 1968.

Nakane, Kinsaku. *Kyoto Gardens.* Osaka: Hoikusha, 1965.

Petersen, Will. *Stone Garden* (*Evergreen Review*, vol. 1, no. 4). Collected in *The World of Zen*, ed. Nancy Wilson Ross. New York: Random House, 1960.

Saito, K., and Wada, S. *Magic of Trees and Stones.* Rutland, Vt.: Japan Publications, 1964.

Shigemori, Kanto. *Japanese Gardens: Islands of Serenity.* San Francisco and Tokyo: Japan Publications, 1971.

Tamura, Tsuyoshi. *Art of the Landscape Garden in Japan.* New York: Dodd, Mead, 1936.

Yoshida, Tetsuro. *Gardens of Japan.* Translated by Marcus Sims. New York: Praeger, 1957.

CERAMICS

Dickerson, John. *Raku Handbook.* New York: Van Nostrand, 1972.

Jenys, Soame. *Japanese Pottery.* New York: Praeger, 1971.

Mikami, Tsugio. *The Art of Japanese Ceramics.* New York: Walker/Weatherhill, 1972.

Miller, Roy Andrew. *Japanese Ceramics*. Rutland, Vt.: Tuttle, 1960.
Rhodes, Daniel. *Stoneware and Porcelain: The Art of High-Fired Pottery*. New York: Chilton, 1959.

Tea Ceremony

Carpenter, Francis Ross, trans. *The Classic of Tea*. Boston: Little, Brown, 1974.
Castile, Rand. *The Way of Tea*. New York: Weatherhill, 1971.
Fukukita, Yasunosuke. *Tea Cult of Japan*. Tokyo: Hokuseido, 1932.
Fujikawa, Asako. *Cha-no-yu and Hideyoshi*. Tokyo: Hokuseido, 1957.
Okakura, Kakuzo. *The Book of Tea*. New York: Dover, 1964 (reprint).
Sadler, A. L. *Cha-no-yu, The Japanese Tea Ceremony*. Rutland, Vt.: Tuttle, 1963 (reprint).

Zen Archery and Swordsmanship

Acker, William. *Japanese Archery*. Rutland, Vt.: Charles E. Tuttle, 1965 (privately published, 1937).
Gluck, Jay. *Zen Combat*. New York: Random House, 1962.
Herrigel, Eugen. *Zen in the Art of Archery*. New York: Pantheon, 1953.
Ratti, Oscar, and Westbrook, Adele. *Secrets of the Samurai*. Rutland, Vt.: Tuttle, 1965.
Robinson, B. W. *The Arts of the Japanese Sword*. London: Faber & Faber, 1961.
Sollier, André, and Györbiro, Zsolt. *Japanese Archery: Zen in Action*. New York: Walker/Weatherhill, 1969.

Flowers and Food

Carr, Rachel. *Japanese Floral Art*. Princeton, N. J.: Van Nostrand Reinhold, 1961.
Herrigel, Gustie S. *Zen in the Art of Flower Arrangement*. London: Routledge & Kegan Paul, 1958.
Richie, Donald, and Weatherby, Meredith, eds. *The Master's Book of Ikebana*. New York: International Book Society, 1966.
Sato, Shozo. *The Art of Arranging Flowers*. New York: Abrams, 1965.

Sparnon, Norman. *Japanese Flower Arrangement: Classical and Modern.* Rutland, Vt.: Tuttle, 1960.

Steinberg, Rafael. *The Cooking of Japan.* New York: Time, 1969.

Tsuji, Kaichi. *Kaiseki: Zen Tastes in Japanese Cooking.* Tokyo: Kadonsha, 1972.

Ueda, Makoto. *Literary and Art Theories in Japan.* Cleveland: Press of Case Western Reserve University, 1967.

Nō Theater

Hoff, Frank, and Flindt, Willi, trans. *The Life Structure of the Noh.* Racine, Wisconsin: Concerned Theatre Japan, 1973.

Keene, Donald. *Nō, The Classical Theatre of Japan.* Palo Alto, Calif.: Kodansha, 1966.

Keene, Donald, ed. *Twenty Plays of the Nō Theatre.* New York: Columbia University Press, 1970.

Nippon Gakujutsu Shinkokai (Japanese Classics Translation Committee). *The Noh Drama,* Rutland, Vt.: Tuttle, vol. 1, 1955; vol. 2, 1959; vol. 3, 1960.

O'Neill, P. G. *A Guide to Nō.* Tokyo: Hinoki Shoten, 1953.

Pound, Ezra, and Fenollosa, Ernest. *The Classic Noh Theatre of Japan.* New York: New Directions, 1959 (reprint).

Sakanishi, Shio. *The Ink-Smeared Lady and Other Kyogen.* Rutland, Vt.: Tuttle, 1960.

Waley, Arthur. *The Nō Plays of Japan.* New York: Grove Press, 1957.

Ze-ami. *Kadensho.* Kyōto: Sumiya-Shinobe, 1968.

Zen and the Ink Landscape

Awakawa, Yasuichi. *Zen Painting.* Palo Alto, Calif.: Kodansha, 1970.

Binyon, Laurence. *Painting in the Far East.* New York: Dover, 1959 (reprint).

Bowie, Henry P. *On the Laws of Japanese Painting.* New York: Dover, 1952 (reprint).

Fenollosa, Ernest F. *Epochs of Chinese and Japanese Art.* 2 vols. New York: Dover, 1963 (reprint).

Fontein, Jan, and Hickman, Money L. *Zen Painting and Calligraphy.* Boston: Museum of Fine Arts, 1970.

Lee, Sherman E. *Chinese Landscape Painting*. New York: Harper & Row, 1954.

——. *A History of Far Eastern Art*. Englewood Cliffs, N.J.: Prentice-Hall, 1964.

——. *Japanese Decorative Style*. New York: Harper & Row, 1972.

——. *Tea Taste in Japanese Art*. New York: Asia House, 1963.

——. "Zen in Art: Art in Zen." *Cleveland Museum of Art Bulletin* 59 (1972): 238–259.

Maeda, Robert J., trans. *Two Twelfth-Century Texts on Chinese Painting*. Ann Arbor: University of Michigan Papers in Chinese Studies, No. 8, 1970.

Matsushita, Takaaki. *Ink Painting*. New York: Weatherhill/Shibundo, 1974.

Morrison, Arthur. *The Painters of Japan*. New York: Stokes, 1911.

Nakata, Yujiro. *The Art of Japanese Calligraphy*. New York: Weatherhill, 1973.

Noma, Seiroku. *Artistry in Ink*. New York: Crown, 1957.

Sirén, Osvald. *The Chinese on the Art of Painting*. New York: Schocken, 1963.

Shimizu, Yoshiaki, and Wheelwright, Carolyn, eds. *Japanese Ink Paintings from American Museums: The Muromachi Period*. Princeton, N.J.: Princeton University Press, 1976.

Sugahara, Hisao. *Japanese Ink Painting and Calligraphy*. Brooklyn, N.Y.: Brooklyn Museum, 1967.

Sze, Mai-Mai. *The Way of Chinese Painting*. New York: Random House, 1959.

Tanaka, Ichimatsu. *Japanese Ink Painting: Shubun to Sesshu*. New York: Weatherhill, 1972.

ZEN AND HAIKU

Bashō, Matsuo. *Monkey's Raincoat*. New York: Grossman, 1973.

Blyth, R. H. *Senryu: Japanese Satirical Verses*. Tokyo: Hokuseido, 1949.

——. *Haiku*. vol. 1: *Eastern Culture*; vol. 2: *Spring*; vol. 3: *Summer-Autumn*; Vol. 4: *Autumn-Winter*. Tokyo: Hokuseido, 1949–1952.

——. *A History of Haiku*. 2 vols. Tokyo: Hokuseido, 1963–1964.

Bownas, Geoffrey, and Thwaite, Anthony, eds. *The Penguin Book of Japanese Verse*. Baltimore: Penguin, 1964.

de Bary, Wm. Theodore, ed. *The Manyōshū*. New York: Columbia University Press, 1965.

Giroux, Joan. *The Haiku Form*. Rutland, Vt.: Tuttle, 1974.

Henderson, Harold G. *An Introduction to Haiku*. Garden City, N.Y.: Doubleday Anchor, 1958.

Honda, H. H. *The Kokin Waka-Shu*. Tokyo: Hokuseido, 1970.

Isaacson, Harold J., trans. *Peonies Kana: Haiku by the Upasaka Shiki*. New York: Theatre Arts Books, 1972.

Issa. *The Year of My Life*. 2nd ed. Translated by Nobuyuki Yuasa. Berkeley: University of California Press, 1972.

Janeira, Armando Martins. *Japanese and Western Literature*. Rutland, Vt.: Tuttle, 1970.

Keene, Donald. *Japanese Literature*. New York: Grove Press, 1955.

———, ed. *Anthology of Japanese Literature*. New York: Grove Press, 1955.

Miner, Earl. *An Introduction to Japanese Court Poetry*. Stanford, Calif.: Stanford University Press, 1968.

Rexroth, Kenneth. *One Hundred Poems from the Japanese*. New York: New Directions, 1964.

Ueda, Makoto. *Literary and Art Theories in Japan*. Cleveland: Press of Western Reserve University, 1967.

———. *Matsuo Basho*. New York: Twayne, 1970.

Yasuda, Kenneth. *A Pepper-Pod*. New York: Knopf, 1947.

———. *The Japanese Haiku*. Rutland, Vt.: Tuttle, 1957.

Yuasa, Nobuyuki, trans. *Bashō: The Narrow Road to the Deep North and Other Travel Sketches*. Middlesex, England: Penguin Books, 1966.

Glossary

amado: sliding, removable panels around exterior of traditional house.

Amida: widely worshiped figure in Buddhist pantheon and central figure of adoration in Jōdo and Jōdo Shin Buddhism.

Ashikaga: dynasty of shōguns (1333–1573) whose patronage inspired great classic age of Zen culture.

ātman: Hindu concept of the "soul" or a personal element in the larger god-head.

aware: aesthetic concept which arose in Heian era, originally meaning a pleasant emotion evoked unexpectedly but later evolving to include poignancy.

Bashō (1644–1694): foremost Haiku poet of Japan.

Bodhidharma: Indian monk who appeared in China around 520 and laid the basis for the Ch'an sect of Buddhism, becoming the First Patriarch of Zen.

Brahman: supreme god-head of Brāhmanism.

Brāhman: priest caste of Brāhmanism.

bugaku: ancient court dances in Japan, imported from Asia.

Buddha: historic figure from sixth century B.C. in northeast Asia whose teachings became the basis for Buddhism.

chabana: spare and elegant flower arrangement prepared to accompany the tea ceremony.

Ch'an: belief system founded by Bodhidharma in the sixth century in China, combining elements of Indian Buddhism and Chinese Taoism and known in Japan as Zen.

Ch'ang-an: T'ang Chinese capital which was the model for the original Japanese capital at Nara.

cha-no-yu: Japanese tea ceremony, which became the vehicle for the preservation of Zen aesthetic theory.

chigai-dana: decorative shelf system in traditional Japanese houses which was borrowed from storage cabinets in Ch'an monasteries.

chinzō: realistic polychromatic character studies of Zen masters.

Chōjirō (1515–1592): first great *raku* potter and founder of *raku* dynasty.

choka: early Japanese poetry form, longer than Haiku.

Chuang Tzŭ: traditionally a fourth century B.C. Taoist.

daimyō: feudal governor of a domain, who often retained a force of *samurai*.

Daisen-in: temple which is the site of a famous Zen stone garden in Kyōto.

Daitoku-ji: major Zen monastery in Kyōto, site of Daisin-in temple.

dharma: term denoting the universal order of the universe.

dhyāna: Sanskrit term for meditation, corrupted to "Ch'an" in Chinese and "Zen" in Japanese.

Dōgen (1200–1253): priest who introduced Sōtō sect of Zen to Japan, founding a temple in 1236.

Eisai (1141–1215): founder of Rinzai sect of Zen in Japan (1191).

en: Heian aesthetic term meaning charming, sprightly.

engawa: outer walkway around traditional Japanese house, between *amado* and *shōji*.

eta: formerly outcast class in Japan because of association with meat and hides industry.

fusuma: sliding partitions in the traditional Japanese house.

Gautama: original name of the Buddha.

genkan: portico in the traditional house where shoes are removed.

Ginkaku-ji: "Silver Pavilion" built by Yoshimasa in 1482.

Godaigo: ill-fated emperor who reigned from 1318 to 1339 and attempted to restore genuine imperial rule.

Gozan: five most important Zen monasteries, or "Five Mountains," which in Kyōto were Tenryū-ji, Shōkoku-ji, Tōfuku-ji, Kennin-ji, and Manju-ji.

haboku: "broken ink" style of monochrome painting.

haikai: Early name for poetic form now known as Haiku.

Haiku: verse form consisting of seventeen syllables.

Hakuin (1685–1768): Zen teacher of Tokugawa period who revived Rinzai sect.

haniwa: clay sculpture of the pre-Buddhist period.

harakiri: ritual suicide, more politely known as *seppuku*.

Heian: Period of indigenous aristocratic culture.

hibachi: small brazier heater in the traditional Japanése house.

Hideyori (1593–1615): son of Hideyoshi, committed suicide when defeated by Tokugawa Ieyasu.

Hideyoshi (1536–1598): general who assumed control of Japan after Oda Nobunaga was murdered and who inspired Momoyama age of Japanese art.

Hīnayāna: more traditional form of Japanese Buddhism, which is practiced in Southeast Asia.

hinoki: Japanese cypress.

Hōjō: regents who dominated the Kamakura period of Japanese history

hokku: first three lines of a *renga*, or linked verse, which later came to be written alone as a Haiku.

Hōnen (1133–1212): founder of the Jōdo or Pure Land sect (1175).

Hosokawa: clan which served as advisers and regents for the Ashikaga.

Hsia Kuei (active ca. 1180–1230): Southern Sung Chinese painter whose style strongly influenced later Zen artists in Japan.

Hui-k'o (487–593): Second Patriarch of Chinese Ch'an, said to have cut off his arm to attract Bodhidharma's notice.

Hui-nêng (638–713): Sixth Patriarch of Ch'an and founder of the Southern school of Ch'an which was transmitted to Japan.

Hung-jên (605–675): Fifth Patriarch of Ch'an and teacher of Hui-nêng.

Ieyasu (1542–1616): founder of the Tokugawa shōgunate, which ruled Japan from 1615 to 1868.

Ikebana: Japanese flower arranging.

Jōdo: sect of Japanese Buddhism based on chant praising Amida Buddha which was founded in 1175.

Jōdo Shin: rival sect of Japanese Buddhism also based on chant praising Amida which was founded in 1224.

Jōmon: prehistoric culture in Japan.

Josetsu (active 1400–1413): leading artist in Japanese Sung revival.

kaiseki: special cuisine associated with the tea ceremony.

Kamakura: effective capital of Japan during period of warrior domination (1185–1333).

kami: Shintō spirits inhabiting the natural world.

Kamikaze: "Divine Wind" that sank the Mongol fleet attacking Japan in 1281.

kamoi: crossbeams in the traditional Japanese house.

Kanō: family of painters dominating much of Japanese painting since the sixteenth century, replacing Zen artists as the official stylists.

kare sansui: stone gardens in "dry landscape" style.

Kinkaku-ji: "Golden Pavilion" built by Yoshimitsu in 1394.

kōan: illogical conundrums used in Rinzai Zen to induce enlightenment.

koicha: powdered green tea used in the tea ceremony.

Kokinshū: anthology of Japanese poems from the year 905.

Kūkai (774–835): introduced Shingon Buddhism to Japan in 808.

Kyōgen: farces performed as part of a program of Nō plays.

Kyōto: capital city of Japan from 794 to seventeenth century and site of classic Zen culture.

Lankāvatāra: sūtra believed by Bodhidharma to best express Ch'an philosophy.

Lin-chi (d. 866): leading figure of the "sudden enlightenment" school of Ch'an, whose teachings were much of the basis of Japanese Rinzai Zen.

Mahāyāna: Buddhism which spread to China and Japan.

mandala: esoteric diagrams purportedly containing the key to cosmological truths.

Manyōshū: early anthology of Japanese poetry (780).

Ma Yüan (active ca. 1190–1224): Chinese Southern Sung painter whose works strongly influenced Japanese Zen artists.

Minamoto: warrior family of the Heian and Kamakura eras.

Minchō (1351–1431): Japanese priest and one of the first Japanese artists to successfully adopt and revive Chinese styles of paintings.

miso: fermented soybean paste used in Japanese cooking.

miyabi: Heian aesthetic term signifying subtleties only a connoisseur could appreciate.

Momoyama: period of Japanese history from 1537 to 1615.

mondō: Zen question-and-answer session in which a novice must respond immediately and without reflection to questions posed by a Zen master.

Mu-ch'i (ca. 1210–ca. 1280): Chinese Ch'an painter whose works strongly affected Japanese Zen artists.

mūdra: sacred hand signs.

Musō Soseki (1275–1351): Zen scholar and adviser to Ashikaga Takauji, who is traditionally thought to be the designer of several early Zen landscape gardens in Kyōto.

Nageire: style of Ikebana.

nageshi: decorative element in the ceiling of a traditional Japanese house.

Nara: site of the first capital of Japan, which was consecrated in 710 and abandoned by the court in 784.

nembutsu: chant to Amida Buddha used by Jōdo and Jōdo Shin sects.

Nichiren (1222–1282): founder of Buddhist sect based on Lotus Sūtra.

Nichiren Shōshū: name of the sect founded by Nichiren.

Nō: theatrical form reflecting Zen ideals, which came to prominence during the Ashikaga era.

Nobunaga (1534–1582): military ruler who began the movement to unify Japan.

Oribe: style of Japanese Zen-influenced ceramics.

pi-kuan: "wall-gazing" meditation practiced and extolled by Bodhidharma.

raku: style of ceramics invented by Chōjiro.

ramma: open latticework in the traditional Japanese house.

renga: "linked verse" form of Japanese poetry, in which different participants must contribute alternate stanzas.

Rikka: an early style of formal flower arranging.

Rinzai: Japanese sect of Zen stressing sudden enlightenment and use of *kōans*.

roji: "dewy path" leading through the Japanese tea garden.

Ryōan-ji: temple in Kyōto with a famous *kare sansui* flat garden.

sabi: aesthetic term signifying the dignity of old age.

Saichō (767–822): introduced Tendai Buddhism into Japan (806).

Saihō-ji: temple in Kyōto and site of early Zen landscape garden.

Sākyamuni: the Buddha, "sage of the Sākyas."

samurai: Japanese warriors, who were the first converts to Zen.

Sanskrit: original language of much Buddhist literature.

sarugaku: theatrical form which was forerunner of the Nō.

sashimi: raw fish.

satori: Zen term for enlightenment.

Sen no Rikyū (1521–1591): proponent of *wabi* aesthetics who strongly influenced the evolution of the tea ceremony.

seppuku: ritual suicide.

Sesshū Tōyō (1420–1506): greatest Japanese Zen painter.

Seto: site of medieval Japanese pottery production.

Shao-lin: Chinese monastery where Bodhidharma reportedly first went to meditate.

Shên-hsiu (606–706): traditionally said to have been rival of Hui-nêng at monastery of Fifth Patriarch and later much favored by Chinese ruling circles.

shibui: important term for later Zen aesthetics which means understated, simple good taste.

shin: type of ink-painting technique.

shincha: type of tea.

shinden: Heian architectural style borrowed from China.

Shingon: esoteric sect of Buddhism introduced into Japan by Kūkai in 808.

Shino: style of Japanese Zen-inspired ceramics.

Shinran (1173–1262): founder of the Jōdo Shin sect in Japan (1224).

Shintō: original Japanese belief system, which preceded Buddhism.

shite: leading character of a Nō drama.

shoin: name of the writing desk in Ch'an monasteries, which gave its name to the classic style of the Zen-inspired Japanese house.

shōji: Rice-paper-covered latticework used as windows in the traditional Japanese house.

Shūbun (fl. 1414–d. ca. 1463): painter-monk at Shōkoku-ji in Kyōto.

Siddharta: the Buddha.

sō: technique of Japanese ink painting.

Sō'ami (1472–1525): Japanese ink painter and garden artist.

Sōtan (1414–1481): Zen painter at Shōkoku-ji, none of whose works are definitely known to survive.

Sōtō: Japanese Zen sect emphasizing "gradual" enlightenment through *zazen*.

sukiya: later style of Japanese architecture which evolved from the *shoin*.

sumi: Japanese black ink.

sūtra: works supposedly reporting discourses of the Buddha or his disciples.

Taira: warrior clan instrumental in ousting Heian aristocracy and ending Heian era.

Takauji (1305–1358): founder of the Ashikaga shōgunate.

Taoism: native Chinese belief system which influenced Ch'an philosophy.

tatami: woven straw mats used for carpeting in the traditional Japanese house.

Tendai: sect of Chinese Buddhism introduced into Japan by Saichō (806).

Tenryū-ji: important Zen temple in Kyōto and site of early Zen-style landscape garden.

toko-bashira: decorative, unpainted tree trunk used in traditional house as part of art alcove.

tokonoma: special art alcove in the Japanese house, which was originally derived from the shrine in Chinese monasteries.

Tomi-ko: wife of Ashikaga Yoshimasa.

Toshiro: thirteenth-century potter who visited China and brought back important Chinese ceramics technology.

usucha: a thin tea served as part of the tea ceremony.

wabi: aesthetic term meaning a sense of deliberate poverty and naturalness.

waka: thirty-one-syllable Japanese verse popularized in the Heian era.

waki: supporting actor in the Nō drama.

Yayoi: pre-Buddhist culture in Japan.

Yoshimasa (1435–1490): Ashikaga shōgun and staunch patron of Zen arts.

Yoshimitsu (1358–1408): Ashikaga shōgun whose patronage sparked the classic era of Zen culture.

yūgen: most important term in Zen aesthetic vocabulary, meaning among other things that which is mysterious or profound.

zazen: meditation, a mainstay of the Sōtō sect of Japanese Zen.

zenkiga: style of Zen painting.

Index

ABOUT THE AUTHOR

Thomas Hoover, who has made a lifelong study of the differences between Eastern and Western modes of perception and creativity, began the notes for Zen Culture *some eight years ago while on an extended visit in Japan and finished the book in New York City, where he now lives and works. He holds a Ph.D. degree in the natural sciences and has been an on-and-off student of the Japanese language for well over a decade. He has published articles in a variety of technical and popular journals, on topics ranging from basic scientific research to the history of technology.*

VINTAGE WORKS OF SCIENCE AND PSYCHOLOGY

VINTAGE ASIAN STUDIES